Tom Never's Ghost

Jack Warner

Tom Never's Ghost

*An eyewitness account
of the past 350 years
on Nantucket Island and in its
little known Southeast Quarter*

As told to

JACK WARNER

Copyright ©2006 by Jack Warner

Cover Illustration: "Manor House—4:00AM" by John F. Lochtefeld ©2000

The author is deeply grateful to the distinguished artist, Mr. John Lochtefeld of Nantucket Island, for his kind permission to reproduce his wonderful etching— "Manor House 4:00 AM"—on the cover of this book.

Published by
Quatrefoil, Inc.
P.O. Box 819, Siasconset, MA 02564

ISBN No. 0-9778056-0-3

For Anne Hibbard Warner
— With Love and Gratitude —

Contents

Figures

Tom Never's Ghost

How this story came to be told . . .

The fog was the thickest I'd ever seen, that June morning just three years ago. I had headed out from my Tom Nevers home in full sunshine, with the thought of walking a mile or so to the beach. But suddenly—almost from nowhere—up came a fog so dense that I could scarcely see more than ten feet ahead.

As I groped my way back to my property, I realized that there was a man standing quietly at the end of my driveway. I didn't know him, but his kind smile and relaxed manner made me comfortable enough to ask him if he'd like to wait out the fog at my house. He nodded "yes," and we inched side-by-side up the long gravel drive, using the tall scrub oak on either side to guide our way.

I asked if he lived in Tom Nevers. And he said yes, that he lived out near the Head. He said his name was Thomas and I told him mine was Jack. Other than that, we had no chance for any conversation until we were seated safely inside and I put on the coffee.

Nothing about his appearance prepared me for what he was about to tell me that morning. He was fairly tall, a bit lean, and deeply tanned—about 70 years old I would guess. He had a faint accent, but too faint to place. His clothes were dark, but not much different than my own. I simply assumed that he was a retiree, like so many of us with homes in the area.

As we started to sip our coffee, he looked intently at me, smiled a bit, and said that he had heard I was interested in learning the history of Nantucket's Southeast Quarter. That didn't surprise me too much because I had been asking everyone in sight for the past month what they knew of the area.

My curiosity had come from a conversation at one of those cocktail parties that start off each season and give Nantucket summer people the chance to renew their friendships with each other and with the growing number of year-rounders. At the party I had asked how many of us now live in Tom Nevers? The answer was, "Well over a thousand." I then asked if a history had ever been written on the area? Here, the answer was, "Not that I know of." The consensus being that except for 'Sconset, nothing much had ever happened in the Southeast Quarter—that the place had always been wild and fully undeveloped before the 1970s. This surprised me. How could an area large enough to be called the Southeast Quarter be totally by-passed in Nantucket's long and rich history? Surely the Southeast Quarter had some story to tell. And if it did, why had it escaped notice and faded from memory?

But try as I may, I could find nothing in print covering this part of the Island. Perhaps nothing did happen out here. Perhaps we were just a deserted scrub oak-covered piece of land south of the old Milestone Road—stretching between mile marker number 4 and 'Sconset.

That's why I perked up so when my visitor brought up the subject of the Southeast Quarter. "What can you tell me?" I asked. "I'm eager to hear everything and anything you can tell me."

He smiled and warned me that what he was about to say might surprise me. Then he asked if I'd promise to just listen without judgement and without interruption. "Absolutely," I agreed. But within ten or twelve minutes, I feared that this was a stranger I should never have invited into my home. Yet his calm manner, and my curiosity about what he might tell me, forced me to sit nervously quiet without revealing my sense of growing concern.

Right off, you should know that I have never believed in ghosts—at least not the kind that you read about in spook stories. So I more than half suspected that this man's visit and his story were part of an elaborate prank played on me by one or more of my neighbors. But if this was a prank, the thing I still can't explain is how this man knew so much about a subject that even the Island's leading historians had never before written about.

For nearly three hours he wove a fascinating tale full of colorful detail. And when he concluded, he simply rose from his seat, said goodbye, and headed out into the still clinging fog. I have never seen him again. And no one I know could remember someone of his description.

Was what he told me true and valid? Or was it all just a concocted tale? I had to know. So I went back to the Atheneum and to the Nantucket Historical Association research library, reviewing hundreds of books and documents. I traced old deeds and court records, and dug back into the microfilm files of the Nantucket "Inquirer and Mirror." Only this time, I back-searched by specific event, date and name.

Fact after fact was verified, and event after event was confirmed. Then I started interviewing the Island's historians and people who had long connections to the Tom Nevers area and the Southeast Quarter. And remarkably, I could find nothing that appeared contradictory to what my visitor had told me. Even a broadened search to include several major museums and libraries, some private collections, and the Internet, revealed no flaws in his story. (In the back of this book, you'll find a partial list of the many sources I consulted, and the people I spoke with.)

Yet clearly, some of the things he told me can simply never be verified—only because they had never before been written down. Things like why the Indians finally allowed the English to settle here, and what the English really hoped to achieve. Things like how Tom Never got his name, and why so many places in the Southeast Quarter now bear that name. Things like how Nantucket managed to eclipse other ports in whaling wealth, and what ultimately caused its fortunes to fall. Things like how a single naval battle off Tom Nevers turned the tide in the War of 1812. Things like Jared Coffin's long forgotten luxury garden just west of 'Sconset. And things like why the Southeast Quarter remained the last part of Nantucket to be developed.

Even without complete documentation in some of these areas, I now fully believe them. But I'll leave it to your judgement as to what to accept or reject.

Far more demanding is the leap-of-faith necessary to believe that the stranger that visited me that foggy June morning was indeed who he claimed to be—the still present ghost of Tom Never. This I can never prove—or disprove.

Jack Warner
Tom Nevers
Nantucket Island
October, 2005

FIGURE 1   Nantucket Island—Key Locations—

1. Madequecham Valley
2. Sachem Wanackmamack
3. Tom Nevers Head
4. Tom Nevers Pond
5. Tom Nevers Swamp
6. Philip's Run
7. 'Sconset
8. Occawa
9. Bloomingdale
10. Plainfield
11. Sankaty Light House
12. Gibbs Pond
13. Altar Rock
14. Bean Hill
15. Squatesit
16. Shimmo

17. Quaise
18. Polpis Harbor
19. Wauwinet
20. Squam
21. Sesachacha Pond
22. War of 1812 Sea Battle
23. Nantucket Beach Properties
24. U.S. Navy Base
25. Tom Nevers Airfield
26. Surfside
27. Miacomet
28. Hummock Pond
29. Wesco (Nantucket Town)
30. Sherburne Bluffs
31. Cappamet (1st settlement)
32. Madaket
33. Warren's Landing
34. Tuckernuck
35. Muskeget

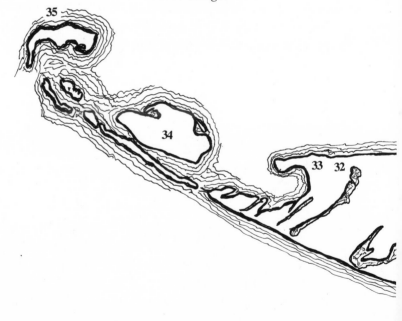

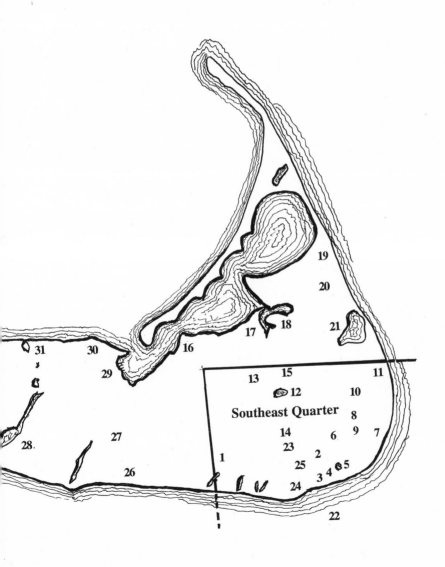

Southeast Quarter

All that follows was told to me by a stranger who visited my Tom Nevers home on a foggy June morning three years ago. It is not my story, it is his. Compiled from my notes and recollections of that day, it gives what appears to be an eyewitness account of the history of Nantucket's Southeast Quarter—as witnessed by someone who claims to have seen it all happen. And since his story spans more than 350 years, this does suggest something pretty strange indeed. So quite reluctantly, I've come to accept the notion that the stranger visiting me that day was indeed the ghost of Tom Never.

1

In Search of Paradise . . .

Y ou wanted to know about Nantucket's Southeast Quarter. So let me start at the very beginning. It's about land. It's always been about land. And I'll tell you why.

Those of us who came to this island and settled in its Southeast Quarter did not come here by accident. We were drawn here, displacing those who came before us—just as we all will be displaced by those yet to come. That shouldn't upset you. It's an inevitable characteristic of our human nature.

From that ancient time when our parents were expelled from Eden, our kind has searched endlessly for a Paradise here in this world to replace that which was lost to us. Our search has taken us to the coldest and hottest places on earth, to the driest and wettest of terrain. And always, our compulsive goal has been the same. To find a place where we can not only sustain our bodies and spirits, but also a place where we can live exactly as we wish—safe from "outsiders" who might once again take our happiness away.

Scientists have often remarked that we humans are the most adaptable of earth's creatures. They point out that no other species can survive in such a broad range of altitudes and climates, in places of such population density or remoteness. The reason goes far beyond our physiology, far beyond our skills in creating clothing and shelter, far beyond our ingenuity in husbanding food and water, far beyond our ability to fashion tools and machines. It comes instead from that inner compulsion we share to find for ourselves a place that can become our exiled Eden. And our search for that place has driven us to every portion of this globe.

Some believe that they've found their Paradise in teeming cities, others in small villages or in the verdant countryside. Some believe they've found it in dense forests, or in ancient deserts, or in mountain heights. Some see it in the lush tropics, or in places of majestic cold. And then there are those, like we, whose search for Paradise has brought us to an island far away.

And when we find our Paradise, we attempt to stake out our claim— by possession, or purchase, or agreement that says this place is ours. Just as other animals mark out their territory, we set boundaries intended to keep the uninvited away. But of course, this is illusory. Others will come, perhaps not for a very long time. But they will come. Because they, like we, are compelled to do so. And just as we displaced others, they will displace us too.

You are not the first generation to make the Southeast Quarter of Nantucket your earthly Paradise. People have settled here for many thousands of years, even before Nantucket was an island. But as the melting glaciers gave up their cold waters and the oceans rose by nearly 400 feet, this prominence—like a great ship—was set adrift from the mainland. Nantucket became a place apart, protected from the easy incursion of outsiders.

With time, the Southeast Quarter did become a physical Paradise. The warming waters of the Gulf Stream moderated its climate and incubated small marine life, which in turn attracted squids and vast schools of fish—bluefish, sea bass, cod and sturgeon of gigantic size. The southern shore became the fall and winter feeding grounds for roaming whales— which when stranded, washed up on the beaches in abundance. Shellfish of every description thrived—oysters, crabs, clams, scallops, lobsters, quahogs, periwinkles, and mussels. And birds of every type chose this place in their annual migrations north and south.

The sandy soil began to richen and gave forth plants and flowers of great diversity, many with healing powers. And small game flourished, because their natural predators on the mainland could not reach them.

When my ancestors first came to this place more than 1,000 years ago, they selected the southeastern portion of the island for their home. From its high rolling hills they had great vistas of *both* the rising and the setting sun. The mighty ocean, with its abundance of sea life, lay directly at their feet. The soil here was far more productive for planting than that of the soggier lowlands to the west. Ponds and springs gushed forth water that was pure and sweet. And the shallow valleys gave them protection from the cold winter winds and storms, when they came. Here they settled and here they prospered, growing stronger and taller with each passing generation.

But alas, their Paradise was challenged when others finally came—a covetous band of Indians from the west.

My people had come to Nantucket from the north, from the area we now call Cape Cod. The new ones came from the west, from the island now called Martha's Vineyard. At first, the new ones came only in the summer—to gather shellfish at the west end of the island and to harvest dead whales that washed up on the southwestern shore. But with each passing year, more and more of them came—until eventually they outnumbered us and desired all that we had. Fierce people they were, and they plotted to make this entire island their own.

But we vowed never to be driven from our land—from this Paradise that was ours. We would fight them with all of our power and resolve.

Ancient legends told us of a great battle between two gods that once ruled this island. Giants they were—one a kind and gentle Good Spirit from the east—the other a wicked Evil Spirit from the west, with many heads and arms, and with hissing serpents for legs.

The Evil Spirit envied the Good Spirit and plotted to kill him to take possession of the island's eastern half. With cunning, he lay in wait and then attacked with all his monstrous furry.

The battle raged for many days, back and forth across the central moors. At first, Evil seemed the stronger. But then the Good Spirit delivered a decisive blow. The Evil One fell to earth with such a thunderous crash that the ground split in two—creating a deep valley into which he was swallowed up for all time beneath the sand. That valley—which runs from north to south—is today called the Madequecham Valley. And it was here and along its extension to the north that my people decided to make their stand. This would be our western territorial boundary for the wars to come.

For untold years, any of the new ones who dared to cross that line faced a certain death. Their heads and hands were cut off from their bodies and mounted on poles as a warning to others that might also dare to cross. And we lived that way for generations.

Eventually, peace between our people came. We began to live in harmony and even intermarried. And as we grew in numbers, our culture changed and several new sachems were established across the island— each with its own elder. But as before, the largest and most powerful sachem was here in the southeast.

But this time of peace would grow uneasy. For we knew with growing certainty that one day the English would invade our shores.

❦   ❦   ❦

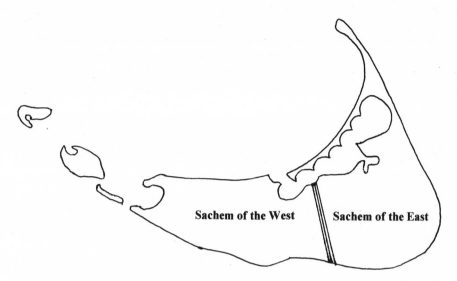

Sachem of the West   **Sachem of the East**

FIGURE 2   Nantucket Island—Circa 1400

For untold generations, the Madequecham Valley formed a natural boundary between the warring Indian tribes of the west and east. Legend said two giant gods once ruled the Island—the Good God of the east and the Evil God of the west. In a great battle, the Evil One was defeated by the Good Spirit and was swallowed up beneath the sands at this place, forming a deep fissure in the ground. As time passed, this valley which we now call the Madequecham Valley became a "no man's land" between hostile tribes. To cross this place meant certain death.

2

1630 . . . Beware the English

For more than 25 years we had been warned of their coming. The great Wampanoag Confederation—comprised of more than 30 settlements on the mainland—had sent news of the white man's first arrival and had alerted us each year to the steadily growing danger. Trade with the Wampanoag sachems on the mainland had long been our custom. Each spring and throughout the summer, their canoes would arrive with skins, flints and pottery—to return home filled with dried clams, crabs, tubers and melons. And with each passing year, they'd bring us ever more troubling news of English avarice and brutality.

As early as 1524, Verrazano of Italy had explored the coast of the mainland. This was our Confederation's first glimpse of the outsider's giant ships. Ships the size of floating islands, with masts like the tallest of trees and sails billowing out like clouds. And with guns spewing fire and giving forth a terrifying noise like thunder. Though very short in stature, these strangers were wrapped in vests and hats made of iron to make them strong. And their faces were covered with thick hair, like the wild beasts. Yet while ferocious in appearance and weapons, they seemed respectful of our dominion and claimed to come only in peace. We would see!

In 1602, Gosnold the Englishman explored and named Cape Cod and Martha's Vineyard. And he built a small fort and trading camp on

Cuttyhunk Island. A delegation of fifty Wampanoags—led by Massasoit's father, the most powerful of the sachems—arrived in nine canoes from the mainland. At first, relations went well. But suspicions were growing. It appeared that the English had more in mind than just trade!

The year after Gosnold left, Martin Pring built a stockade and trading post on Cape Cod's northern shore. To enforce his will, he unleashed two viscous mastiffs trained to bite and kill. And he became the first to fire his guns directly at our people.

Then in 1605, we learned that a man named George Waymouth kidnapped five of the Abenaki people in Maine—for what purpose we did not know. Thus began a period of open hostilities along the entire New England coast and onto Cape Cod.

But it was Captain Edward Harlow in 1611 who brought the first direct taste of the English threat to Nantucket's shores. Sailing south from Monhegan Island off the coast of Maine, Harlow traced the mainland to Cape Cod. There he lured three Wampanoag aboard, presumably to trade. But his true plan was to chain them up and bring them back to London, to be put on paid display as savages. A Wampanoag named Pechmo wrestled free and swam to shore, but the other two—Monopet and Pekenimme—were taken captive. With a furious group of Wampanoag, led by Pechmo, in pursuit—Harlow lifted anchor and hastily sailed away, heading west along the lower coast of Cape Cod's arm, hungry for more "savages" to capture.

But news of his deceit had spread quickly before him. He was repulsed at his next stop, with several of his men being downed by a hail of Wampanoag arrows. Harlow then turned directly south to search for an uncharted but long rumored island. And he thus became the first of the English to find Nantucket. Some will tell you that Gosnold or others predated Harlow in finding Nantucket, but that is simply not the case.

As Harlow's ship sailed into Nantucket's great harbor, my people were about to see firsthand that which they had long been told of. Though still unaware of Harlow's specific treachery, they cautiously ringed his ship with their canoes and stood off as his men tried to entice them aboard—dangling beads, bracelets and gleaming hunting knives before them. It was left to Sakaweston—an elder of our southeastern sachem—to determine Harlow's intentions and to measure his honor. Sakaweston climbed aboard and soon villainy revealed itself. Harlow's men seized him and immediately began firing their guns to repel all who might approach to free him. Harlow quickly set sail again—the same day he arrived—without ever setting foot on the island.

We never saw Sakaweston again, although some say that it is his image the English portrayed on their Massachusetts Bay Seal of 1629. Others say that after many years in England, Sakaweston escaped and became a fierce warrior in Bohemia during the Thirty Years War. Of all that, we do not know.

After leaving Nantucket, Harlow sailed to Martha's Vineyard where he captured two more Wampanoag. One, the tall Epenow, he displayed in London for years as "a savage wonder"—reaping a great fortune off the indignity and misfortune of our people.

With this bitter taste of the English still fresh in our mouths, we reflected on the legend of Roqua—the son of the old sachem who once ruled a place at the eastern end of this island, in a time before our long years of war. The Roqua legend foretold the coming of white men from the sea and the ultimate death of our people. This is that legend, as I learned it as a boy—

One night, while Roqua and his people slept, a raiding party from a western tribe attacked his village near Sesachacha Pond and set it ablaze. With his village in flames, Roqua and his warriors chased the invaders into the moors, unaware that a second raiding party was laying in wait behind the village to strike after Roqua left. Throughout the night, Roqua fought with strength and courage across the moors, until he was the only man left standing.

Returning to his village at daybreak, Roqua was horrified to find total devastation. His father, his wife, his daughter, and all his people had been annihilated.

After burying their bodies and wrapping up his wounds, Roqua waited for darkness. Then armed only with a club and single spear, he set off for the enemy stronghold in Miacomet. When he found them, they were all sleeping after celebrating their victory. Roqua entered the sachem's wigwam and crushed the leader's skull with his war club. Then he set fire to many wigwams and cried out for vengeance.

Illuminated by the bright blaze of the fire, Roqua fought with the fury of ten men, slaying dozens before they could subdue him. Finally, bristling with arrows, Roqua fell to his knees and spit out this prophecy before dying, "I see a storm approaching from the north. The canoes of white men with white sails will come to these shores. All will die and be buried in a single grave." We began to worry that perhaps the days of Roqua's prophecy might be close at hand!

1614 brought us further warnings of the English. Captain John Smith led an expedition along the mainland coast to map the region and to lay the groundwork both for trade and for an English settlement. While well intentioned, Smith could not control his men. One of them, Thomas Hunt, abducted twenty four of our people—including Squanto—from Plymouth and Cape Cod, taking them to Spain to be sold as slaves.

Then in 1616, a Frenchman put a curse upon our people. After a shipwreck on the mainland, he and his fellow seamen were taken prisoner in retaliation for the English cruelty. They were paraded from sachem to sachem all along the coast. And the last of them, before being put to death, said to us *in our own language* . . . "God is angry with you for your wickedness. He will destroy you and give your country to another people." The prophecy of Roqua was heard anew!

Within a year of the Frenchman's curse, our people began dying all along the coast. A plague—some say bubonic—raged for three years from Maine to Narragansett Bay, killing nine out of ten.

It was 1620—immediately after the end of the plague—when the Pilgrims came. They were led by a cruelly aggressive man named Miles Standish. He desecrated our burial sites, looted our storage pits, and shot any of our people who dared to come near him. Settling the Pilgrims in the then deserted Plymouth, he left them ill prepared for the harsh winter that was to come. By spring, more than half had succumbed to cold, starvation, and diseases common to the English.

Taking pity on these suffering Pilgrims, Squanto stepped forward to help them. Newly returned from his own captivity in Spain and England,

Squanto knew that these austere Puritans had left England because of religious persecution. He spoke their language and offered to become not only their interpreter with the Algonquian people, but also their advisor in raising crops and building winter stores.

But even as the Plymouth colony stabilized and treaties were signed with the sachems of the mainland, of Cape Cod and of Martha's Vineyard, Miles Standish took an action that would throw all of the Algonquian people into panic and eventual despair.

Using as his justification false reports of a planned uprising—reports cunningly provided by the supreme sachem Massasoit to consolidate his own power over rival sachem leaders—Miles Standish invited the sachem Wituwamet and his men to a feast at Wessagusset, a place that is now called Weymouth. There he killed them with their own knives. Later that same day, he repeated the deception and massacred even more. Racing back to Plymouth, Standish impaled Wituwamet's severed head on a ten-foot stake and displayed it as a sign of his invincibility.

Yes, this is the same Miles Standish that Longfellow immortalized some 230 years later in his narrative poem—*The Courtship of Miles Standish*—as a noble leader, but bashful suitor, who sought the hand of Priscilla Mullins through the intercession of his old friend John Alden. While a cherished part of today's Pilgrim folklore, Longfellow's tale bears no resemblance to the real Miles Standish—a cruel, wicked and feared man, whose brutish acts brought chaos to the entire region.

All the broken treaties, the unprovoked slaughter and the betrayal by their own supreme sachem, so terrified and shocked the Algonquian people that they abandoned their homes and villages and ran about like men distracted. They left their crops, concealed themselves in swamps and other hidden places, and soon fell victim to sickness and new diseases. As a result, many died, including the three Cape Cod sachems—Canacum, Aspinet, and Ianough. But before dying, Ianough—for whom Hyannis would be named—lamented, "It is now clear that the God of the English is offended by our people and will destroy us all in anger."

❧ ❧ ❧

More and more of the English came. And with them came more death. Soon after the Puritans settled in Boston in 1630, smallpox raged out of control among our people. The plague of 1616–1619 had killed nine in ten. This new plague destroyed many of the rest. As one of the English noted, "The Algonquians die like rotten sheep."

❧   ❧   ❧

Yet throughout all this time, on Nantucket we enjoyed a good and peaceful life. We were as far distant from Cape Cod and the mainland as France was from England. And the shoals were still a treacherous mystery to the English, keeping them far away. Save for that one day in 1611 when Harlow kidnapped Sakaweston, we had no other direct contact with the outsiders.

But we grieved for all the others in the once great Wampanoag Confederation. And we welcomed their refugees to our shores. Year after year, they came in great numbers to escape English cruelty and the threat of slaughter and disease. So that gradually our numbers swelled to become nearly 3,000 by 1650—giving us a population density as great as western Europe, and *ten-times* as great as our density on the New England mainland before the 1616 plague.

This island—Nantucket Island—was still our Paradise, but we feared that it would not remain so for long. We knew that the outsiders would one day surely come. Their god was angry with us and would take our land away. We had no other shores to flee to. And our legends told us that we "Would all be buried in a single grave."

❧   ❧   ❧

3

1659 ... At the Sachem Wanackmamack

My story now jumps ahead to 1659—the year when the English first came to start a year-round settlement on Nantucket. A full 48 years had passed since Harlow's raid, 43 years had passed since the Frenchman's curse, 39 years had passed since the great plague ended and the Pilgrims had landed at Plymouth, and 29 years had passed since the Puritans settled in and around Boston. Only now, after all this time, did Nantucket's sachems grant the English permission to come. What finally persuaded them to do so? As surprising as it may sound today, it was a desire for the English "technology." I know this to be true because I was then 17 years of age and witness to it all. Here's how it all happened and the central role played by the Southeast Quarter—

❦ ❦ ❦

Less than an hour after the English settlers came ashore in the autumn of 1659 at the place now called Warren's Landing in Madaket Harbor, the runner reached Wanackmamack with the news of their arrival. As sachem of the Island's southeastern territory, Wanackmamack was considered the Chief Sachem of all of Nantucket Island.

In the Massachusett language spoken by the Wampanoag, the word "sachem" is both a person and the land ruled by that person. As a sachem, Wanackmamack was not a king or lord in the English sense. Rather, he was a leader or elder who ruled with the advise of his senior men—managing his region's affairs by means of wisdom, fairness, love, and occasionally by the redistribution of possessions. If a sachem's people ever grew to doubt his leadership, they could replace him by consensus. But at age 65, Wanackmamack had kept his peoples' trust for more than 35 years.

The Sachem Wanackmamack extended from the Madequecham Valley east to the sea. Its northern boundary ran to stone markers about a half-mile north of Altar Rock. And it contained two major villages— "Occawa" about a mile west of 'Sconset, at the head of the wetlands now called Tom Nevers Swamp—and the village of "Squattest" near Altar Rock.

Nearly 800 people lived in the Sachem Wanackmamack—132 families with 202 adult men, 214 adult women, and 367 children. As was our custom, we spent the warmer months closer to the southern shore where we could harvest the bounty of the sea, sky and land. Then during the harsher winter months, we moved north into the more protected hills and valleys of the Sachem Wanackmamack. Some of us lived in the villages or close by, but most preferred dwelling on one of the small house lots that were scattered all across the countryside.

The people of Sachem Wanackmamack built rectangular barrel-domed wigwams that we called "wetu"—with typically two or more generations living together. Low sleeping platforms, storage baskets and pots, and a central fire pit dominated the interior.

A grid of bent saplings gave the wetu its support, and woven grass mats covered and enclosed the structure. The sapling grids were left standing year-round; only the mats had to be moved to ready a family's seasonal home in the north or in the south.

Each family group planted and harvested their own crops in common areas—with corn, beans, squash and gourds the main staples. Wild groundnuts, wild lettuce and wild berries were also abundant. The groundnuts, a potato-like tuber, were dug out of the soft soil in Tom Never's Swamp. Wild bearberry was also harvested. Its small gray berries were ground into meal, mixed with fat, cranberries and sweet fruit berries, then dried into small cakes—as a convenient food for the men during their long days of fishing and birding.

While the men would help with the spring planting, generally it was the women and children who tended and harvested the crops, ground the corn into meal, and gathered all manner of shellfish and useful plants and berries.

Because fish and birds were more abundant than land animals, they were our main source of food. And hunting them was a man's chief duty. Assisted by the older boys, the men fished along the shore and in the ponds using hooks and spears made of bone. And twice each year we would dig open the tidal ponds to the sea—herding fish into weirs constructed of saplings, twigs and reeds. Weirs were also placed in the tidal estuaries to trap fish coming in to feed.

Beached whales provided us with an abundant source of rich meat and fat. Several men would work together to butcher one of the beasts, dividing large slabs of flesh and blubber amongst them. The bones were left to dry and whiten in the sun, to be distributed later for fashioning into tools.

Birds were hunted for both their meat and their feathers. They were flushed out of the low grasses and bushes with the help of small dogs trained for that purpose. As the birds began to rise into the air, they were brought down with arrows shot from short bows.

To attract large numbers of birds during their migrations each year—and to hunt them effectively—the grasses and berry-laden bushes had to be kept low and the fields and nesting areas kept open. To accomplish this, the men set fires each year to burn off the old growth. You'll read that this practice of burning was to prepare the fields for planting. It helped there too, but it was birding—and not agriculture—that was the primary reason for the burning.

Cooking pits were used to bake the fish, birds, vegetables and shell-fish all together, using a technique similar to today's clambake. A pit was dug in the sandy soil and lined with large flat stones. A fire was set and fueled for several hours to heat the stones thoroughly. Then the food, wrapped in wet seaweed, was added and covered by a thick layer of sand. After several hours of baking and steaming, the pit was opened and the food distributed. The roasting and boiling techniques, commonly used by the English in their cooking, were rarely if ever used by the people of Sachem Wanackmamack.

Hot stones and seaweed were also used in preparing our sweathouses that restored both health and strength and cleansed the body, the mind, and the spirit.

With large animals relatively scarce on the Island, skins and furs were seldom worn as everyday garments. Rather, reeds and grasses were woven into overlapping panels that were tied about the waist and draped over the shoulders. Both men and women wore their hair long, with a double or single braid. Holidays were celebrated with feasts and were highlighted by competitive games played by the men on the wide sandy beach.

The powwow, or shaman, played an important role in our community—healing the sick, casting spells, seeing into the future, and interceding with the gods. The Wampanoag people had thirty-seven gods. The most powerful was Kiehtan, the creator who dwelled in the heavens and who would welcome all good men to his side when they died. Other gods ruled the sun, the moon, the sea, the winds, the rains, the fish, the birds, the harvest, and other elements of life upon which the people depended. Some gods were evil, especially Hobbamock, the god of darkness who had to be appeased.

Wanackmamack and his senior men held their councils in the meetinghouse at Occawa. Here they discussed petitions and options, followed by the smoking of a shared stone pipe of pokeweed to give them wisdom and to achieve consensus. The stone pipe was made of the same blue clay we used for pottery. Pokeweed was smoked because there was no tobacco grown on the Island. And it was preferred because it brought forth the dreamsleep visions that carried the insights of our beloved ancestors and our gods.

Several times during the years before the English settlers landed at Madaket Harbor, Wanackmamack and the five other sachems of the Island held councils in Occawa to consider if and when to allow them entry. All agreed that over the past fifteen years a different kind of English had settled on the mainland, on Cape Cod and on Martha's Vineyard. These English no longer killed or made captives of the Wampanoag people, they honored and lived by their treaties, and they seemed to be deeply religious. It appeared that peaceful co-existence with the English was perhaps possible.

But the council talked even more of the amazing English "technology" that they had seen during their visits off-Island, and of their need to bring it to Nantucket. The English had iron plows that could turn more earth in an hour than the four strongest men of the sachems could till in a day. They had firearms that could kill more birds in an afternoon than the most expert bow hunter could bring down in a month. They had fishhooks, knives, hatchets and tools of superior strength and effectiveness. They had nets large enough to harvest large quantities of fish from the seas and ponds. They had blankets and all types of body garments stitched from warm woven wool to provide protection from the cold winds and rains. The council agreed that all these advances were greatly needed by the sachems to cope with the expanding requirements of their large and ever growing populations.

And particularly encouraging was the fact that the English now freely offered to share with the sachems on Nantucket the love and mercy of their own powerful God. A certainty of Paradise in the afterlife was the English promise—rather than the "death and burial in a single grave" that had been prophesied so often to the Wampanoag in the past.

For nearly five years, news of this beneficent God had been brought to Nantucket by the kindly Thomas Mayhew, his saintly son Thomas, and an eloquent Wampanoag Christian missionary named Hiacoomes. They preached the existence of a single, all powerful, all loving God— and the concepts of personal sin, individual guilt, and redemptive life through the intercession of Christ. And these were not just the spoken words of the English; it was all written down for eternity in a black book they carried with them—a book containing the true words of God. They also introduced the concept of personal prayer. With prayer, each man could speak directly with God as often as he wished to atone for his sins and to gain forgiveness, without the intervention of others.

These teachings so moved the Wampanoag of Nantucket that a number of us had already embraced the English religion through baptism, and more were becoming what the English called "Praying Indians" each month.

But still, caution was called for. While an alliance with these English seemed beneficial, once the floodgates were opened it would be very hard to close them again. For this reason, Wanackmamack endorsed a plan proposed by the next-most-powerful sachem—Nickanoose.

Nickanoose was sachem of the eastern territory north of Sachem Wanackmamack—including today's Squam and Wauwinet. Young and willful, Nickanoose—who had only recently succeeded his father—was also quite canny. He proposed that any English presence be limited to the less desirable lands at the far west of the Island. Homesteads of very small size would be leased to the English, with broader grazing rights provided on a year-by-year basis. In this way, the English and their actions could be watched carefully. If problems arose, the leases would simply not be renewed.

Spotso, the sachem of the central territory to the west of Wanackmamack, agreed. His sachem included today's Shimmo and ran south to the sea. It was bounded on the east by the Madequecham Valley and on the west by Weweeder Pond.

Attapeat, the sachem to the west of Spotso felt he had nothing to fear. Known as an aggressive warrior, he had close ties to the Wampanoag headquarters in Mount Hope and its Supreme Sachem—Massasoit's son and heir, Metacom—known by the English as King Philip. Attapeat's sachem extended from Monomoy southwest to the head of Hummock Pond, and along Hummock Pond south to the sea.

The sachem Pattachohonet, who had originally come from Martha's Vineyard, knew he would be directly affected by Nickanoose's plan. His territories covered the island of Tuckernuck and extended east from Madaket to Hummock Pond, and encompassed most all of the area north of Attapeat's sachem. This included Wesco, the present site of Nantucket Town. Pattachohonet was troubled, but was finally compelled to agree by the sheer force of the more senior sachems' persuasion.

The sachem Seiknout, also originally from Martha's Vineyard, felt he had no choice but to agree. He controlled the far western island of Muskeget. All the others were for the plan, so he simply gestured "yes" without further comment.

So the decision was made. The English would be allowed to come, but only in a very much-controlled way.

❦ ❦ ❦

As early as 1641, Thomas Mayhew had asked if he might graze sheep on the Island. For more than thirteen years his request had been emphatically denied. Then in 1654 he was allowed to do so, but only on a seasonal basis near Madaket Harbor at the western end of the Island—with the understanding that only a few temporary shelters be built.

From 1654 to 1659, relations with Thomas Mayhew proved excellent. He conducted himself with dignity and together with his son Thomas and their aide, Hiacoomes, shared the knowledge of their God with the Island's people. So early in 1659, the sachems announced to Mayhew their final decision. Mayhew could bring English settlers to establish a year-round Nantucket community.

Wanackmamack empowered Nickanoose to represent all the sachems and personally handle negotiations and supervise relations with the English. The always-shrewd Nickanoose—aware that to the English it was always the written word that superseded the spoken word—had formal lease documents drawn up some months before their arrival.

Now in October of 1659, they were here. And it was time to go forth and greet them.

❦ ❦ ❦

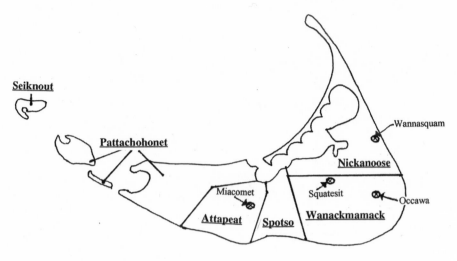

FIGURE 3   Nantucket Island—Circa 1650

Six Sachems ruled the Island when the English came (Wanackmamack, Nickanoose, Spotso, Attapeat, Pattachohonet and Seiknout). Wanackmamack ruled
the Southeast Quarter and was the Chief Sachem among them all. This map
shows their respective territories in 1659 and also shows the four principal
Indian villages—Occawa, Squatesit, Wannasquam, and Miacomet.

4

1659 . . . At Warren's Landing

When Nickanoose reached Madaket Harbor, he had every reason to feel superior and in full control. Near a single small open boat, he saw that the English landing party consisted of just eleven people—two aging men, a gray-haired woman, a gawky lad, six children, and a frail young boatman. The second oldest man he had met before—Thomas Macy, who had come to Nantucket in June with his cousin, Thomas Mayhew, and two other English to open the way for a year-round settlement. But Mayhew and the others were not here today.

Nickanoose asked about them and Macy told him that the others would not come until next year. Only these eleven would form the first Nantucket English settlement.

Macy, at age 51, was the leader of the party and his immediate family made up seven of the eleven. Neither he or any of the others could speak Massachusett, but using English and gestures he introduced his wife Sarah and his five children—Sarah, Mary, Bethia, Thomas and John—ages 13, 11, 9, 6 and 4. Next he introduced Edward Starbuck, age 55, who was a full partner in the venture. Then James Coffin, who while only 19 was a partner representing himself and four others—his father

Tristram Coffin, his brothers James and Tristram, Jr., and his brother-in-law Stephen Greenleaf. Next came Isaac Coleman, a boy of 12, whose role was not explained. And finally, the boatman Daggett who lived in Martha's Vineyard and acted as their pilot.

Seeing that they were cold, tired and hungry after their difficult crossing from Martha's Vineyard in rough seas, Nickanoose instructed his men to help settle them into two temporary lean-to structures near the beach and to prepare food and drink. Tomorrow he would tell these English the terms of the lease documents he had drawn up. This would be easy. They were in no position to disagree. And the terms of the lease agreement they struck now would bind all the English that followed. But little did Nickanoose realize the full extent of their plans for his Island. And even if he did know, he could never have envisioned the eventual impact of those plans on his people.

🦋   🦋   🦋

Thomas Mayhew was without doubt a patient man. He had invested a full eighteen years of effort to realize this day.

Mayhew had first visited Nantucket back in 1641 and had decided then and there to make it his home. He was thrilled by the Island's beauty and excited by its abundance and potential. But most of all, he saw it as a haven from the growing turmoil and repression throughout the Massachusetts Bay Colony, where the Puritan authorities were beginning to exercise an iron-fisted rule.

Immediately upon his return home to Watertown—where he was a respected textile trader and landowner—Mayhew contacted James Forrett, the Boston agent of William, Lord of Sterling. Lord Sterling held the British Royal Patent for all the lands from the Hudson River to the islands off Cape Cod. After some negotiation, Mayhew secured a deed for the whole of Nantucket and for the two small islands adjacent to it. The deed was in his name and the name of his son and all their future associates. As was common at the time, the deed gave them "full power to plant and inhabit the land forever . . . provided that they render *and give yearly* to Lord Sterling, his heirs or assigns, such an acknowledgement as shall be thought fit" by Lord Sterling's appointed representatives.

Under English law, this gave Mayhew titled ownership to Nantucket, but exercising that right was provisional upon Mayhew securing separate rights from the native population. This practice of securing separate rights from the natives was considered both necessary and just, all across New England.

Early the next week, Thomas Mayhew and his son Thomas, Jr. sailed to Nantucket to secure what they called "indian rights." They began by asking permission to graze a few sheep on the Island. But things did not go well and they were abruptly turned away.

Not to be dissuaded, Mayhew decided that a gradual approach was called for. He again visited Lord Sterling's agent and within ten days signed an expanded agreement—adding both Martha's Vineyard and the Elizabeth Islands to his Nantucket deed rights. He immediately dispatched his son to Martha's Vineyard, instructing him to take as much time as needed to court and win over the native population.

The process took nearly two years; but during that time the Mayhews learned the way to secure the Wampanoag's trust and cooperation. It was through a display of dignity, evenhandedness and a generous sharing of the word of their God. The Mayhews comported themselves as true senior sachems, not as brash Englishmen plotting to claim the Island for their king.

In 1643, Thomas Mayhew joined his son in Martha's Vineyard on a full time basis and established a settlement on the eastern end of the Island. From this base they gradually expanded their "indian rights" across the entire Vineyard—while also making frequent missionary trips to Nantucket. But it was to take a full eleven years of this constant effort before the Nantucket sachems would even consider granting Mayhew's original request for a sheep grazing station.

At last in 1654, they told Mayhew that this would be permitted, but only on a seasonal basis, with temporary shelters for a few sheepherders. A man named Captain Humphrey Allerton was appointed by Mayhew to supervise this effort, because Mayhew knew he could be trusted to make sure that nothing went awry.

Then four more years passed—until in 1659, the Nantucket sachems told Mayhew that he would be allowed to establish a year-round settlement amongst them.

Mayhew had always vowed to make Nantucket his permanent home. And he had worked steadily for eighteen years to realize that dream. But now at age 66—as the busy Governor of Martha's Vineyard with large holdings to manage, and still mourning the recent disappearance of his son and heir Thomas, Jr. at sea—Mayhew recognized that he would need the help of younger and equally-motivated men who could be trusted to carry out his mission on Nantucket. Two such men were his younger cousin Thomas Macy and his cousin's friend, Tristram Coffin—both of whom lived well north of Boston in the Merrimack River Valley.

Macy had heard Mayhew speak of Nantucket for many years—about his plans to create a new homeland there that would be free of all economic, religious and political restrictions . . . a new country of his own shaping, inhabited by people of character and kindness . . . solid, intelligent, hard-working people who could create unlimited wealth for themselves and the generations to follow.

Early on, Macy said, "To me, cousin, this sounds like an earthly Paradise." "Indeed, indeed." answered Mayhew, " . . . an earthly Paradise!" And that is how they both expressed it for all those many years.

Macy had mentioned Mayhew and Nantucket often to Tristram Coffin and his other close friends in Salisbury, Newbury, Newburyport, Amesbury and Hampton. Most of them, like he, were Baptists who had come to Massachusetts from England's open west country and other rural regions. Unlike most of their fellow settlers, they were not Puritans from East Anglia. And increasingly, they were bristling over the stern, fundamentalist rule being exerted by the Massachusetts Bay Colony's Puritan government. Things had become so oppressive that there were regulations, laws and fines covering practically ever endeavor—with a harshly repressive stance taken against all religious dissent. Quakers were called "a cursed sect of heretics" and any found entering Massachusetts were jailed and often severely whipped. If they did not agree to permanent banishment and to leave Massachusetts immediately, they were hanged. That was the prevailing culture in Boston and throughout Massachusetts in the late 1650s.

Little wonder that Macy and his friends grew so excited when Mayhew asked if they'd like to share in the settlement of Nantucket with him. None had ever seen it, but if it was as he described it they were willing to abandon Massachusetts and begin a new life in this "virgin land," which did not fall under the jurisdiction of any mainland government.

Tristram Coffin took the lead in mapping out a strategy, organizing the potential investors and handling negotiations with Mayhew. Of them all, he was the most experienced and he and his family were prepared to make the greatest investment in Nantucket. And unlike Macy, he had no conflicting family ties to Mayhew.

Before sitting down with Mayhew, Coffin called together a meeting of the potential investors and proposed a concept he called, "Proprietors Of The Common And Undivided Lands Of Nantucket." Investors would all become Proprietors and own equal shares. Initially, each would receive a private plot of land for his homesite and garden. And all other land on the Island—whether acquired initially or in the future from the native population—would be owned and shared in common. Unlike the small fenced properties favored by the East Anglians across the Massachusetts Bay Colony, this land would be vast and open—like the large estates they had known in their homes in Britain's West Country.

Further, they would be free of the oppressive rule of the Puritans and the Bay Colony Government. They would live as brothers, with no outsiders to tell them what they could or could not think or do. As Proprietors, *they* would be the Government!

Yes, it would require hard work and some patience. But securing the whole Island from the Indians was a near certainty. They had learned how to do this in Massachusetts. And besides, they'd need workers and the Indians would be more than willing to be hired on once they saw the rewards that a good farming and sheep raising economy could bring them.

Questions were asked about how future English settlers would be treated. What about sons, brothers, other relatives and close friends? And surely they would need experienced craftsmen, tradesmen and other specialists as the colony grew. From this discussion they agreed that each of the nine men present could at his discretion select one other partner or associate to become a Proprietor with full rights and privileges. This right to a partner would also apply to Thomas Mayhew, who wished to retain a full interest in the Island.

Thus it was agreed that there would be twenty "full share" Proprietors—Mayhew and these nine—plus ten more "full share" partners, chosen one each by the original ten. It was further agreed that in the future ten other men could be offered "half shares," based on a common agreement among the twenty as to their need and desirability. (In actuality, fourteen "half shares were eventually awarded—adding the equivalent of seven full shares to the original twenty. And this is how it came to pass that all Nantucket lands acquired over time by the English were said to be owned in common by 27 shareholders.)

The next day, Tristram Coffin headed south to Watertown to meet with Thomas Mayhew and to lay out his Proprietorship proposal. After some discussion, Mayhew agreed, subject to three conditions—

First, that in addition to his own full share and extra full partner share, Mayhew receive a set-aside estate of 370-acres in what is present day Quaise. Second, that the Wampanoag be dealt with fairly and be paid full value for their land. And third, that Coffin and the other Nantucket investors pay him £30 plus two beaver hats—one for himself and one for his wife. Mayhew knew the Tristram Coffin's son, Tristram, Jr., was a successful hatter, whose wares he had long admired.

Coffin agreed, with two provisions of his own—

First, because Mayhew was to become a Proprietor controlling two full shares, Mayhew should pay the proportional initial price for these shares—and in the future make additional investments as needed, on an equal basis with the others, to purchase additional land rights from the Wampanoag. And second, before signing any final agreement, that Mayhew secure a written document from the Nantucket sachems permitting an English settlement at the west end of the Island. And further, that the signing of this document should be witnessed by Coffin, Thomas Macy, and their associate John Coleman—none of whom, incidentally, had ever visited Nantucket or understood the Wampanoag language.

Agreeing in principle, Mayhew quickly set sail for Nantucket with Macy, Coffin and Coleman. This was in June of 1659. After a tour of the Island, the three new potential investors were excited beyond words about the Island's natural beauty and economic potential. Clearly, all that Mayhew had told them was true. Anxiously, they watched as Mayhew discussed with Nickanoose buying rights to "the plain at the west end of Nantucket." A deed and crude map were drawn up, and Mayhew paid the Wampanoag £12 in wampum at the signing.

Coffin, Macy and Coleman returned home to the Merrimack Valley to report to the others all that had occurred. They spoke with amazement about the Island and the great respect and fondness that the Wampanoag had displayed toward Mayhew.

Within 12 days, Mayhew drew up a bill of sale awarding his Nantucket rights to the Proprietors. All quickly signed and ceremoniously paid him. Then they all celebrated with a festive banquet hosted by Coffin. After dinner, Tristram Coffin, Jr. presented Mayhew with his beaver hats, one of which Mayhew insisted on wearing throughout the rest of the evening.

The original ten "full share" signers were—Tristram Coffin, Thomas Macy, Christopher Hussey, Richard Swain, Thomas Barnard, Peter Coffin (a son of Tristram), Stephen Greenleaf (a son-in-law of Tristram), John Swain, William Pile, and Thomas Mayhew (the seller who also became a "full share" purchaser).

The ten then chose these ten others, who were close to them, as "full share" partners—Tristram Coffin selected his son-in-law, Nathaniel Starbuck. Thomas Macy selected Edward Starbuck (Nathaniel's father who was also the father-in-law of two of Tristram's daughters). Christopher Hussey selected his friend, Robert Pike. Richard Swain selected Thomas Look (father-in-law of Tristram's grandson). Thomas Barnard selected his brother, Robert Barnard. Peter Coffin selected his brother, James Coffin. Steven Greenleaf selected his brother-in-law, Tristram Coffin, Jr. John Swain selected a neighbor, Thomas Coleman. William Pile delegated his partner rights to Thomas Mayhew, who selected his associate, John Smith. And Thomas Mayhew, exercising his own rights, selected his son, Thomas, Jr.—who although missing at sea for nearly two years, was still named by his father in case he should return.

If you've been keeping track of all this, you'll realize that Tristram Coffin and his immediate and extended family owned eight of the original twenty shares—a 40 percent interest! Mayhew effectively controlled 15 percent more. But their combined dominant majority position would inevitably fall to a minority position with the naming of the "half share" men in the years to come.

With twenty "full share" partners, the price paid to Mayhew—£30 and two beaver hats—was indeed nominal, especially considering that Mayhew himself paid £3 of that amount for his own and his missing son's shares. And considering that he also laid out another £12 in wampum to Nickanoose.

But everyone recognized that their real expense would come later in acquiring usage rights to Nantucket from the Wampanoag over the months and years ahead. And make no mistake, their avowed goal was to own and control all of Nantucket as their homeland. This would require hundreds of pounds of additional investment.

Coffin and Macy were men of considerable experience and means. And that's important to realize. Let me tell you a little about their backgrounds.

Coming from landed gentry in England's Devonshire County, Tristram Coffin emigrated to the Massachusetts Bay Colony in 1642 with his wife, five children, mother and sisters when he was 37 years of age— largely to avoid the Civil War in Britain. He became a successful trader up and down the Merrimack River and started buying up land from the Indians. He also owned and operated a very profitable ferry, and with his wife Dionis ran a popular tavern in Newbury. By 1659, his children were grown and had become successful in their own right. For example, his son Peter Coffin became wealthy operating sawmills in Dover, New Hampshire. His son Tristram Coffin, Jr. was a leading hatter and owned a large house in Newbury. Daughter Elizabeth married well to Captain Stephen Greenleaf.

In 1640, Thomas Macy at age 32 and while still single emigrated with his family from Chilmark in Britain's Wiltshire County to become one of the first English settlers of Salisbury. Three years later he married Sarah Hopcott, also from Chilmark, and began a successful career as a self-described "merchant and clothier." Macy became a selectman and later Deputy to the General Court. He owned more than 1,000 acres of land, a fine house, and considerable livestock. He was an experienced weaver and part owner of a sawmill.

Many stories have been told about Macy and his family fleeing Salisbury to Nantucket in an attempt to escape censure for giving shelter to four Quakers who stopped at his house during a violent rainstorm. These legends of Macy's "escape" were derived from John Greenleaf Whittier's poem *"The Exile's Departure,"* published 167 years after the fact in 1826. The truth is that Macy was indeed asked to appear before the Court to answer charges of sheltering four Quakers—charges that carried a maximum fine of £5. Macy did not appear, but sent a written explanation to the court in late August of 1659, just prior to his already planned departure to Nantucket. While this incident did reaffirm Macy's resolve to leave Salisbury, it did not precipitate it. That all the charges against him were dropped is confirmed by the fact that none of Macy's Salisbury property was ever confiscated. In fact, Macy returned to Salisbury in 1664 to sell his home and land at a considerable profit. Whittier's interest in dramatizing the story of Macy's "escape" may in part be explained by the fact that Whittier was a very active and devout Quaker.

My point in telling you this brief bit of background on Coffin and Macy is to give you a better appreciation of their financial and business sophistication. These were not simple homesteaders looking for a new plot of land to farm in an area free of religious persecution. They were men with the vision, the ability, and the resolve to transform Nantucket into their own personal homeland. Or as Mayhew and Macy often expressed it—"an earthly Paradise."

🌾　🌾　🌾

Nickanoose returned to Warren's landing the next morning to meet with Macy, Starbuck and Coleman. Tracing the shape of the Island on the damp sand, through gestures and the few English words he knew, Nickanoose asked them the extent of their planned settlement. Macy indicated that ten more families would join them the following summer and that each would occupy a small "house lot" here on the Island's west end. Their planting would be done in a common area near their home sites. Eventually, they'd like to raise some sheep on the open land, but always making sure that their animals never encroached on the Wampanoag planting areas. In all, the English community would be limited to 25 partners—which they called "Proprietors"—many of whom were of the same family.

At all this, Nickanoose was surprised—although he concealed it. The size of the planned settlement was far smaller than he had expected, and their intended practices far closer to Wampanoag custom than was common to the English on the mainland. He estimated that at most they were talking about fewer than 100 settlers. And their planned house lots were no larger than the plots of about one-third acre then being allocated to each Wampanoag family. Their common use of the land for planting was also according to Wampanoag custom. And a few more sheep would hardly be noticed on an island this large.

In fact, these plans seemed so modest that Nickanoose decided not to show them the more generous lease document he had drawn up. Instead, he simply expressed that he wished them well and that they should call upon him if they needed his help during the coming winter. Then he returned to the southeastern quarter to tell Wanackmamack and the other sachems that the English would not be a problem. After all, how much harm could 100 settlers and a few sheep cause among 3,000 Wampanoag?

In time, our people would know only too well the answer. Because this day marked the beginning of our total displacement.

5

1672 . . . How Tom Never Got His Name

For more than five generations, my family held a position of special trust in Nantucket's Southeast Quarter. Our land was the highest point on the Island's south shore. At 65-feet, it gave us a sweeping view of the beaches to the east, to the south, and to the west. Back in those times, our beaches were still more than a half-mile wide—with the broadest beach stretching out just below our bluff.

My family's task in the sachem was to find and harvest beached whales—and they were abundant throughout much of the year. At first sight of the beached creatures, we'd sound a signal to the rest of the sachem. The duration of the signal would indicate how many extra men would be needed for the harvest, based on the number of whales to be butchered, rendered and cooked. Two whales of 12-foot size could be processed by two or three members of my family in a single day. But often, there were a dozen or more whales to be processed, and this required the assistance of others from the sachem who were assigned to this task.

We possessed two large iron pots that had been brought from the mainland many years before. In these, the blubber was boiled and rendered into oil which was transferred into clay-lined cisterns, for trade with other sachems and for use by our own people throughout the year. The meat was cooked in steam pits in the sand, or salted and dried to pre- serve it for future use. And the bone, when bleached white by the sun, was fashioned into tools—again, for our own use or for trade.

My father was still living when the English came among us in 1659. But during that first winter he died and Wanackmamack called me to the council meeting house at Occawa. I was my father's second son—18 years of age—and my name was then Tomanonackqua.

Wanackmamack said that he had selected me to become the leader of my family and asked if I would vow to carry out all the responsibilities that had been entrusted by the sachem to my family over many, many generations. I expressed concern that my older brother, Imackqua—five years my senior—rightly deserved this honor and would be most upset if he were passed by. Wanackmamack said that it was his decision who to name and that my older brother had proven himself to be too willful and unreliable to be entrusted with this important task. I loved my brother but knew that Wanackmamack was probably right. Imackqua would often run off hunting with his friends, not returning for his assigned watch times, and claiming not to have heard the signal when there was whale harvesting to be done. And when he was there, he'd be argumen- tative and brusque with us all. (As the years progressed and my older brother descended into a life of rebellion and thievery, I often wondered if I might have changed things if I had spoken up for him that day with Wanackmamack. But I didn't, and that failure grieves me still.)

So on that day in the winter of 1660, I became my family's leader. And I gave Wanackmamack my solemn vow that I would forevermore take personal responsibility for the finding and harvesting of all whales in the Southeast Quarter. Wanackmamack then called in our sachem's se- nior men and asked me to repeat that vow three times aloud to each of them. When I had done so, they welcomed me to their circle and invited me to become a member of their council.

Over the twelve years that followed, many changes came to Nan- tucket—often to the material benefit of our people. But each change exacted a permanent cost—the gradual diminution of our identity, our independence, and ultimately our very existence.

Wanackmamack, in his wisdom, could foresee these threats. But as he told us often, he believed we could keep the English fairly well contained in the Island's western half. The Madequecham Valley had always been our historic western border, and we should view it that way again. The important thing was to maintain our dominion over the Southeast Quarter—our true homeland. And we did succeed in doing this for another hundred years. The Southeast Quarter would be the very last place to fall from our control—and even then, that would occur only after the great plague of 1763 had depleted our numbers to just a few.

But I'm getting ahead of my story. Let's concentrate on the year 1672. By then I was 31 years of age and my family had become so productive in the harvesting of whales that we could sell substantial excess quantities of oil each year to the English for their lamps. And it was to talk about this oil that Peter Folger and Captain John Gardner came to see me.

I had known Peter Folger for several years and considered him to be my friend. He was an intelligent, kind, and highly principled man who had come to the Island in 1663 to serve as an interpreter, miller and surveyor. It was from Folger that I had first learned to speak English. Although he was nearly twice my age, he asked me to call him Peter. And he called me Tom—a shortening of my Wampanoag name, Tomanonackqua.

Captain John Gardner was new to Nantucket and I had not yet met him, although I had heard Peter speak approvingly of his skills. Captain Gardner had come to Nantucket to help the Island develop its fishing trade—particularly for cod. But he had a special interest in whale oil too, because of a unique tax provision he had found in New York law. Under this law, Long Island and Nantucket could export their whale oil tax-free if that oil came from "Indian drift whaling." Exported "English oil" would be taxed—exported "Indian oil" would not. If properly exploited, this tax advantage could be translated into both a larger share of the whale oil export market and greater profits.

Captain Gardner proposed that we form an alliance to export all of the oil that my family could produce. The casks would be marked with my name and sign to certify them as containing "Indian whale oil." Captain Gardner would act as the shipping and export agent, and my family would receive a premium price for our exported oil. We would purchase oil for our own domestic needs from the other sachems. And if they had an excess, we could buy that too and mark the casks with our name for the export market.

Peter Folger encouraged me to consider Captain Gardner's proposal seriously, and if I approved of it, to discuss it with Wanackmamack and the other council members. This could bring extra wealth to the sachem, enabling us to do many things for our people.

That very day we met with Wanackmamack. He knew Peter Folger to be a man of honor and accepted his endorsement of Captain Gardner. After some discussion in the full council, the plan was agreed to and the alliance formed.

The following week, Captain Gardner and Peter Folger returned to draw up the final details of our plan. And at that meeting, Captain Gardner raised an issue that would have a lasting impact upon me and the Southeast Quarter. He repeated the great importance of having a special name and mark on our whale oil casks, to certify their Indian origin. But he said we needed to select a new name—because my Wampanoag name, Tomanonackqua, was far too difficult for the English to read or even speak. And that our sachem name, Wanackmamack, was no easier.

Immediately, Peter Folger proposed that this new name be "Tom Never"—combining the English first name that he had given me, with the vow I had made to *never* desert my whaling responsibilities here in the Southeast Quarter. When I smiled and nodded "yes," Captain Gardner grasped my hand and declared, "Henceforth, to the outside world you shall be Tom Never!" And so it was. From 1672 until 1692—when the New York tax law changed—all the casks of oil that we produced for export were marked "Indian Whale Oil rendered pure by Tom Never."

Our whale oil trade flourished, and my new English name was soon commonly applied to all those areas where my family lived and worked. On early maps you'll find Tom Never's Head, Tom Never's Pond, and

Tom Never's Swamp. As you know well, these locations still bear the Tom Never's name today. But sometime in the early 1900s, the apostrophe was dropped. My name was always Tom Never, and never Tom Nevers! Peter Folger deserves that I clarify this point.

Another point worth noting is that whaling is said to be America's first industry. And if that is so, then to my knowledge "Tom Never" was America's first coined brand name. There may be others to claim that honor, but if there are I have not heard of them.

❧   ❧   ❧

Thus far I have said little about the changes occurring in those thirteen years between the first arrival of Thomas Macy, Edward Starbuck and James Coffin in 1659—and the arrival of Captain John Gardner in 1672. Let me do so now.

The first winter passed quietly and without difficulty. So in the early spring of 1660, Edward Starbuck returned to Salisbury with enthusiastic reports. This cleared away the apprehension of the other Proprietors— and several packed up their possessions and gathered supplies for their move to Nantucket. By summer, the main body of 50 or so settlers arrived, with Tristram Coffin at their head. Immediately, plans for house building began. But not a footing was set before Nickanoose returned to secure extra payment and a signed deed.

Tristram Coffin asked that the signing be delayed for a week until Thomas Mayhew and an interpreter could be brought over from Martha's Vineyard. Felix Kuttashamaquet and Peter Folger were chosen by Thomas Mayhew to act as interpreters, and a deed was prepared by Mayhew and Coffin in accordance with what they said was English law.

This deed gave the English rights to all the land from the Island's western end to today's Hummock Pond, and also rights to the northern strip of land running from the head of Hummock Pond to the Monomoy Creek "provided that none of the Indian Inhabitants . . . shall be moved without full satisfaction." It also gave the English rights to mow grass and secure timber and wood "upon any part of the Island within jurisdiction" and also gave the English "free liberty for the feeding of all sorts of cattle on any part of the Island, after Indian harvest is ended until planting time, or until the first of May."

For all these rights, an extra fee of £14 was to be paid. Coffin, Mayhew and Macy signed the deed and both Wanackmamack and Nickanoose added their marks. Peter Folger, Felix Kuttashamaquet and Edward Starbuck signed as witnesses.

The terms of the deed were pretty much in accordance with Wanackmamack's and Nickanoose's original plan. As they saw it, the sachems had not really given away any of their former rights and the English were fairly well contained in the western end of the Island. Grazing rights seemed of little consequence, and they were strictly limited to the non-growing seasons.

One thing that did surprise the sachems was the size of the house-lots set out by the settlers. While Macy had originally talked about lots of less than an acre, they now decided to assign lots of nearly 23 acres. These lots were clustered along and near Cappamet Harbor—which is now called Capaum Pond because it has long since lost its opening to the sea. That site was chosen for its good moorage, protecting hills, and easy access to fresh water.

The Wampanoag watched with great interest and admiration as the English built their homes and outbuildings and began to till the soil. They watched as the settlers fished and hunted birds and small game. They watched as the sheep were shorn, the wool spun into yarn, the yarn woven into cloth, the cloth cut and sewn into warm and supple garments. And throughout, the English welcomed their curiosity and were happy to show them how all this was done.

Even more, the Wampanoag stood in awe of the goods and livestock arriving steadily from the mainland. Iron tools, candles and lamps, food-stuffs and special seeds for planting, fabrics and clothing, furniture, lumber, leather goods, and containers of every description. Plus the animals—the cows, chickens, pigs, sheep, and most impressive of all, the horses.

The sachems knew that all these imported and manufactured goods would tremendously help their people. And the English offered to supply them, even suggesting ways that the Wampanoag could afford to buy them. One way was to barter corn and other produce, shellfish, oil, and feathers. Another way was to work for the settlers, bartering labor time for goods. And a third way was to sell more and more land usage rights to the English. (In the first five years of the English settlement, most of those Wampanoag who were initially living in the "English territory" chose to sell all of their rights to remain there. They received a total of £75—this in addition to the £26 already paid at the outset by the English for that territory.)

New settlers continued to arrive, primarily the "Half-Share Men" and their families. These were men of special skills, trades and/or talents needed to develop and serve the new community. You'll recall that I said the Proprietors made a provision in their original plan to add 10 "Half-Share Men," but that ultimately 14 half-shares were awarded. That did not mean 14 different people. In some cases, more than one half-share was awarded to a single person, based on his special talents—and in another case, an extra half-share was awarded to one of the original Proprietors.

The first Half-Share man to arrive was William Worth, who in 1662 was granted 1½ half-shares to take charge of all the "sea affairs" for the community. He was the only Half-Share man to be granted rights to participate in all future land purchases throughout the Island. (The Half-Share men that followed Worth were limited to share in land purchases in the original territory only—which their contracts called "The First Plantation.")

Next came Peter Folger, who moved to the Island in 1663 and received a half-share to serve as an interpreter, miller and surveyor. Peter's son, Eleazur Folger, also received a half-share to practice the trade of shoemaker. Thomas Macy, already a full-share Proprietor, received an extra half-share in 1664 to provide expanded services as a weaver.

Then came Joseph Coleman as a tradesman, and Samuel Stretor and Nathaniel Holland as tailors. Richard Gardner received 2 half-shares—one for his work as a seaman and the second for his work as a shoemaker. Later, John Bishop was granted 2 half-shares to build a horse mill.

Later, Richard Gardner's eldest son, Joseph, was granted a half-share as a shoemaker. And Nathaniel Wier was granted ½ of a half-share to act as a timbersmith and woodsmith.

Much as we'd recruit someone to come to the Island today to fill a key position in government or the school system, the Proprietors would screen Half-Share men candidates and make them a contractual offer. These offers would vary, depending on the position and to some degree on the negotiating skills of the candidate. But typically, a candidate would be granted a house-lot, rights to share in all current planting, timber and grazing areas, and limited rights to participate in future land purchases. They would, of course, be required to pay their prorated share of the costs to acquire these future land holdings.

Some formula for their ongoing compensation would often be specified, usually a percentage share of the revenues generated by their efforts.

These contracts were conditional on the candidate moving to the Island and taking up residence by a specified date—and remaining on the Island and practicing his trade for a certain specified number of years. If these conditions were not met, the candidate's house-lot and half-share rights reverted to the Proprietors, who could reassign them. One notable example was Richard Smith, who was initially granted a half-share to act as a seaman. But based on his long absences from the Island, his half-share was forfeited.

Full-Share men had no such restrictions. In fact, a number of them never took up residence on Nantucket. They held their shares as an investment, later selling or bequeathing them to others. Remember, the 20 Full-Share men had paid for their shares, made additional cash investments, and taken all the risks of forming a new colony. Half-Share men had been gifted their shares with no cash outlays. Together they all formed a single community, but this distinction between them would eventually ferment a bitter division called The Half-Share Revolt.

The last Half-Share man to be chosen was Captain John Gardner of Salem, who was Richard Gardner's brother. In 1672, Captain Gardner was offered and accepted a half-share to develop the Island's trade of fishing, with special emphasis on offshore cod fishing. A bright, energetic and forceful man with strong leadership abilities, Captain Gardner would have a profound impact on the Island's next quarter century. I'll tell you more about that later.

For now, let's keep concentrating on the first dozen years of the colony—a period when Tristram Coffin reigned benevolently and without challenge as the Island's English patriarch.

From the beginning, Tristram Coffin took steps to see that the Wampanoag were not angered by his people's actions or by the growing number of their sheep and cattle. The colonists set up their own form of local government and encouraged the Wampanoag to do the same. In this way, all complaints and grievances between the two communities could be aired and settled through established channels. The Wampanoag were left to conduct their own Christian services in their own way—in their own churches and without any interference. (The English built no churches on Nantucket, preferring to hold worship services in their own homes.) And the English scrupulously paid for any damage to Wampanoag crops, caused by their sheep and cattle. And in addition—as I mentioned before—the English shared their knowledge of building, planting, fishing, hunting, and the trade crafts with the Wampanoag—selling them whatever tools, clothing, implements and supplies they desired to purchase or barter . . . even doing so on credit.

These actions impressed Wanachmamack and Nickanoose greatly. They respected Tristram Coffin as a great English Sachem. And they soon developed trusting relationships with Edward Starbuck and Peter Folger. Tutored as he was by Peter Folger, Edward Starbuck was the first of the original Proprietors to learn Algonquian and was a man of special vitality and courage. These qualities the Wampanoag admired. But it was Peter Folger, more than any other, who should be credited with the successful relations between the settlers and the Wampanoag.

In 1635, Peter Folger emigrated from County Norfolk, England at age 20. Sailing aboard the ship Abigail, he met and fell in love with a young servant girl, Mary Morrill, who was indentured to a well-known preacher named Hugh Peters. For the next nine years, Peter Folger worked in Dedham and Watertown as a schoolmaster and at other trades to save the £20 necessary to free Mary from her indenture. They married and soon accepted Thomas Mayhew's invitation to join him in settling

Martha's Vineyard. There he learned the Algonquian dialect of the Massachusett language and became known as "The English schoolmaster who teacheth the Indians and instructs them in the Lord's Day." Throughout all his time on Martha's Vineyard, Peter Folger had close ties to both Thomas Mayhew and his son Thomas, Jr.—assisting them often and making several trips with them to Nantucket.

Briefly, Folger moved his family to Portsmith, Rhode Island. But when in 1663, at age 48, he and his son Eleazur were each offered a half-share to settle in Nantucket, they accepted the offer enthusiastically. Nantucket was to be Peter Folger's home for the next 27 years.

The Folgers had two sons and seven daughters—the youngest of whom was born on Nantucket on August 15th, 1669. She was named Abiah and it was she who would become the mother of the American patriot—Benjamin Franklin.

From the moment of his arrival in 1663, Peter Folger was viewed as the scholar of the Island and a leading religious figure. While he received his half-share to be an interpreter, miller and surveyor—he did far, far more. He acted as the chief go-between in assuring peaceful relations with the Wampanoag—anticipating and heading-off problems and encouraging productive co-operation. He taught English to the Wampanoag and Algonquian to the English. And he baptized many Praying Indians and instructed them in the Word of God. In their eyes, Peter Folger was a worthy successor to the universally admired Thomas Mayhew.

❧ ❧ ❧

Perhaps the most pivotal and certainly the most traumatic event of this whole period occurred in October 1665, just six years after the English arrival.

On a clear moonlit night from my watching post on the bluff now called Tom Never's Head, I saw six dark shapes moving quickly through the surf. At first, I thought it a pod of whales about to beach themselves. But as they came closer, I recognized them as war canoes.

As they came silently ashore, I could count over 40 men—all with weapons. They lifted and carried their canoes to a spot almost directly below my perch before they spoke for the first time. It was only then that I realized this was King Philip, supreme sachem of the Wampanoag, come here with his warriors to kill John Gibbs.

King Philip was the second son of Massasoit—the supreme sachem who in 1622 had manipulated Miles Standish into slaughtering two rival sachems in order to consolidate his power. You'll recall that this act helped trigger panic among the Wampanoag people—prompting many to abandon their homes and plantings to flee into the swamps where they succumbed to disease and starvation.

After Massasoit's death in 1660, his two eldest sons—Wamsutta and Metacom—changed their names to Alexander and Philip, conveying to the English through their choice of names that they should henceforth be viewed as the current and future kings of their people. Alexander was the first to succeed his father as supreme sachem, but he had little time to make an impact. By 1662 he was dead, some say murdered by the English. And Philip succeeded him, adopting the name—King Philip—along with all the resplendent clothing and trappings that he felt his powerful new station warranted.

From his headquarters in Mount Hope—near Bristol, Rhode Island—King Philip embarked on a grand tour of all the mainland sachems in the Wampanoag Confederation to consolidate his "kingdom" and to let the English know in no uncertain terms that he was the Indian leader to be reckoned with. But thusfar he had bypassed Nantucket—perhaps because of its remoteness, but more likely because of the stories he had heard about the close relations here between the Wampanoag and the English.

Then in 1665, two incidents occurred that riveted King Philip's attention on this Island.

In January, during a violent winter storm, a bark from Martha's Vineyard washed up on Coatue. Its shipwrecked passengers included two English seamen and three Wampanoag—one of whom was Joel Hiacoomes, the Harvard-educated son of the Praying Indian missionary who had assisted Thomas Mayhew, Jr. in his godly work on Nantucket. In an attempt to pillage the bark's cargo, three men from Sachem Nickanoose set-upon and killed all five of the bark's stranded passengers.

As news of the murders of two white men by Indians spread across New England, a call for reprisals swelled among the English population. King Philip knew that it was an incident just as this that had ignited the Pequot War nearly 30 years before, so he felt compelled to seize the initiative if he was to maintain his position of power and influence. King Philip ordered Nickanoose to appear before him at Mount Hope for public chastisement. Then he ordered Nickanoose to have the murderers publicly hanged upon his return to Nantucket.

In August of that same year, word reached King Philip that a young Nantucket Wampanoag also studying at Harvard College had spoken out against him—saying that while the hangings were in truth justified, King Philip had ordered them solely to further his own ambitions—making him nearly as treacherous as his father, Massasoit. This young Wampanoag's name was Assassamough, but he was better known by his English name, John Gibbs. His home was here in the Sachem Wanackmamack.

King Philip decided that John Gibbs must be silenced, and he seized upon an old tribal law to justify his killing. Among the Algonquian, it had long been considered taboo to speak the name of the dead, especially the name of a dead Sachem. King Philip declared that by uttering the name "Massasoit," John Gibbs had signed his own death warrant. And now that John Gibbs had returned from Cambridge to Sachem Wanackmamack, the time had come for King Philip to deliver it.

As King Philip and his men crept eastward along the beach to reach the concealing trees of the wetland now called Tom Never's Swamp, where they planned to hide until daybreak, I slipped away from my perch and ran as hard as I could to Wanackmamack's wetu in Occawa village. The question I had then, and now, is why King Philip himself had personally come to Nantucket with his war party. He could have had John Gibbs killed before his return from Cambridge to Nantucket—or simply sent his warriors here to do his bidding. I suspected that he had more in mind for us than simply silencing John Gibbs. And I expressed that thought to Wanackmamack.

Without hesitation, Wanackmamack issued his orders. John Gibbs was to be awakened and sent to hide until being summoned, in a hut near the pond that now bears his name—Gibbs Pond. A runner was sent to Tristram Coffin and Peter Folger to tell them of King Philip's intentions. They, along with a full complement of the English, were asked to join Wanackmamack, Nickanoose and all their council members atop Altar Rock by sunrise. Wanackmamack knew that Coffin and Folger would comply, because Tristram Coffin had personally sponsored John Gibbs' enrollment at Harvard College. And because Peter Folger, as Gibbs' tutor and mentor, regarded the youth so highly that he had given him as his surname the name of Folger's own maternal grandfather—Gibbs.

Shortly after daybreak, King Philip and his party entered Occawa and were told that John Gibbs could be found with Wanackmamack at Altar Rock in the middle moors. As they neared the base of this high prominence, they were much surprised to see such a large assemblage of armed English and Wampanoag atop it—here deep in the Island's interior, at such an early hour of the morning. Before King Philip could ascend the hill, Wanackmamack greeted him loudly and asked why they were being honored with his presence. King Philip snarled out that he had come to put John Gibbs to death for speaking the name of his father.

In a voice strong and steady, Edward Starbuck declared, "John Gibbs is son to us all and our grief would be inconsolable if he were to die." Wanackmamack then suggested that King Philip, "In his mercy and as a sign of compassion for those assembled . . . consider granting John Gibbs a pardon for his great offense." Wanackmamack then put forth the idea that the people of this Island give King Philip silver to atone for Gibbs' error—silver that could be used "to memorialize the memory of King Philip's great and illustrious father."

Then Wanackmamack asked that John Gibbs be brought forth to personally petition for King Philip forgiveness. Surrounded by a phalanx of 12 of the sachem's tallest and most powerful men, John Gibbs emerged from the line of trees near the pond and mounted Altar Rock from the side. There he bowed, and then knelt. Striking his breast three times, he stated his unworthiness and asked for King Philip's pardon.

King Philip stood silently for several minutes there at the base of the hill, with all eyes looking down upon him. The only sounds were those of the crows sweeping hither and yon in the thickets.

Though we'll never know for certain, I believe that the real reason King Philip had come to Nantucket was to use the John Gibbs incident as a test of loyalty. To use it as a means of assessing how fully he could count on the Island's Wampanoag population to obey him in future confrontations with the English. If that was his purpose, the solidarity he saw that day would have given him his answer—"none at all!"

Without revealing any signs of his true emotions, King Philip nodded "yes" and gestured for John Gibbs to leave his presence. Then he sent forth one of his warriors to retrieve from Edward Starbuck the box of silver coins being offered in atonement.

When he counted the number of coins, King Philip stomped the ground and called this an insult—£11 was insufficient. Starbuck said that this was all the silver they possessed, everything else being tied up in crops and animals. This was not true and King Philip suspected it. But the English all repeated, one after the other, that £11 represented the Island's total cash resources. That Wanackmamack and the other Sachems offered nothing was a point not lost on King Philip. (In actuality, Wanackmamack had pledged added lands to the English that very morning, in exchange for the £11 being paid up to King Philip. As such, John Gibbs was being ransomed by his own people.)

After some period of snorting and glowering, King Philip turned on his heel and stomped off toward Occawa. There he traced a swampy stream to the southern shoreline, to retrieve his canoes and return home in silence. From that day on, the swampy stream he followed has been known as "Philip's Run." (The double meaning of the "Philip's Run" name was most intentional.) It connects the cranberry bogs to Tom Never's Pond and it is used to drain the flooded bog each October—although today it flows beneath the Milestone Road through a large conduit pipe.

King Philip never returned to Nantucket and the Island completely escaped the devastation of King Philip's War, which was to rage on the mainland ten years later. Escaping that bloody war was a direct result of our solidarity on that momentous day in 1665 when King Philip came to kill John Gibbs. That day also stood as a powerful symbol to us all—of the bond of common dependence existing between the Wampanoag and the English of Nantucket. We were becoming one people.

❀   ❀   ❀

But lurking behind all this apparent harmony was the relentless appetite of the English animals—especially their sheep. As their numbers grew, they began to strip bare more and more of the land. This prompted the Proprietors to place special restrictions on the number of animals that could be owned—beginning with horses, which required the most forage. By reducing the number of horses, it was hoped that more grazing land would be available for sheep

In June of 1667, those men without property rights were ordered to remove all their horses from the Island. Settlers with property rights were restricted to one horse per household. And all further sales of horses to the Indians on the Island were prohibited.

In 1668, further restrictions were introduced. For each "full-share" owned, a property-owner could keep no more than 40 sheep, 3 cows and one horse—or any combination of them based on an agreed-to formula—with each cow considered the equivalent of 8 sheep, and each horse the equivalent of 16 sheep. Applying this formula, a "full-share" property-owner could own as many as 80 sheep, if he got rid of his horses and cows. (If the holders of all 27 shares chose to keep the specified mix of sheep, cows and horses, the Island would then have a maximum population of 1,080 sheep, 81 cows and 27 horses. But if they all chose to keep only sheep, there would then be a maximum of 2,160 sheep Island-wide.) Of course, all of these calculations were based on the amount of land already purchased from the Island's sachems. Double the amount of land, and a "full-share" property-owner could own twice as many animals!

To enforce these so-called "stinting rights," the animals of each shareholder were "earmarked" and counted at least annually by the Proprietors. Animals in excess of the allotted number were herded into a pen and confiscated.

These new rules caused some grumbling among the property-owners and prompted many lively discussions within families about the need to expand the common land holdings eastward. That would, of course, eventually happen—raising the Island's sheep population to over 15,000. But that overwhelming animal density would not be reached for another 100 years. For the present, Tristram Coffin's stinting rights plan seemed to work—keeping the animals from becoming a major problem in maintaining good relations with the Wampanoag.

But in spite of all good intentions, the sheep would keep breeding and keep eating.

❊   ❊   ❊

6

1700 . . . Sheep, Horses & Whales

When the first eleven English settlers came ashore in Nantucket in 1659, they found 3,000 Wampanoag. By the time that Captain John Gardner arrived in 1672, our native population had halved to just over 1,500—and the English population had grown to over 100. By 1700, the Wampanoag population had almost halved again to fewer than 800, while the English now numbered more than 300. Our people were leaving even faster than the English were coming. They were not forced out; rather they chose to depart as the Island changed in ways not to their liking.

As one scans the history of civilization, it's easy to conclude that the displacement of one group by another occurs most often by violence or force. Yet a closer reading of history teaches us that these tales of war and invasion are the colorful exceptions. Most displacements occur far more slowly, often with the willing compliance of those who are displaced. The newcomers are embraced—or at the very least tolerated—for the short-term benefits that they bring, with a naïve belief that they can be kept in check. But nature shows us that once given a foothold, an invasive species will almost always overwhelm the incumbent. That is the very nature of living things, and in my experience it is just as true for human cultures and societies as it is for animals and plants. And that also is the story of Nantucket—past, present and future.

Even though the Wampanoag would remain on Nantucket for another 150 years, by 1700 we were effectively displaced. We had welcomed the English somewhat reluctantly, accommodated them, and gradually took on many of their ways. But we were not English, so we never fully understood what drove them—the accumulation of wealth for their families. Wealth in the form of animals, which translated directly into the accumulation of all our land.

Tristram Coffin and the first settlers also thought that they could make Nantucket their permanent ancestral home—shaped in their own image and sealed-off from change by outsiders. But through their own doing they brought in others who would effectively displace them—most notably, the group of Half-Share men led by Captain John Gardner. This pattern of gradual displacement has been repeated again and again over the centuries as each new wave of settlers have come to our shores. Just as the sea takes away some of our beaches and adds to others, Nantucket's shape as a community is forever changing. And there's no human power that will stop it. This is not a complaint; it's a sad realization that you'll understand more fully when you hear the rest of my story.

🜨   🜨   🜨

As I described to you earlier, the Proprietors only owned land at the western end of the Island. And this land was held in "common and undivided shares." With the exception of their personal home-sites and the promised Mayhew parcel at Quaise, no private ownership was permitted. Even their farming was conducted in common plots.

Each year, the Proprietors would select a sizeable tract and fence it off for farming. Each shareholder would then be assigned a section for planting. After the harvest, the common plot would be abandoned and a new tract would be selected for the following season. There was no attempt to rotate crops or enrich the soil—save for the practice of "sheep shitting." At the start of a new season, sheep would be herded into the fenced plot and the English would terrify them with loud noises and by waving firebrands throughout the night. By the next morning, the planting area would be strewn with sheep droppings. The sheep were then released and the freshly fertilized soil turned for planting.

With farming practices of this type, it's little wonder that over the years the once-fertile Nantucket soil would yield fewer and fewer bushels of crops per acre. Certainly, proper planting techniques were known by the Proprietors. But they chose not to follow them because their focus was on sheep farming as the source of wealth for their families. They had little interest in agriculture as a business and, in fact, thought it counterproductive to use valuable grazing land for farming. Beyond that, with stinting rights limiting the sheep population to one sheep per 1.5-acres of land in "common and undivided ownership," they obsessed over the fact that future wealth absolutely demanded that they increase their land holdings to include the eastern end of the Island.

To that end, the Island's English government—with Tristram Coffin as its chief magistrate—instituted a number of new regulations shortly after that time in 1672 when I first entered into my partnership with Captain Gardner to brand and sell my whale oil for export. All were designed to pave the way to give the English more land for sheep grazing.

The Proprietors' desire to expand their sheep holdings persuaded them to put further restrictions on the ownership of horses. Remember that under the Island's stinting rights regulations, a horse was considered to be the equivalent of 16 sheep. Therefore, for every horse that could be eliminated, 16 extra sheep could be added. This made the horses owned by the Wampanoag an irresistible target.

Over the years, the sachems had purchased a number of horses from the English. But now they were being told that they no longer had a right to graze them, even on their own land. The justification was that in the original deeds, the sachems had sold to the English all rights to animal fodder anywhere on the Island. Under the new regulations, the sachems were given two choices—either sell off their horses, or let them starve. As you might expect, the sachems objected vehemently. And when they did, an attempt was made to impound their horses and fine them if they resisted. Also, a stiff fine was levied on any Englishman attempting to sell additional horses to the Indians.

After a tense standoff, a compromise was reached. The sachems were allowed to "purchase" the rights to own up to 87 "horse commons" of land in their own territory, if they deeded over an equivalent amount of land to the Proprietors. Combined, this added about 2,000 acres to the English holdings. This maneuver also effectively froze and then reduced the number of horses owned by the Wampanoag. Eventually, the English repurchased 64 of the sachems' horse commons for £423, adding another 1,500 acres to the Proprietors' holdings.

Other regulations were instituted to stem the tide of Wampanoag departures and to keep those remaining financially dependent on the Nantucket English community. One regulation forbade all off-Island merchants from conducting "any trade or traffic with any Indian or Indians anywhere on the Island without first obtaining the permission of the Island's general court." This effectively meant that only resident Nantucket English traders were allowed to trade goods with the Island's Indians, giving these traders the power to set prices for all goods sold *and* bought. And a system of credit and debt-servitude was instituted to enlarge the Wampanoag's dependence.

Beyond selling some grain for local Island use, the Indians traded mainly in fish and feathers—which the English then sold into the export market. In return, the Indians purchased shoes, coats, woolen cloth, fishhooks, lines, powder, shot and plowshares—mostly on credit. As an Indian's credit debt grew, he tried to resolve it by increasing his output of fish and feathers. But as he fell behind, he was required to work off his debt through a system of debt-servitude, supervised by the court. Following the example of the General Court on Martha's Vineyard, it also became common practice on Nantucket to sell a debtor's obligation—or to pass it on to one's heirs as "owned property." While not strictly speaking slavery—as practiced widely on the mainland—this form of enforced servitude gave the English on Nantucket a pool of cheap labor and acted as a powerful incentive in persuading the Indians to sell their remaining land rights in order to buy their freedom.

During this time, the English began selling rum and hard cider to the Indians, which accelerated their accumulation of debt. While frowned upon by Tristram Coffin as "a risky business," little was done to effectively stop this practice—except to outlaw the sale of liquor to the Indians by off-Islanders.

Much has been written about the Indian's weakness for liquor. It's true, we are very susceptible to alcohol addiction. But it should also be noted that part of the attraction is that like the pokeweed pipe, liquor brings forth dreamsleep visions—visions considered to carry insights from our ancestors and gods. With liquor, our people could achieve that mystical experience as frequently as they wished—whereas smoking of the pokeweed pipe was reserved only for important times and was limited largely to the senior men of the sachem.

The Island Court dealt even more firmly with what today we'd call petty theft. Conviction carried heavy fines, well beyond the means of most offenders. If unable to pay, they were sentenced to long periods of servitude to the injured party. For example, when Alewife was found guilty of stealing three pails of beer, one gallon of molasses, and two gallons of rum from Nathaniel Starbuck and Peter Coffin, he was sentenced to become their servant for a period of six years. When Moab was convicted of stealing two sheep, he was condemned to serve John Macy for three years. When an Indian from our sachem confessed to stealing eighteen sticks of whalebone from Thomas Macy, he was sentenced to serve Macy for seven years. Sentences of this type were not limited to men. Damaris, an Indian girl accused of "stealing sundry goods" valued at less than £5, was condemned to return the goods, pay £10, be whipped ten stripes, and to serve John Gardner for four years.

Any servant caught trying to run away from his master was whipped and then returned to servitude, often with an added fine and an extended sentence. Chronic offenders were at times branded on the forehead or hands. And the Island was effectively sealed off from escape through a regulation stating, "If any person English or Indian shall at any time carry in any vessel any Indian servant . . . off the Island without orders from his master, he shall be fined twenty shillings." While all this may sound terribly cruel or harsh, I should point out that these measures were considered quite fair and just by the English—in contrast to the practices then being carried out elsewhere throughout New England. But do recognize that since most of the English settlers on Nantucket were related by birth or marriage, justice in those days was more than a little swift and biased in favor of the plaintiff.

These practices provided a ready source of cost-free labor—but more importantly, they contributed to the acquisition of more land for sheep by the English. A convicted Indian's sachem or family could choose to pay the fine to gain his or her freedom. Or they could earn the money to do so by deeding more of their land to the Proprietors.

In all this I was fortunate. With income from my whale oil partnership with Captain John Gardner, I was in a position to purchase on several occasions the freedom of my older brother Imackqua. You'll recall that I said he had fallen into a life of rebellion and thievery after Wanackmamack had named me the leader of my family. This worsened considerably after I formed my partnership with Captain Gardner. And as if to embarrass and mock me, my brother adopted the name Jack Never.

Again and again Jack was brought before the court and I paid his fines. On one occasion, he and an Indian named Will Cowkeeper (so named because his job was to drive the cows to and from town for milking) were convicted of "breaking into a warehouse of Nathaniel Starbuck and carrying away several goods." Jack Never and Will Cowkeeper were each fined nine bushels of Indian corn and twenty-two shillings and six pence. I paid their fines to preclude Nathaniel Starbuck claiming them both for servitude.

Though I had many heated discussions with my brother in an attempt to reform him, Jack Never remained a persistent thief and was frequently called before the court. Finally, I warned him that I would no longer pay his fines. If he stole again he would have to face the full consequences of his actions.

That very night—it was May 23rd in the year 1677—Jack broke into the house of my partner, Captain John Gardner, to show his contempt toward me. He was seen leaving the house and was captured almost immediately. The court declared Jack Never to be, "an incorrigible Indian thief who, not having the fear of God before his eyes but instigated by the Devil, did break into Captain John Gardner's house in the middle of the night and took out of Mr. Gardner's pocket by the bedside five shillings and also opened a case and carried away a bottle with about a pint of liquor in it." He was sentenced to be whipped twenty stripes upon his naked body, and then fined £6. If the fine was not paid, he was to be turned over to Captain Gardner for five years of servitude.

With the help of several of his rough friends, Jack Never broke out of the cell where he was being held and fled into the night fog. For several days, men searched for him all across the Island, particularly here in the Southeast Quarter. There were reports of his sighting, but he was never found. Eventually, it was believed that he had somehow escaped to the mainland. I never saw or heard from my brother again.

The English Court, while quite active, did not wish to become involved with disputes *between* the Wampanoag. We Indians were encouraged to establish our own courts to punish crimes and determine penalties. And in truth, the penalties in our courts were just as harsh as those meted out by the English. So I must freely admit, the sentences placed on my brother were both fair and just.

There were of course exceptions, times when the English Court claimed jurisdiction over Indian affairs. One such case was the May 14th 1704 murder in Madequecham of a Wampanoag squaw named Margerett. Witnesses claimed the Margerett's husband Sabo had threatened several times to kill her for keeping company with an Indian man named John.

When Margerett's badly beaten body was discovered in Sabo's wigwam, both the Indian and English authorities were notified. Because of the seriousness of the crime, the English Court was given jurisdiction. In a one day hearing and trial, eight witnesses were called—revealing an incriminating pattern of behavior on the part of Sabo. In fact, both Sabo and Margerett had earlier appealed to the Indian Court—he claiming that Margerett had betrayed him with John, and she claiming that he had several times threatened her life. A succession of witnesses testified that they had heard Sabo's threats and confirmed his deep jealousy. One witness, Edward Coffin, testified that he had seen Sabo attempting to bury two paddles and a hatchet near Long Pond, on the day following the murder. When asked what he was doing, Sabo ran off toward Madaket Harbor. Others reported seeing Sabo on Tuckernuck and Muskeget Islands, a few days later. An arrest warrant was issued and Mark Indian Constable took Sabo into custody near Capaum Harbor.

On July 14th 1704, a Grand Jury of 14 English and 4 Indians indicted Sabo for murder. When asked how he pled, Sabo said "not guilty." And a trial jury of 12 English men was immediately convened. They found Sabo guilty and sentenced him to death by hanging, a sentence which was carried out that very same day.

🦋   🦋   🦋

As I mentioned earlier, Captain John Gardner was asked to come to Nantucket to develop a cod fishery. For many years, the Indians and the English had fished for cod from small boats off the eastern end of the Island—near Sesachacha and Siasconset. The Proprietors felt that a more organized effort using larger boats could increase yields for export significantly. And Captain Gardner was offered a Half-Share to spearhead this effort.

But as I also told you, Captain Gardner's interest soon turned to whales. Shortly after his arrival, a large gray whale swam into the Great Harbor and thrashed about for several days as the English debated how to capture and kill it. Captain Gardner, who had built his house near the Great Harbor, commissioned a blacksmith to forge points for several long lances to use in spearing the whale. He took a small fishing hook, bent it straight, and gave it to the blacksmith as a model for what he wanted forged. He asked for "a hook that can be lashed to a thick wooden lance and thrown . . . with weight great enough and a point sharp enough to pierce the beast's skin . . . and with barbs broad enough so that the hook wont pull back out."

Gardner's plan was to sail out into the harbor in his boat and tack to a position close enough to plunge lances into the whale's body. Thick wooden beams tied to the lances' lines would act as floats, tethering the whale and preventing its escape. It could then be killed by firing a shot through its eye and into its brain. Using the lines still fastened to the lances, the dead whale could then be pulled up onto the beach for slaughter.

The attempt proved a failure. Captain Gardner could not maneuver his boat close enough to pull within spearing range of the whale. Two hurls missed entirely, and a third simply glanced of the beast's back. Before further attempts could be made, the whale turned tail and swam out of the harbor—circling once as if to scoff at the audacity of its tiny, would be, hunters.

From this experience, Gardner concluded that several oar-powered boats would be needed to maneuver close enough to surround a whale and spear it from three or four sides. With refinement, the lances could be effective, but practice would be needed to perfect a man's spearing skill. To this end, several more lances were commissioned and competitions were held, with all invited to participate. "Harpoon" was the name we used for these lances and for the competition itself—derived in part from the Wampanoag name for whale, which was "pawana." But it would be more than a year until the men got to prove out their new skills at sea. (Some books say that the word "harpoon" comes from the old Basque word "arpoi," which means to grasp or to hold. They say that this became the Spanish word "arpon," which led to the English word "harpoon." That's wrong. Harpoon is a word that was first coined here!)

That first encounter with a whale in the Great Harbor prompted Captain Gardner to meet with some whale oil merchants during his next visit to New York. From them he learned the potential profits that whale oil could bring, and that oil from Indian drift whaling could be exported tax-free—and that led directly to his partnership with me.

Initially, we harvested only drift whales. Then using lightweight 20-foot boats built for and owned by Captain Gardner, we harpooned small whales as they were feeding off-shore. Since they were towed in for harvesting on the beach, they could be classified as drift whales. This added considerably to our production. Each boat had a five-man crew, with an English harpooner and four Indian oarsmen from the Sachem Wanackmamack. To his great credit, Captain Gardner gave all who participated an opportunity to share in the profits. Depending on the whale's size and the current export market, a value was placed on each whale. As the boat owner, Captain Gardner received three shares, the harpooner received two, each of the boatmen received one, and I received one—this in addition to the profits my family earned for harvesting the whales and rendering them into oil. In just a few weeks of successful off-shore whaling, even a single-share boatman could earn more than a full-years worth of wages from working ashore. This is why the people from the Sachem Wanackmamack who were involved in the whaling trade prospered, while those in other parts of the Island were far less fortunate. And this explains why the Southeast Quarter remained ours until long after the rest of the Island had been sold to the English.

Our success on the beaches of the Southeast Quarter drew the attention of Tristram Coffin and others in the English community; and they too decided to enter into the whaling trade. They signed an agreement with James Lopar to move from Long Island to Nantucket "to carry on a design of whale catching on the Island"—offering him a one-third share of the proceeds, ten acres of land, and rights in the commonage to graze three cows, twenty sheep, and one horse. They also offered land and annual grazing rights to John Savage to set up a cooperage on the Island. After a brief stay on Nantucket, Lopar decided to return home. But not before advising the Proprietors how and where to set up whaling stations along the south and east shores.

The Proprietors at that time owned the south shore from Smith Point to Hummock Pond, but not beyond that point. So they undertook an effort to buy up strips of beachfront land to the east, at places considered by Lopar to be key spots for whale sightings. The Proprietors offered a fair price and the sachems agreed, but only after they were assured that their people would be hired on at full shares to man the whaling boats.

In little more than a year, whaling stations were established near Hummock Pond, at Madequecham, at Siasconset and Sankaty Head, and at Smith's Point. At each location, lookout masts were erected and small huts were built—with each hut large enough to sleep the full crew of a single whale boat. Each of these five whaling stations was manned nearly year-round—and was made self sufficient with its own tryworks (to boil out the blubber) and clay-lined oil collection and storage cisterns. In contrast to our system at Tom Never's Head, six man crews were used. The boat owner received half the proceeds and the other half was divided into eight shares—with two shares each for the helmsman and the harpooner, and one each to the four oarsmen. If you're good at math, you'll see that at Tom Never's Head, our harpooners and oarsmen received 60 percent more than their counterparts at the stations owned by the Proprietors. That's why we remained independent. Still, with hard work, we could all prosper. And increasingly, the entire Island turned its energies to whaling.

🦋 🦋 🦋

With a new source of income from whale oil exports, the Proprietors mapped out a plan to acquire more common land for sheep farming. But these plans excluded Captain Gardner and the other Half-Share men. The Full-Share Proprietors insisted that the Half-Share men could participate only in the common lands that existed before their coming. All new lands would be owned by the original Full-Share Proprietors only.

This infuriated Captain Gardner and all the other "newcomers." And it brought to a head a bitter conflict that had been brewing between Tristram Coffin and John Gardner since Gardner first arrived on the Island. Called the "Half-Share Revolt," this conflict raged for more than five years—splitting the English community into two hostile factions, until the aging Tristram Coffin finally conceded.

It would take hours to tell you all the ins-and-outs of the Half-Share Revolt. But these few highlights will give you some feel for its bitterness—

Up until 1672, The Full-Share men had the majority vote at town meetings. But that changed soon after Captain Gardner arrived, as the newcomers eligible to vote outnumbered the original settlers. Tristram Coffin tried to prolong his control by exercising a proxy vote for those original shareholders who lived off-Island—most notably his son, his son-in-law, Thomas Mayhew and others. This tactic mobilized the newcomers to elect John Gardner as a selectman and his brother Richard as a delegate to New York. In addition, the town then appointed both of them to go to New York to confer with Governor Lovelace.

The Gardners returned with four surprising documents signed by the Governor. In one, Richard Gardner was named Chief Magistrate and Captain John Gardner was appointed Chief Military Officer. In another, they had received a grant from the Governor allowing them to purchase land directly from the Indians. And in the third, they had the makings of a complete reversal of the Full-Share men's exclusive claim on all future purchases from the Indians. In this document, Governor Lovelace declared, "All ancient and obsolete deeds, grants, writings or conveyances of land upon said Island shall be esteemed of no force and validity. But the claim or interest shall bear this date (1673) from first divulging of the patent granted to the inhabitants by his Royal Highness . . . but not before the date thereof." This meant that all Half-Share grantees were to be included in the proprietary—with full rights to share in all future land purchases—notwithstanding any past agreements or the votes of any off-Island Proprietors. And in the fourth document, the Gardners had secured Governor Lovelace's seal on papers that officially incorporated the Nantucket settlement as the town of "Sherburne"—not coincidentally the same name as the Gardner's ancestral village in England.

The Coffin forces were outraged. But they could do little because the majority at the town meeting supported the Gardner' initiatives. Peter Folger was appointed clerk of the Island's General Court and all documents passed into his possession.

Thwarted at the Island level, the Coffin group appealed to the newly appointed New York Governor, Edmund Andros. (Lovelace had fled from New York just before it was overrun by the Dutch. When the English retook the city, Andros was named as the new Governor.) The Gardner group persuaded Andros to issue a document declaring that the original rights and privileges of the Proprietors should "be preserved unto them." It also gave them the power "to call to account and punish according to law all such persons as have been ring leaders or capital offenders or transgressors against the established government." But since the Gardners and their supporters claimed that they were in fact the "established government," they refused to take any action. The Coffin group again appealed to Governor Andros and the entire New York Council to settle the matter, but the colonial government in New York had far bigger concerns. King Philip's War had just broken out on the mainland. (I'll tell you more about that bloody war in a minute.) However, Andros did appoint Nantucket's first settler, Thomas Macy—who was a Gardner ally—as Chief Magistrate.

As the war progressed on the mainland, more and more of the original Full-Share men moved to the Island. Together again, they persuaded Macy to switch sides and join their cause. Once more the Coffin group had the majority and voted in their own slate of town officials. Peter Folger was ordered to turn over to them all the original deeds and town documents. But suspecting that the Coffin group intended to alter them, Folger refused and he was promptly imprisoned. They then stripped the Gardners of most of their authority and tried to convict them for defying the courts.

At this point, Captain Gardner and Peter Folger played their trump card—their friendship with the Wampanoag, who still outnumbered the English nearly five-to-one. Captain Gardner came to a gathering of all the sachems at Sachem Wanackmamack and asked for their support. They were all well aware of the split among the English and they considered Peter Folger's imprisonment totally unfair. Also, they had little respect for the newly-appointed town officials, who were largely the sons of the original Proprietors and fairly new to the Island. When Captain Gardner told them of the new regulations being planned by the magistrates—and told them of his suspicion that the magistrates planned to forge new deeds to further encroach upon Indian rights—they pledged to Gardner that they would sign no further agreements with town officials until Folger was freed and until a rightful government was reinstated. Their high regard for Tristram Coffin had ended.

The Coffin faction grew increasingly nervous as the Wampanoag publicly displayed their obvious allegiance to Gardner. While there was as yet no violent insurrection or even one minor disturbance, visions of the bloody Indian war raging on the mainland gave many in the Coffin faction sleepless nights that began to weaken their resolve. The two exceptions were Tristram Coffin and Thomas Mayhew, who voted to press on—even ignoring new orders from the Governor and Council in New York instructing them to suspend all sentences against both Gardner and Folger.

As Coffin and Mayhew grew even more vindictive, they began to lose their supporters. Peter Folger was freed after 17-months in prison. He still resolutely refused to surrender the deeds and town documents, as an assurance that they not be altered by those in power or coming into power. In fact, these original papers were never found, although historians to this day have searched widely across the Island. To prevent their discovery and capture, they had been taken to New York by Captain Gardner and entrusted to a council member there, who eventually transferred them—one by one, as separate documents—into the government storage vaults in Albany. Over the years, Folger also placed copies of all these documents into the Nantucket town records. They have not been lost; they were concealed in plain sight as individual documents.

Finally in June of 1678—more than five years after it all began—the majority of Full-Share men conceded that all Half-Share grants "shall not be confined to the first township . . . but shall, according to proportion, extend throughout the whole Island." They declared that all Half-Share holders were to be "partners with ourselves." John Gardner was elected as a selectman and within two years became Nantucket's Chief Magistrate. Two years later, new "winter feed" deeds were signed with the Indians—providing full proportional benefits to both Full-Share and Half-Share men. In these new deeds, the Wampanoag retained grazing rights to keep a prescribed number of cattle, horses and sheep. This set the stage for future land sales that would follow in the new century.

Old bitterness began to fade as a new generation came to leadership. By 1683, seven of the original settlers had died. Both Tristram Coffin and Thomas Mayhew died in 1681—Coffin at age 76 and Mayhew well into his 80s. Wanackmamack died in 1678 at age 84. Nickanoose died in 1682 at age 47. Peter Folger died in 1690 at age 75. Thomas Macy survived until 1701, when he died at age 93. Captain John Gardner outlived them all, dying in 1706 at age 82.

Intermarriages also healed old wounds. Perhaps the best remembered here on Nantucket was the 1686 marriage of Captain Gardner's daughter Mary to Tristram Coffin's grandson Jethro. She was 16 and he was 23. And their father's built for them one of the finest houses on the Island. It still stands today on Sunset Hill and it is called the "Oldest House."

❧　❧　❧

Few people today know anything of King Philip's War, but it was one of the most devastating in New England's history. All of the New England colonies were drawn into a desperate fight for their very survival. And before it was over, forty of New England's ninety towns were severely damaged and sixteen more were burned to the ground. Thousands of English settlers—men, women and children—were slaughtered. And many thousands of Indians perished. In fact, by the time it was over, the Indian defeat was so total that Indian tribal life in Southern New England was virtually eliminated—clearing the way completely for unimpeded white settlement from that point forward.

King Philip's War began in June 1675, when King Philip ordered a surprise raid on the Massachusetts/Rhode Island border settlement of Swansea—followed within days by a coordinated series of brutal raids on other New England towns. All were left in ashes with few survivors. King Philip's stated goal was to annihilate the English and to take back all the territory that he said they had stolen from his people.

Almost from the time he left Nantucket in 1665 after the John Gibbs incident, King Philip had been smoldering over the increasing number of land sales forced upon the Wampanoag by their growing dependence on English goods. Then in 1671 he was publicly humiliated before an English court that interrogated him, fined him, and demanded that the Wampanoag surrender all their firearms. He acquiesced, but vowed silently that one day he would avenge this insult and have satisfaction. Secretly he began to build a cache of weapons—preparing for the moment, far in the future, when he could incite all his people to rise up in decisive action.

That moment came in 1675 when the English hanged three Wampanoag for the murder of a Christian Indian—an informer that the English had placed in King Philip's headquarters at Mount Hope, near today's Bristol, Rhode Island. Knowing he was a spy, King Philip had ordered the man killed—hoping for just such a public retaliation by the English. King Philip had prepared the fuse and the English lit it! By their actions, they had given him a fully incensed Indian nation ready to explode into vengeance under his leadership. And he now had all the firearms he needed to wage total war.

The colonists had a well armed militia, but they were unable to draw the Indians into a major battle that would pit them face-to-face. Frustrated, the English launched retaliatory hit-and-burn raids on individual Indian villages. Because these raids were not limited to Wampanoag villages, the Nipmuck and Narragansett Indians were drawn into the war and soon all of the New England colonies were in fierce combat. To enlarge the war, King Philip tried to persuade the Mohawk to join him. But they refused. They trusted King Philip even less than they trusted the English.

The turning point came in April 1676 in Rhode Island, at a battle called "The Great Swamp Fight." It still stands as the bloodiest battle ever fought in New England. In a single day, the Narragansett were completely defeated—with more than two thousand slaughtered, including the Narragansett supreme sachem Canonchet. The English losses were also very substantial, including eight militia company commanders.

King Philip continued to lead the Wampanoag and the Nipmuck on attack missions, but his initiative began to loose momentum as he encountered larger and larger forces of militia laying in ambush. Finally, in August 1676 at Mount Hope, the end came with a single shot from the gun of an Indian turncoat in the service of Captain Benjamin Church. King Philip was assassinated in his own secret camp by one of his own.

King Philip's body was drawn and quartered, and his head was carried to Plymouth where it was displayed on a pole for the next twenty years for all to see. His wife and son and his chief lieutenants were captured and sold into slavery in the West Indies. The English vowed never again to allow the Indians of New England have a supreme sachem.

Of course none of these mainland horrors came to Nantucket. We had turned our back on King Philip at Altar Rock more than ten years before. But perhaps now you can understand why the English here were extremely nervous, especially since we were well armed and outnumbered them five-to-one. Unlike the Wampanoag on the mainland, the English had never tried to take away our guns. And no one wanted to take the risk of demanding that now.

✣   ✣   ✣

With King Philip's War and the Half-Share Revolt behind us, all attention refocused on raising sheep and harvesting whales. Almost the entire adult male population—both English and Indian—was now involved in these two pursuits, with the greatest emphasis on whaling because of its superior profits.

In 1690, the Proprietors persuaded Ichabod Paddock to come from Cape Cod to school us in his whaling techniques. He showed us how to build more maneuverable lightweight boats made from cedar strips, better ways to approach and harpoon whales, and faster ways to try out the oil. He also persuaded us to add three more lookout stations on the south and east shores. I spent considerable time with Paddock and found him to be as abrasive as he was wise. But the things we learned from him proved essential, because in 1692 the Crown transferred the jurisdiction of Nantucket from New York to Massachusetts. This ended our export tax exemption on "Indian Oil" and increased our need for greater productivity to maintain profits. Captain Gardner and I continued our partnership in much the same way as before, although his time and attention were more focused now on other matters.

I have not said much about religion. And that's an especially curious issue. By 1700, the vast majority of the Wampanoag on Nantucket were "praying Indians" We kept the Sabbath at three Indian churches—two Congregational and one Baptist—with our main church at Occawa here in the Southeast Quarter. John Gibbs, our first pastor, kept the word of God alive among us and brought us Bibles in the Massachusett language. And we also had our own Island schools, with four Indian teachers to educate our children in language and other matters. The largest of these schools was also in Occawa.

In contrast, the English had built no churches and had no schools. They met privately on the Sabbath in small groups and taught their own children at home. For some reason they seemed adamantly unwilling to spend money to employ ministers and teachers. One excuse was their religious diversity. Thomas Macy and Edward Starbuck were Baptists. Peter Folger was an Anabaptist. John Gardner was a Puritan archconservative. Some others were Congregationalists. And most of the rest were lapsed Quakers or lapsed Puritans. But certainly the prime factor in not building churches was the Coffin clan's lack of interest in organized religion. They were said to be proud "Nothingdarians." Sheep and whales were their sole priority.

❧   ❧   ❧

7

1770 . . . An Island Empire

T
he Nantucket of 1770 would have been totally unrecognizable to the English who first settled here. They had dreamed of a serene pastoral paradise, protected from the intrusion of outsiders. But in just a few generations, Nantucket had transformed itself into a teeming urban center of wealth and world commerce.

With over 530 houses, a population in excess of 5000, and more than 200 sailing vessels manned by over 2000 seamen of all colors and races, Nantucket had become one of the largest and richest communities in the colonies.

The sprawling town now bordered the great harbor and was encircled on the land side by a sturdy fence, with its main gate near the present day traffic rotary where the Milestone Road begins. Most of the houses from old Sherburne at Capaum Pond had been moved into the new town—which at first retained its original Indian name of Wesco. As it grew in size, the town was renamed Newtown and then Sherburne. (But it would not be until 1795 that it would be renamed as the Town of Nantucket.)

The harbor bristled with masts. Three long docks—each 300-feet or more—jutted into the harbor, and many short docks flanked them. Over 300 sailing vessels could be moored at the same time. And each day saw new arrivals and departures—bound for the mainland, or England, or the

African coast, or the Indies. Surrounding the docks were dozens of warehouses and workshops, boarding houses and taverns—and other places that I'd prefer not to mention.

High on the hills, beyond the town's winding streets and brightly colored houses, stood four windmills to grind corn and other grains. And outside the town fence grazed the animals. More than 15,000 sheep roamed free across most of the Island, effectively stripping the land of all but a whisper of vegetation. (I expect you know by now that I absolutely hated those sheep because of what they did to the beauty and fertility of our once primeval land.) Over 500 cows also grazed in fenced common lots. And other large common lots were fenced off for the raising of crops. There were a few scattered farms and outlying houses, but over ninety-percent of the Island's population lived within the fenced-in town.

Truly, Nantucket had become an Island Empire. And as you know, it was whaling that made it all happen. To understand how and why that all came about, we have to pick up our story back at the start of the 1700s. And I can tell you, I can remember it all unfolding as if it were yesterday.

❧   ❧   ❧

Whales roamed far and wide across the seven seas. So why and how, you may ask, did the tiny Island of Nantucket become the world's foremost whaling power? Like most events in history, the answer is a combination of things—and in this case, it's things spiritual, economic and cultural. Let's begin with the spiritual—

Quakerism came to Nantucket in 1702, in the form of a preacher from England named John Richardson. He—and later a Quaker missionary named Thomas Story—had such a profound impact on the Island's most prominent woman, Mary Starbuck, that she enthusiastically championed Quakerism to the point that it became the Island's almost universal religion. By 1737, nearly ninety-percent of Nantucket's population had become Quaker. Their Great Meetinghouse—one of the largest buildings in all of New England—was so immense that it could seat more than 1000 members in worship. And by 1755, their membership had swelled to over 2000, requiring a doubling in size of the building.

Quakerism was the driving force that united the people of Nantucket into a single, cohesive community with shared values and a common purpose. The shipowners, sea captains, merchants, shopkeepers, bankers, and all the other townspeople and ship hands saw themselves not as competitors, but rather as a "Society of Friends." Quakerism also provided the framework for alliances that bridged families and generations—and opened financial and business alliances with Quaker leaders in Newport, Philadelphia, and elsewhere in the colonies.

Nantucket Quakers led a life of stoic simplicity, hard work and frugality. And though sober in deportment, dress, speech, architecture and possessions, they greatly prized building their personal wealth—almost every penny of which was reinvested back into their businesses. One ship led to two and then four. This was repeated generation after generation, compounding their material success and giving them protection from financial ruin as setbacks inevitably occurred from time to time in the always risky whaling business. Their heirs—being Quakers too—were rarely tempted to divert their legacies into creature comforts and leisurely pursuits. Also, because Nantucket Quakers were both pacifists and adverse to all political activities, they had no interest in the governmental affairs of the outside world. All this provided an almost unprecedented level of reinvestment in the Island's economy—which was, of course, by then based on whaling.

In 1712, by accident or through an act of Providence, the Nantucket Quakers discovered the economic potential of the mighty sperm whale—with its huge head containing the world's finest oil. Blown off course in a sudden storm, Captain George Hussey encountered a pod of this rich prize in the waters beyond the shoals south of Tom Never's Head. With an average yield of nearly 1900-gallons per animal, this was a beast so valuable that it was worth taking greater risks to hunt. Bigger and bigger boats were built. Longer and longer voyages to more distant whaling fields were undertaken. Daring new whaling techniques were attempted, refined and perfected.

With their focus on hunting the sperm whale, a willingness to embark on sea voyages for as long as three years, and a daring born out of religious zeal, Nantucket whalers soon became the masters of the seas—eventually even traveling to the Pacific in 1791 and to the waters off Japan in pursuit of their goal.

And fueling all this was the Island's singular cultural heritage. It was said that Nantucket lads were born to be whalers and that Nantucket girls were born to be whaler's wives—so single-minded was Nantucket's focus on whaling during the 1700s. A boy's education in the craft began at the earliest age. And each one of them dreamed of one day becoming a whaling captain, much as boys today dream of becoming a star athlete or a musical superstar. Boat handling, barrel making, early apprenticeship as a cabin boy, signing on as a crewmember—all occurred before a boy was out of his early teens. Then a steady progression with the goal of commanding and then owning one's own ship. A Nantucket boy knew innately that his honor as a person, his success as a provider, the admiration in which he was held by the Island's young women, and the respect of other men, were all linked to his career in whaling. Little wonder that he pursued it so enthusiastically.

This is not to say that everyone in Nantucket was destined to go to sea. But virtually every social and business activity on the Island revolved around whaling. Nantucket was a whaling town, pure and simple, and everyone knew it.

So it was all of these factors—the spiritual, the economic, and the cultural—that converged to make Nantucket the number one whaling port in the world. And it was indeed something to see! But I must tell you that from both the Quaker and Indian point-of-view, it was far from a peaceful transition.

ℋ   ℋ   ℋ

As you can well appreciate, the money to be made in whaling was a powerful magnet drawing thousands of new comers to the Island. And among them were some of less than admirable character. Also, after long months at sea, returning whaleship hands could be, shall we say, "rowdy!" All this proved very upsetting to the Quakers and prompted them as early as 1723 to hire constables and "stout men" to patrol the town to enforce the peace, especially at night. They were also empowered to keep young

Quakers away from those places where music, dancing and other inappropriate behavior occurred. Later, when our Wampanoag population had shrunk to a minority, the constables and stout men were used to enforce an Indian curfew. At 9:00PM, all Indians not living within English houses as full time servants were rounded up and expelled through the town gate, which was then padlocked for the night. By this time, most of the poorest Indians were living in a rather squalid settlement near Miacomet.

But while the English turned their attention to the sea, their hunger for more land did not abate. Wool was an important secondary source of income that required little effort until sheep shearing time. And the women and girls of the Island could spin the wool into yarn and weave cloth while their men were away at sea. So relentlessly, the Proprietors bought up or claimed "debtor's rights" to more and more grazing land—but not without encountering strong and ongoing resistance from the Wampanoag, especially here in the Southeast Quarter.

As early as 1700, Wanackmamack's grandsons Cain and Able—together with other eastern-end sachems—petitioned the Massachusetts General Court. And in response, Governor Belmont agreed that the English land claims were "a circumvention and fraud." But still the English persisted, breeding more sheep and turning them loose. In 1722, Chief Justice Samuel Sewall wrote a harsh letter to Quaker leader Jethro Starbuck criticizing the grazing practices being used by the English. But still they persisted, breeding more sheep.

By 1738, relations between the Indians and the English had reached such a low point that rumors of a massacre plot began to spread. These rumors proved false, but they chastened the English to be a bit more cautious. Even so, they continued to breed more sheep. The English attitude was that with a shrinking number of Indians on Nantucket, we Indians neither needed nor really deserved all the land we still had.

Frustrated by a growing inability to protect our land rights, the Wampanoag here in the Southeast Quarter decided to take action. In 1741, we called a special council meeting at Occawa and expelled our sachem, Benjamin Able—the great grandson of Wanackmamack—accusing him of selling our land without permission. We chose John Quaap as our new sachem, and under his leadership embarked on a decade-long effort in the courts to regain our land. Old documents were uncovered to support our claim that we rightly still owned the eastern half of the Island. Year after year, petitions were filed, but the English sidestepped or ignored them—knowing that they would win in the end by simply out-living the Indians. And so they did.

🦋   🦋   🦋

There's a rise on the Milestone Road, part way between the fifth and sixth stone markers, where the village of Siasconset first comes into view. This is Bean Hill and it's the place where Benjamin Tashama lived for many years, and where he died in great sadness during the cold winter of 1770. Nothing remains of Benjamin Tashama's house—the boards, windows and beams were soon scavenged and even the 1,800-pound porch stone was carted away. It now rests at the entrance to the old Fair Street Museum, next to the Society of Friends Meetinghouse.

That nothing remains of Benjamin Tashama's Bean Hill house is symbolic. It represents the total disappearance of Sachem Wanackmamack and the effective end of the Island's native culture. While a handful of Indians did survive Benjamin Tashama, they were largely of mixed race and by 1770 almost fully assimilated into the English way of life.

Benjamin Tashama, the grandson of Sachem Autopscot and a direct descendant of the great Wanachmamack, was Nantucket's last sachem. For many years, he had taught and preached in the tribal village of Occawa. But after the great plague of 1763, fewer and fewer of his people came to hear him. Soon Occawa was deserted and eventually no one even came to his house on Bean Hill. The once proud Wampanoag nation of Nantucket remained alive only in his memories.

The true cause of the 1763 plague was never determined. Some say it was yellow fever brought to the Island on a brig from Ireland. Others say it came on a Nantucket whaling ship returning from the west coast of Africa. But these theories have been largely discounted. Others say it was smallpox or typhus. And modern medical scientists theorize it was yellow famine fever, carried by lice. All we really know is that it selectively targeted the Island's native population—with devastating results. Of the 324 full-blooded Indians then living on the Island, 222 died—most within 48-hours. Of the 102 who escaped the sickness, 18 were at sea whaling, 40 were servants in English houses, and the remaining 44 lived apart in small family clusters in the outlying countryside.

The only ones to contract the disease and recover were of mixed Indian blood. Not a single white or black Nantucketer even became ill. Truly, this was the "Indian Sickness" foretold in Wampanoag legend. And the first to perish were Benjamin Tashama's daughter Sarah and all her children.

The plague also claimed the last seven members of my own family— Zachara Never and his wife and two sons, his brother Jonathan Never, and his two sisters Susanna and Betty Never.

On February 16th 1764, the plague ended as suddenly as it came— but not before spreading to Martha's Vineyard and Cape Cod. That year it killed thirty-percent of the Indians on the Cape and Islands. But nowhere was the impact of the plague as great as on Nantucket.

Four months later—in early summer—the bluefish stopped coming to Nantucket, and they would not return for another seventy years. Bluefish had been plentiful in Nantucket waters from the spring through the fall for untold generations. Their departure was another sign that an era had ended. And Benjamin Tashama's death in the winter of 1770 finally sealed it.

✤　✤　✤

Despite all this turmoil, life had somehow remained fairly tranquil in the Southeast Quarter. Far from the noise and strong smell of the town, we still had the beauty of the open land and sea to sustain us. And it was common for the townsfolk to travel out to the east end by horse cart or by foot to picnic. A series of rutted cart paths snaked across the land, converging at a point in Tom Never's Swamp where a relatively dry crossing to Siasconset could be made. The old fishing shacks in Siasconset numbered nine in 1770, and some had been enlarged a bit to become fair weather houses for the sickly. One English family lived there year-round, engaging in farming.

Another English family had a house and small farm near Tom Never's Head. The husband had retired from whaling to tend the land and keep a few cows. His wife prepared meals for the townsfolk and visitors who wanted to enjoy the vistas from Tom Never's Head on their return trip from Siasconset—which everyone now called 'Sconset.

The northern route to 'Sconset skirted Polpis Harbor, where a house for dining and refreshment became a popular destination in itself. You may recall that Saint-John de Crèvecoer—in his widely published "Letters from an American Farmer"—told of dining here and at the Tom Never's farmhouse.

Despite the still waging dispute over land, people remained civil in the Southeast Quarter. As always, the Quakers were reserved and polite, and the Indians accommodating. Incidentally, as you know from their writings, the Quakers spoke like the Bible—using words like "thou" and "thee." But you may not realize why they wrote and spoke dates as they did. For example, "the second day of the fifth month." They did so because the Romans had named the weekdays and months for their gods. And the Quakers believed that the names of pagan gods should never be written or spoken.

❧ ❧ ❧

You may wonder what role I played during this time period? And how can it be that I am still here with you now? The answer to the first question is "very little" and to the second question, "I'm really not sure."

On a mild October day in 1709, at age 68, I decided to complete the crew of one of our whaling boats because my eldest son Peter was ill with a fever. The day was wondrously clear and the water unusually calm as we rowed past the shoals to the offshore whaling grounds. A perfect day! But then with great suddenness and absolutely no forewarning, the southwestern sky darkened to indigo. At breathtaking speed, the darkness raced toward us, consuming more and more of the sky. In a matter of just seconds, gale force winds engulfed us, then torrents of rain mixed with stinging salt spray. The sea churned in fierce anger as massive waves broke down upon us, seemingly from all directions—flipping over our whaleboat and cracking wide its fragile seams. Gasping for air, I struggled for a time in the water, trying to find my boat and my crewmen. Then darkness closed in all around me.

It was dawn the next morning when I awakened on the beach beneath Tom Never's Head. Seeing no other survivors or signs of our shattered boat, I climbed the bluff to my house. As I entered, I found my wife and children sitting in a circle and mourning my death. I called out to tell them I was safe. But for some reason they could neither see me nor hear me. It was then that I realized that I had passed over—but that somehow my spirit still remained in this place.

Why this is so I can only guess. Perhaps it was my vow to Wanack-mamack long ago never to leave this land. Perhaps my love of this place was simply too great, and never to leave it is both my blessing and my curse. Perhaps the creator chooses one of us to watch over each part of his earth, and this place is my post. I'd like this last possibility to be true. But if it is, I don't really know why I've been chosen rather than another. I find that I have no power to protect this place or to change things. All I can do is to observe and then tell people like you my story—hoping that you will tell others. Perhaps the creator's message to us all is simply this— that man's search for a substitute eden on this earth will always be frustrated and always prove futile.

I think you'll see this even more clearly as the rest of my story unfolds.

8

1783 . . . New Glory

I watched as the whaleship *Bedford* set sail from Nantucket with a full cargo of oil in early September of 1783. Her destination—London. She would be the first American ship to sail into a British port since the peace treaty had been signed in Paris, officially ending the seven-year-long War of American Independence.

As the English pilot boarded the *Bedford* to take her up the Thames to her berth, Captain Mooer gave the signal to run up his ship's colors. For the first time, the "Stars and Stripes" of the United States of America flew in a British port. Snapping smartly in the morning's brisk wind, the *Bedford's* flag proudly proclaimed a new nation and a new age. Hundreds on the docks and along the shore gawked and pointed to the new flag. They would remember this day well!

❦   ❦   ❦

The Revolutionary War had taken a heavy toll on Nantucket, virtually destroying our economy and bringing our people to near starvation. More than 1500 Nantucket vessels of various sizes were confiscated or lost at sea. Over 1200 Nantucket seamen were captured or killed. The Island's population declined by nearly 35-percent. And of those who remained,

202 had become widowed and 342 were left orphaned. The estimated losses in whaling and shipping exceeded $1,000,000. And the Island's sheep population had fallen to little more than 3000, compared to 15,000 at the war's start.

Before the American Colonies declared their independence in 1776, the vast majority of Nantucket's people were firmly against any break with England. As Quakers they were pacifists and strictly apolitical. In fact, when the Colonies organized a meeting at Boston's Faneuil Hall to debate how best to protest the Revenue Acts of Great Britain, Nantucket refused to even send delegates. Throughout, they looked with growing alarm at the heated rhetoric and provocative actions of the Patriots.

London was Nantucket's principal market and the people of Nantucket considered themselves to be more English than American. And as a seafaring Island Empire, they feared that if a war were to break out, they would be prey to both sides

Nantucket was not alone in its aversion to a break with England. Across the American Colonies, a full third of the people were strongly opposed and one-third more were very uncomfortable with the idea. But event layered upon event to make an American Declaration of Independence inevitable. And ultimately, a small group of Nantucket Patriots became convinced that they too should take "rebellious actions."

It should come as no surprise to you that it was money that played a key role in shaping England's policies toward its American Colonies. They viewed their American possessions mainly as a source of cheap commodities and a market for English manufactured goods. While the Colonies were permitted to make finished products for their own internal consumption, it was illegal for one American Colony to sell its finished goods directly to another Colony. Their goods had to be shipped first to England, where they were taxed and then—with large profit mark-ups added—shipped back to another American Colony where they were taxed again. All this was designed to keep the American Colonies dependent on Britain for both exports and imports, and to maximize the wealth that the Colonies generated for the Royal purse.

This long-standing policy increasingly infuriated many in the Colonies, but it would take Britain's confiscatory Stamp Act of 1765 to actually trigger the American Revolution. Here's how that "final straw" tax came about—

In fighting the French and Indian War (1754–1763) to thwart France's claim to the American Colonies, England had doubled its national debt. As a result, Parliament voted to sharply increase the duties imposed on American trade by enacting the Stamp Act of 1765. They argued that since the war was fought on behalf of the Colonies, the Colonies should rightly pay its cost. This outraged the American Patriots and gave rise to their growing cry—"Taxation without representation."

The voice of the crowd grew steadily louder and their anger came to a head on March 5th 1770, when a squad of British troops fired into a crowd killing five demonstrators. This was the famous Boston Massacre and the first to die was one Crispus Attucks, a seaman of mixed race off a Nantucket whaler.

News of the massacre spread, the resistance stiffened, and dozens of retaliatory plots were hatched. But the flash point came on the night of December 16th 1773, when more than 150 Patriots made a frontal attack against Great Britain's interests—an attack not against troops, but against taxation. This was, of course, the legendary Boston Tea Party. And it took place on two Nantucket ships—the *Dartmouth* and the *Beaver*—and on a third ship named the *Eleanor*.

All three ships had sailed from London, where they had unloaded full holds of whale oil and bone. Their return cargo was tea—the *Dartmouth* and *Beaver* alone carrying 342 chests of tea valued at over £18,000. On Sunday, November 8th, the ships reached Boston Harbor and were ordered to tie up at Griffin's Warf, where they became unwilling parties in a standoff between the Patriots and the British.

As the ships docked, a group of 25 armed men came aboard warning, "Unload at your peril. Return to London with your cargo or face the full consequences." It was said that Paul Revere himself stood watch on the dock.

The *Dartmouth* was owned by Francis Rotch and the *Beaver* was under charter to his brother William. These were Nantucket's most successful whale oil merchants and shipowners. They were also staunch Tories. And it was money and not politics that shaped their course of action. According to Boston Port regulations, any ship not unloaded within 20 days could have its cargo confiscated by the British Authorities. This gave the British little reason to protect the Rotch brothers from the Patriots. By simply waiting, the British could seize all £18,000 worth of their tea, cost free—plus that of the *Eleanor*. Only then would British troops confront the Patriots, to secure their prize.

Between the Patriot ultimatum and the Port regulations, the Rotch brothers felt they had no alternative but to return to sea and seek another port. But before they could do so, British Governor Thomas Hutchinson issued an edict ordering His Majesty's soldiers on Castle Island to fire upon and sink any ship attempting to leave Boston Harbor with a cargo of tea. The standoff continued for nearly three weeks, during which time Francis Rotch attempted to negotiate a compromise. With the help of Samuel Adams and other prominent Bostonians, Rotch appealed to both the Port Authorities and Governor Hutchinson for a special clearance or extension. Day after day they were told that their case was being considered. Then, with just one day left, they were told that their request was denied. Confiscation of their cargo would take place the very next day.

Word spread to the Patriots and they decided to take immediate action. Some favored burning the ships, but that was opposed by John Hancock. So instead, they agreed to destroy only the taxable tea and not the American ships that carried it.

The many paintings and engravings that memorialize this historic event show a rollicking band of Patriots dressed as Indians—hollering out war cries and brandishing flaming torches. But in truth, the whole affair was conducted with stoic determination. As hundreds watched silently from the shore, about 150 men went aboard the *Dartmouth*, then the *Beaver*, then the *Eleanor*. Systematically, they moved all the tea boxes to the open decks, pried them open, and dumped their contents into the harbor's fetid waters. There was no rioting, no horseplay, no shouting. Only one ship hatch lock was broken open and the Patriots later repaired it. And while it is true that most of the boarding party had blackened their faces to conceal their identities, only a small handful dressed themselves as Indians.

In prompt retaliation for this rebellious act, a furious British Parliament issued the Boston Port Bill, which closed that city to trade. But this ban had little impact on Nantucket—which during this period actually increased its shipments of whale oil and spermaceti candles to London. (To meet greater demand, the Island's candle factories increased their production to over 4,560,000 candles that year.)

However, this bonanza was short lived. In February 1775, the Massachusetts Bay Restraining Bill was issued—which prohibited Massachusetts, New Hampshire and Rhode Island from trading with England and her possessions in the West Indies. Seeing this Restraining Bill as potentially devastating, Nantucket appealed for immunity directly to England—ignoring the Massachusetts government, under whose jurisdiction they fell. In doing so, Nantucket characterized itself as a neutral Island with long and close ties to London. But the British considered Nantucket as far from neutral. Indeed, the Island had long been thought a center of contraband trade between Holland and New York. And in fact, Nantucket was a principal entry point through which gunpowder was being smuggled into the Colonies. So it came as no surprise that Britain ignored the Nantucket appeal.

Two months later, the Battles of Lexington and Concord were fought. And 15-months later, the Colonies declared their independence. Full-scale war was now a certainty.

Nantucket was caught in the middle. With its location 30-miles out to sea, the resource-strapped Colonial Government knew that it could not protect the Island—and more than that, doubted the Island's true loyalties. Many even viewed Nantucket as a Tory colony whose pacifist pleadings conveniently masked a greedy desire to keep trading with the enemy. For their part, the British wanted to neutralize the Island as a conduit of both income and gunpowder to the rebellious Colonies. So as a result, both sides effectively blockaded the Island throughout most of the Revolutionary War.

Nantucket ships were seized at sea by both British and American privateers. Only a few small sloops under rigid restrictions were permitted to sail to and from the mainland to transport emergency supplies. And several times the Island was plundered by landing parties from both sides—

including a raiding party of the so called "refugees," a ragtag roaming army of American Tories who had been driven off their farms and out of their towns by angry Patriots.

In 1781, after an extremely severe winter that froze over the harbor for three months, a near starving Nantucket appealed directly to British Admiral Digley for relief. In return for a solemn pledge of neutrality from Nantucket, Digley agreed not to invade the Island and to grant permits for a very limited number of small craft to bring in emergency supplies. This helped the Island survive, but confirmed the worst suspicions of many on the mainland that Nantucket was not truly loyal to the American cause.

It is true that during the American Revolution, no shots were fired on Nantucket. But in full fairness, it must be recognized that innumerable acts of individual heroism did occur beyond our shores—as hundreds of Nantucket men left the Island to fight as Patriots on the mainland and at sea. The arrogance and brutality of the British both before and during the war transformed many Nantucket men from pacifists into Patriots.

❦   ❦   ❦

You may wonder why a blockade proved so devastating to Nantucket. After all, we had lots of potential farmland and many thousands of sheep. The reason is that before the war, Nantucket had brought in the bulk of its foodstuffs, firewood and supplies by boat from Cape Cod and the mainland—finding this far more convenient and cost-efficient than producing them on the Island. But with the blockade, virtually all these imports were cut off. Now—faced with very limited agricultural resources—the Islander's were forced to forage as best they could. We had sheep, but little else.

The Island's soil had become so depleted over the years that harvests proved inadequate. An acre of cultivated land yielded not much more than 20-bushels of corn. Fifty years earlier, the yield had been over 250-bushels per acre. This forced the Town Officials to expand the planting areas significantly. In 1775, for the first time, the Southeast Quarter was laid out for planting. Along-shore fishing was also re-instituted on a far larger scale. Twenty more fishing shacks were built in 'Sconset and a well was dug to support them. Birds were hunted on an organized basis and shellfish were gathered by teams assigned to that task. Firewood became so scarce that peat was dug in Tom Never's Swamp and in the bogs along Philip's Run. By 1780, most of the Island's few remaining trees had been cut down—and even old roots were being dug out and dried, to be burned for warmth. Times were extremely difficult. And the Islander's managed to survive only by learning to live off the land—rediscovering and adopting many of the techniques used long ago by the Wampanoag.

And throughout all this time, there was a sense of growing apprehension—because there was little reliable news on how the war was progressing and who was winning. The sole consolation was a belief that after the war finally ended—regardless of who proved victorious—Nantucket's whaling skills could once again return the Island to prosperity and greatness. That was, of course, assuming that Nantucket could hold on that long!

Then came the bitter winter of 1781. Thick ice covered the land, beaches and harbor—all but preventing fishing, shellfish gathering and peat digging. Sheep died by the thousands, both from exposure and from an inability to penetrate the ice shield covering their grazing lands. The Islanders were reduced to eating seagulls and other shore birds. Grain stores from the last harvest were entirely depleted. Finally, in desperation, the Town Officials voted to seek relief from the British with a written pledge promising, "To take no part in the contest and give no cause of offense to either of the contending forces." All they asked in exchange was limited rights to transport emergency food supplies and firewood from the Cape and the mainland to Nantucket. There was no reply from the British until after the spring thaw.

Bracing for another potentially devastating winter, all of Nantucket worked together throughout the spring, summer and early autumn of 1781 in an attempt to stockpile their scarce provisions. Then one evening a small sloop sailed into Nantucket Harbor with an announcement that absolutely electrified the Island. On October 19th 1781, General Cornwallis had surrendered to General Washington at Yorktown. The United States of America had successfully defended and won its liberty as a new nation—defeating the most powerful Empire on earth. Celebrations broke out across the Island. Nantucket's seven-year-long ordeal was over at last.

Immediately, Nantucket laid plans to reclaim its role in the whale fishery. A number of ships returned from South America and other distant ports where they had waited out the war to avoid capture. And the Rotch brothers and the other Island shipowners sought the return of many of the 134 whaling ships that had been confiscated by the Royal Navy and American privateers. In addition, a fleet of new ships was commissioned. With the war ended, Nantucket whaling captains were anxious to return to sea, and they had their pick of hundreds of able-bodied seamen who were ready to sign on—both at home and in the Ports of Boston and New Bedford.

But after seven years of hardship, many whaling men of Nantucket found themselves too old and too worn out to return to the sea. They took jobs in the spermaceti candle factories, ropewalks, cooperage shops, ship chandlers and other support trades. And a number retired to family farming, especially here in the Southeast Quarter.

The once mighty Sachem Wanackmamack was soon replaced almost in its entirety with a scattering of small planting fields and tiny homesites.

9

1814 . . . Victory At Sea

s I recall it, October 10th was an uncommonly busy day in the
Southeast Quarter. Hibbard Rae had brought in extra hands to
help with the fall harvest on his 40-acre farm near Tom Never's
Head. And at his house—not quite a quarter-mile back from the shore—
Hibbard's wife Lydia and their four daughters were preparing several
pots of thick chowder, and baking beans and flat corn bread to feed the
hungry workers who would be staying in their barn for most of the next
week.

At the same time, a crew of other workers was erecting a mile-long
fence along the Southeast Quarter's northern edge—the first leg of more
than 7-miles of fences that would fully enclose a new privately-owned
2,124-acre "set-off" called "Plainfield"—which ran to the north toward
Polpis. The old rutted roads to 'Sconset that had meandered across Plainfield were already closed off. These would be replaced permanently by the
even older rutted road just south of the new fence. To make this old
route sound like an improvement, they decided to call it the 'Sconset
Turnpike.

That same day, more than 200 fishermen were at work in 'Sconset,
organized into 5-man boat crews. The village had grown to 42 houses,
aligned in three rows. These tiny houses, called "fishing stages," were lit-

tle more than seasonal fish shacks—with rough boarded sides, shingled roofs and wood chimneys. But they could sleep a 5-man crew, plus a boy or two hired on to help with the work ashore. The men cooked and ate mainly out of doors, but just about all the fishing stages had a large board table hinged to the wall, that could be folded down for use if the weather outside proved foul.

Not far north toward Sesachacha—which still had 12 fishing stages left at that time—60 more fishermen were at work. The catch was good this October. But even so, two more boat owners decided that they'd haul their fishing stages to 'Sconset before the next season. With the old roads to Town being closed, 'Sconset was the place to be. In fact, by 1820 all the remaining fishing stages would be moved to 'Sconset and Sesachacha would be abandoned.

Lest I give you the impression that life was idyllic on Nantucket that October of 1814, let me contrast the above with events in Town. The United States was again at war with Great Britain. The Island's economy was in shambles. Hungry people begged at almost every street corner. Soup lines stretched along upper Main Street to Gardner, where an aid station was set up each afternoon. The Town's wells were now bringing up water containing grit and foul-smelling saline clumps. Even though Great Britain had granted Nantucket neutrality, everyone was growing fearful that the King's forces were poised to attack and burn the town at the least provocation. Rumors of pending disaster were rampant. Bitter divisions existed at almost every level—political, social and religious. Nantucket's once great optimism had fled the Island.

Against this backdrop, you can imagine the fear that ran through Lydia and Hibbard Rae and the others on their farm—when they were awakened from a very deep sleep on the night of October 10th by the sounds of gunfire and not-too-distant screams. At first, they looked toward Town, but could see nothing through the dense fog. Then a sudden yellow glare brightened the sky to their south, just above the ocean. Two tremendous booms—followed by nearly 30-minutes of sporadic gunfire and screams—brought a full realization that a fierce naval battle was being waged just off the south shore of Tom Never's.

❦   ❦   ❦

Few Americans today remember much about the War of 1812—except perhaps that it earned the *U.S.S. Constitution* its name "Old Ironsides." Or that the British invaded Washington, DC and burned both the White House and Capitol Building. Or that our valiant defense of Fort McHenry inspired Francis Scott Key to write his poem "Star Spangled Banner," which became our National Anthem. Far fewer today realize that the War of 1812 represented a critical coming-of-age for America. That it so challenged the resolve of our still fragile nation that it almost precipitated the internal break-up of the Union. Or that by ending British ambitions in the Northwest Territories, it opened our full expansion to the West. And almost lost from memory is the daring naval battle off Tom Never's that played a decisive role in bringing the War of 1812 to its final end.

The War of 1812 was largely about trade, and as such it was fought mainly at sea. It began officially on June 18th 1812, but was nearly twenty years in the making as a neutral United States played a delicate game at the edges of the bitter wars between England and France—first during the French Revolution (1793–1801) and again during the Napoleonic Wars (1803–1814).

For many years, American shipowners had exploited a loophole in an old British law, which forbade neutral countries from transporting goods *directly* between Europe and the French and Spanish West Indies during wartime. But by simply putting into a U.S. port en route and issuing new documents, American shipowners effectively sidestepped this prohibition against direct shipments. The result was a boom in U.S. shipbuilding. Profits soared. And the wages paid to experienced seamen doubled and then tripled. The European Wars had made America a dominant force in Trans-Atlantic trade.

To block the flow of goods to France and her allies, Great Britain began to challenge American ships, and in 1805 officially eliminated the law's loophole. Widespread seizures of American ships followed, as Great Britain instituted a blockade of the European coast and let loose scores of

British privateers to target American vessels. In turn, Napoleon retaliated with his own blockade of the British Isles. Now both France and England threatened to confiscate any American ships that attempted to supply their enemies. Still, a remarkable tonnage of American cargo made it through. The potential profits were so enormous that the risks in running the blockade seemed worth taking.

Most wars have a flash point that riles public outrage. And in this war it was the "Chesapeake Affair." On June 22nd 1807, the British warship *H.M.S. Leopard* fired upon and captured the *U.S.S. Chesapeake*—not only looting it but also impressing its sailors into servitude in the Royal Navy. The British claim was that most of these American sailors were still British subjects. Now it was no longer just a matter of lost ships and cargo, the sacred sovereign rights of American citizens had been violated!

Backed by an angry Congress, President Thomas Jefferson tried to exert economic pressure on both Great Britain and France through an escalating series of total trade embargoes against them. By cutting off all U.S. trade with both countries, he hoped to demonstrate the importance of American shipping to their national interests—and as a result force both countries to negotiate. But they wouldn't. And even when these "total embargoes" were in effect, American foreign-trade dropped by only one-third. Huge potential profits and the difficulties of enforcement rendered these trade embargoes porous. Meanwhile, the number of American ships lost at sea kept growing for another four years after the *U.S.S. Chesapeake*'s taking.

In 1811, President James Madison thought he had solved part of the problem, based on a commitment from the French. If the U.S. would re-impose a trade embargo against Great Britain, France said it would open all its ports to American commerce. Madison announced the embargo, only to find that he had been tricked by Napoleon. Further negotiations with Great Britain broke down and a declaration of war now seemed inevitable.

Unencumbered trade with Europe was not the only factor driving America toward a war with Great Britain. The American frontiersmen wanted free access to all of the lands under British-sponsored Indian control in the West—and they had long dreamed of expelling the British from Canada. At the same time, the Southern "war hawks" wanted to take control of West Florida from Great Britain's ally Spain. And all agreed that it was vital to head off any possible British interference near the New Orleans Delta and the Gulf of Mexico. The Louisiana Purchase in 1803 had doubled America's territory—adding all the land from the Mississippi River to the Rocky Mountains—from the Gulf of Mexico to British North America. But the value and success of this vast new heartland absolutely required the unimpeded flow of commerce through the Delta. A British blockade could end that, and a British victory over Napoleon might even lead Great Britain to claim that the Louisiana Purchase from the French was illegal—based on disputing the legitimacy of France's ownership of this territory. Those were the rumors, and those were the great fears.

On June 18th 1812, Henry Clay, John C. Calhoun and their fellow Southern "war hawks" joined forces with the radical Western contingent in Congress to override the votes of the moderates. America's second war with Great Britain was declared—just 28 years after the War of Independence had ended.

Almost immediately, America realized that it was ill prepared to wage a major war against the British. Attempts to gain a foothold in Canada failed, with American troops surrendering to a much smaller force at Detroit. And on the Niagara River, an American incursion was quickly beaten back. Initially, things went better at sea—with the victory of the *U.S.S. Constitution* over the *H.M.S. Guerrière*, and the capture of the *H.M.S. Macedonia* by the *U.S.S. United States*. But American warships were vastly outnumbered and the newly recruited American privateers couldn't make up the difference.

In 1813, the British Navy struck back aggressively. The *U.S.S. Chesapeake*—commanded by Captain James Lawrence of "Don't give up the ship!" fame—was defeated by the *H.M.S. Shannon*. And one by one, most of the American warships were captured or bottled-up in port. With Napoleon's forces now checkmated in Europe, Britain poured more and more resources into the American campaign. Ultimately, more than 500 British war vessels plied the U.S. coastline in a brazen display of superior British seapower.

While America still showed some fight in the north—notably with Admiral Oliver Perry's victories on Lake Erie, the retaking of Detroit, and the turning back of British land and naval forces on Lake Champlain, thwarting their move south in an attempt to take control of the critically important Hudson River Valley—things were going so badly elsewhere in the war that dissension was spreading quickly. The Federalists in New England, the Democrats in the South, and the Republicans in the West all advocated different strategies based on their still differing objectives. New England depended on the Atlantic trade and that was now nonexistent. They pleaded—"Peace at any cost!"—and became openly hostile to the rest of the Union. Secession was actively debated at their special Hartford Convention. And unconditional surrender to Great Britain was being advocated.

Then in August of 1814, the British scored a major military victory that ultimately proved to be a strategic blunder. Massing ships in Chesapeake Bay, they launched a ground assault on the Nation's Capitol. Not content with simply occupying Washington, DC, they torched both the White House and the U.S. Capitol Building to humiliate America. Then they turned north for a full-scale bombardment of Fort McHenry—designed to clear the way for their seizure of Baltimore. But here they were halted by a heroic defense, immortalized in Francis Scott Key's epic poem—"Star Spangled Banner."

Word of these events raced across the country, and like the smoldering White House and Capitol buildings, set Americans everywhere aflame. Within days, the "Star Spangled Banner" appeared in virtually every newspaper and was sung proudly to the suggested tune of the old English hymn—"To Anacreon in Heaven." A divided America came together, discovering in itself a renewed spirit of patriotism and resolve. It was becoming increasingly clear to the British that this war was far from over.

Not long after, Great Britain agreed to enter into talks to negotiate a settlement. And finally, on December 24th 1814—following months of hard bargaining led by John Quincy Adams, Henry Clay and Albert Gallatin—a peace treaty was signed, with no real gains for either side. Fifteen days later, Andrew Jackson soundly defeated the British forces at New

Orleans, later claiming that he had not been "officially informed" that the war had already ended. With his victory, the Mississippi Delta was now secure. And in the Northwest and South, defeats suffered by the Indians during the war forced them into treaties that opened up their lands for future American expansion. So remarkably, most of America's objectives for the war had been achieved!

🕊　🕊　🕊

But let me take you back to Nantucket on October 10th of 1814, before the eventual outcome of the war was known. And let me tell you why things had deteriorated so badly since the boom days at the beginning of the century.

In 1803, oil and candle prices achieved record highs. One reason was fewer ships in the trade, another was soaring demand in Europe and in a growing America. So in 1804, most Nantucket ship owners increased both the number and the size of their ships, and they also began to use Martha's Vineyard and New Bedford as ports—even then the sand bar at the mouth of the harbor was becoming a problem for the larger ships.

But in 1806, the whaling economy sharply reversed. Supply exceeded demand and large inventories began to build up. Then 1807 brought the first U.S. trade embargoes, further reducing oil and candle exports. And at the same time, ship insurance rates soared, and then insurance became no longer available regardless of price. Some owners took their ships out of service, and employment for laboring men on the Island nearly dried up. Nantucket was in a deep recession.

Finally, in 1809, the Island's shipowners thought that the threat of war had subsided enough to risk a return to full scale whaling. After all, they would be sailing to South America and the Pacific, not Europe. So after a frantic period of refitting, all 161 Nantucket whaling ships were sent out—a massive exodus that had never happened at one time before. But there was a harsh downside. With all the ships gone, there would be no jobs on the Island to service and supply them for at least another three years. And the shipowners would see no income until their ships returned safely.

With an empty harbor and no jobs, anxiety grew. More and more families decided to leave, but found that their houses could not be sold. By 1810, the Island's population dropped to 6,807—with 1,322 families, 379 widows, and 474 fatherless boys. Nantucket became even more a two-class society—with some still wealthy, but most of the laboring class destitute.

The Island's solid Quaker ties also had frayed. Over the years, the Friends had "disowned" large numbers of their members as being "too worldly." These former Quakers moved on to become Congregational-ists, Unitarians, and Methodists. And even the remaining Quakers began to argue and splinter. To use today's term, the Island's once unified pop-ulace was becoming dysfunctional.

The situation remained grim and tipped toward desperate, when in 1812 it began to look like war was inevitable. Many on Nantucket were old enough to still remember the harsh impact of the War of Independ-ence—the hunger, the cold, the poverty, and the fear brought on by the total blockade of the Island by the British. But now the Island was even more vulnerable—with poverty at home and the full whaling fleet out to sea, unarmed and providing an easy target for capture.

In May 1812, Nantucket sent a protest to Congress—an urgent ap-peal to avoid war with Great Britain. There was no reply. Then on June 24th, word reached the Island that war was already declared.

In a rush to prepare for a British blockade and for possible looting, food supplies were brought in and stockpiled—and the Island's banks sent their money to the mainland for safekeeping. Obed. Mitchell set up a wool factory on the North Wharf to spin yarn for warm clothing and to give work to 200 unemployed people. A petition was also sent to Presi-dent Madison, asking him to draw-up stipulations with Great Britain that exempted the whale and cod fisheries from the hostilities. Again, there was no reply.

Soon the entire coastline was infested with British frigates and their tenders. British privateers were everywhere, plundering and sinking coastal craft at will. Boats from the *H.M.S. Nimrod* threatened to land upon and burn Nantucket. And all attempts to run the blockade were either thwarted or forced to pay large bribes to get through. For example, the

British sloop *Chebocco* patrolled the outer harbor for months, demanding cash payments for safe passage. This drove the cost of flour to $14 a barrel, corn to $1.80 per bushel, and wood to $17 a cord—several times their pre-war prices. But at least some supplies got through. Other tenders off the frigate *H.M.S. Nymph* were not so "kind and compassionate."

Throughout 1813, word reached the Island that Nantucket whaling ships were being captured or burned in both the South Atlantic and Pacific—and that that others had put into port in South America to wait out the war. How many, if any, would return to Nantucket was uncertain.

Though no one back home yet knew it, the Nantucket whaling ships *Lima* and *President* and 10 others had put into Talcahuano Harbor in Chile for resupply and refitting. Away from America for more than a year, they were totally unaware of the war or that the royalist Peruvian government—which then controlled much of Chile—had allied itself with Great Britain. Upon entering the harbor, all 12 ships were seized and their crews imprisoned. The Peruvians planned to sail the ships to Lima and to march the Nantucket crews over 2,000 miles to the capitol, in chains.

In a daring raid, an American diplomat named Joel Robert Poinsett led a band of 400 Chilean patriots in an attack to free the Nantucket seamen. President Madison had appointed Poinsett to be U.S. Consul General for Argentina, Chile and Peru. But his true mission was to persuade these South American countries to throw off European influence and become U.S. allies. His bold rescue allowed all 12 of the Nantucket ships to escape. And ultimately, five of them would make it home safely to America. But in rescuing the Nantucket seamen, Poinsett compromised his position in South America. This ended his diplomatic career there, but led to other key positions in the U.S. government—first Congressman, then War Minister to Mexico, and then Secretary of War under Martin Van Buren. If his name sounds at all familiar to you, it may be because the poinsettia plant was named in his honor.

At the beginning of 1814, the noose around Nantucket tightened even further, when President Madison ordered a total halt to the movement of all American vessels to prevent their capture or destruction. This completely cut off Nantucket's contact with the mainland and prevented even the most meager resupply of bread, flour and fire wood for nearly four months until the embargo was lifted.

During this time, the Island's leaders hotly debated what was necessary for the Island's survival. The Federalists feuded bitterly with the Democratic Republicans. In the end it was decided to make a direct appeal to the Commander-in-Chief of the British blockade, pledging the Island's neutrality in an exchange for a grant of safe passage for the Island's whaling ships and coastal vessels. In late July, a delegation aboard the sloop *Hawk* set off under a white flag of truce to find Admiral Alexander Cochrane. In Chesapeake Bay they were told he had sailed to Bermuda. Arriving there, they were told he had just sailed back to Chesapeake Bay—so they retraced their course to find him. It was August 29th—more than a month after they left Nantucket—when they finally met with Admiral Cochrane aboard his flagship *H.M.S. Surprise*. He listened to their petition sympathetically, but told them he could offer them no relief before consulting with the Admiralty. Under a letter of safe passage from the Admiral, they departed for home, with uncertainty tinged with some degree of optimism.

Upon their return to Nantucket on September 10th, they learned that the Island had already signed an agreement of neutrality. Three weeks earlier, the captain of the *Nimrod* had arrived with a letter from the area commander, Admiral Henry Hotham. Under the proposed terms, the Island would be given permits to bring in firewood and necessary provisions from the mainland. In exchange, they must agree—"*not* to take up arms against British forces, *not* to defend any public property, *nor* to make any opposition against British vessels coming into the harbor to refresh." No reference to the whaling fleet was included.

At a special town meeting, the Islanders had agreed to these terms, feeling that they had no alternative. A delegation was dispatched to finalize the papers of neutrality with Admiral Hotham aboard his flagship *H.M.S. Superb*. There they learned that two more conditions had been added, presumably at Admiral Cochrane's insistence. First, that Nantucket agree *not* to pay any taxes assessed upon them by the U.S. government—and if they did pay any U.S. taxes, that double that amount be paid to Great Britain. And second, if any counterfeit permits for the safe passage of supply boats were issued or used, all Nantucket vessels of every kind would be captured and destroyed.

Nantucket reluctantly signed its agreement to all these final terms on August 28th—the day before the *Hawk* party had petitioned Admiral Cochrane in Chesapeake Bay, and two weeks before the *Hawk* had returned to Nantucket. Clearly, Admiral Cochrane had played them for fools.

Quickly, the Island's sense of relief turned to alarm. The permits issued by the British were highly restrictive and totally inadequate—just 3 passports to Delaware for bread, 3 passports to New York for provisions, and 15 passports to the mainland for firewood. No fish or oil could be brought to market. No vessel could take part in fishing or whaling. No passengers could be transported. Permits could not be transferred to any vessels other than those specifically named.

The great fear was that the British had set up Nantucket for failure— that they would contrive a passport violation and then use it as an excuse to burn the Island's vessels and occupy the town. Fear turned to near panic as reports spread that the British had burned Washington, D.C. to the ground and had the same fate planned for Baltimore.

Now, less than two weeks later, the sound of a major gun battle could be heard just off Tom Never's Head.

❦   ❦   ❦

The Tom Never's naval battle was one of the fiercest and most heroic of the war. And it restored the lost hope and lost pride to the people of New England. The valiant American privateer *Prince de Neufchatel*—under its plucky commander Captain Jules Ordronaux—had outsmarted and outfought a far larger British force intent on its destruction. Against all odds, the *Prince de Neufchatel* had prevailed!

This victory said even more to the people of Nantucket. We were children of the sea, who had been deprived of the sea's blessings for the three long years since our ships had sailed away. That privation had eaten away at our very souls, depleting us in ways we had not even realized. Now, all that life force came rushing back. The sea had not forgotten us; it had given us a great victory as a sign!

❧　❧　❧

The *Prince de Neufchatel* was the first of its kind. Built by Christian Bergh in New York during the winter of 1812–1813, she featured a radical design—a sharp lean hull, two very tall raked masts, and innovative rigging that allowed hoisting vast spans of sail. She was a 310-ton brigantine, officially classed as a hermaphrodite schooner. Measuring 173-feet stem-to-stern, nearly 26-feet abeam, and 123-feet to the tip of her topgallant—she could berth a crew of 150 men and wield a punishing barrage of firepower through her 22 gunports. And she was a beauty, with the shiny black of her hull enriched by the terracotta red and pale yellow of her bulwarks and deck houses.

One look, and Captain Ordronaux knew that she was the ship he had been looking for. Apprenticed in the French Navy, he was the commander of the sloop *Marengo*—which the French had placed at the disposal of the U.S. government as a privateer just days after America's declaration of war with Great Britain. Captain Ordronaux had already distinguished himself with the audacious capture of the cargo-rich British brig *Lady Sherlock*, the first treasure of war brought into New York Harbor. And his reputation kept growing.

Now here was a ship with the size, speed, and attitude to teach the British a real lesson right in their home waters. Captain Ordronaux knew he must have it, and he persuaded the owners to back him and secure a letter of marque as a privateer from the U.S. government. He signed on a crew and set sail for France on July 4th 1813—destination Cherbourg, where the *Prince de Neufchatel* would be outfitted as an American privateer to Captain Ordronaux's personal specifications.

Sixteen of the ship's cannons were replaced with custom-designed 12-pound carronades—squat guns with huge breaches for fighting close-in. Loaded with bags of musket balls, langrage or metal scrap, they could cut away an enemy ship's rigging or sweep her decks clear. Loaded with solid or charged cannonballs, they could stove in an enemy ship's gunnels and take out entire gun crews. The very sight of them in such an array would cause any enemy she got close to to think twice about resisting.

To act as chase guns, two extra-long 18-pounders were installed toward the bow and another long gun was mounted on a swivel in the bow to cover either side. That left four unused gunports—where the 18-pounders could be repositioned if the tactics of engagement required.

The *Prince de Neufchatel* set sail from Cherbourg and almost immediately wreaked havoc on British shipping. In March 1814, she took 9 prizes in the English Channel—escorting them to French ports, with their crews confined below decks and her own men at the helm.

In June, she captured 6 more British ships in 10 days, all of which were escorted to Le Havre. Each time, she immediately headed back out for more.

As word spread, the names *Prince de Neufchatel* and *Captain Ordronaux* began to take on mythic stature. She was called "The Terror of the Seas" and he was called "The Sea Wolf" by British seamen. Bounties were posted and more and more British vessels were deployed to capture or kill them. But as always, Captain Ordronaux eluded them.

In August 1814, Captain Ordronaux moved west into the Irish Channel. There he immediately encountered a brig that wouldn't surrender, so he sank her. In September, he captured 8 brigs, 2 sloops, and destroyed a cutter. During that summer, the *Prince de Neufchatel* was chased over twenty-times by British warships. But she always outran them, at times slowing her speed just to taunt them.

It had been fourteen months since the *Prince de Neufchatel* had first left America and it was time to return. The lock boxes and holds were full of treasure taken at sea or received in France from the sale of confiscated cargo and vessels. The crew was reduced by more than two-thirds as they were transferred a few at a time to sail captured ships into port. And more than a dozen prisoners-of-war were confined below decks. Now, Captain Ordronaux wanted to bring his fight home to the American coastline, where the British naval forces were inflicting the most harm. His plan was to run the blockade and put into Boston Harbor for refitting, resupply and the signing-on of at least 100 more men—then back out to sea to pluck off cargo-rich British supply ships, one-by-one.

As she approached America, the *Prince de Neufchatel* encountered an irresistible prize—the *Douglass*, a 429-ton British merchantman riding very low in the water, a sure sign that her cargo holds were full. The *Douglas* put up little resistance and when boarded revealed a cargo of rum, sugar, molasses, coffee and cotton—worth at least $75,000 in America. She was en route from the West Indies to Liverpool. But now, she and her rich cargo would be escorted to Boston, adding profits and glory to the *Prince de Neufchatel*'s arrival. The entire crew of the prize ship was transferred to the privateer and confined below decks. And Captain Ordronaux assigned eight of his men to take charge of the *Douglass*. This reduced his onboard crew to just 35 men and increased his prisoners below decks to 37.

On the late afternoon of October 9th—less than a day out from the American mainland—the *Prince de Neufchatel*, with the *Douglass* in her wake, spied an American sloop and came alongside to ask how the British had deployed their warships to blockade the coastline and Boston Harbor. On board the sloop was a Nantucket pilot, Charles J. Hilburn, who told Captain Ordronaux that the only wise course was to sail through the unmarked shoals south and east of Nantucket—which the British avoided for fear of running aground. Then a nighttime dash due north along Cape Cod would put them in the best position for a north-by-northeast run into Boston Harbor. Hilburn agreed to pilot the privateer, and came aboard. His younger brother, Tom, went aboard the *Douglass* to pilot her if she became separated in the shoals during the night. Both ships made their way directly to Nantucket's south shore, and the sloop continued on toward Block Island.

As they approached Nantucket early the next day, the *Prince de Neufchatel*'s lookout sounded an alert that a large British warship was on the horizon, off their port beam. She was the *H.M.S. Endymion*, a 40 gun frigate with a broadside of 24-pounders and a crew of 350 men. Commanded by Captain Henry Hope, the *Endymion* was returning from repairs in Halifax to her station in the blockade of New York Harbor. She was fully armed, and her men were rested and eager for action

Captain Ordronaux knew that he could outrun the *Endymion*, but that the *Douglass* could not—and he was unwilling to give up his prize. Above all, he had to keep both ships together and beyond the frigate's cannon range, because her firepower so greatly exceeded his own. So putting Charles Hilburn at the helm, he ordered a direct course toward the Nantucket shoals.

The *Endymion* came about in hot pursuit and by mid-day had nearly halved the distance to its prey. Two more hours and she would be within range to unleash her broadsides. But to Captain Hope's surprise, the *Prince de Neufchatel* and the *Douglass* did not change course to skirt the south edge of the shoals. They plunged directly into them, forcing Captain Hope to stand off, considering his next move. He could sail east to intercept them after they had traversed the shoals—or remain here to prevent them backtracking to the southwest. The odds, of course, favored their running aground. And if they did, he could safely sail close enough to launch boarding parties in his barges to seize both ships. As he weighed these alternatives, the along shore wind suddenly died down and both the *Prince de Neufchatel* and the *Douglass* slowed to a halt in a dead calm. They were now stationary targets and Captain Hope knew he could put them in cannon range in less than an hour—if his faltering wind held at all.

Captain Ordronaux hoisted flags to signal instructions to the *Douglass*. He could see that a thick bank of fog rolling in from the southeast would soon envelop them both, cutting off visual contact and concealing their position from the British. He then ordered long oars put out to coax his own ship forward, looking for a breeze no matter how small.

As the fog closed in around them, the *Prince de Neufchatel*'s sails began to gently flutter and then softly fill. Hilburn ordered them reset to catch the recovering breeze and steered a course due north—aimed directly at the Nantucket coastline, which could no longer be seen. When at last he could hear the sound of the pounding surf, he muttered a rhyme silently to himself to count down several extra minutes. Then he turned the ship sharply to the east a full 90 degrees. By dead reckoning, he had found the narrow channel between the treacherous Old Man Shoal and the beach. Guided only by the sound of the breaking waves, he continued running parallel to the shoreline for another several minutes. Then he ordered the sails dropped and set the aft anchor. Here, the *Prince de Neufchatel* would make her stand until the fog lifted—just 200-yards off Tom Never's Head in 8 fathoms of water.

Captain Ordronaux knew that the *Endymion* would not give up the hunt easily. And he did not expect her to simply wait out the fog at sea. He fully expected that during the night she would deploy a boarding party attack force. Certainly, she had the manpower and the barges to do so. Getting ready to repel them was now his topmost priority. If he was wrong and they did not attack, so much the better. From his current position, he knew he could outrun the *Endymion* to Boston, perhaps even keeping his prize ship, the *Douglass*.

The prisoners were double locked below decks, and all 36 remaining crew members began to make ready. The *Endymion* probably expected a full force of 150 men aboard the *Prince de Neufchatel*, so any boarding party they sent would no doubt equal or exceed that number. Grease and oil were swabbed down the privateer's sides to make securing a foothold more difficult. Nets were strung from the bulwarks to the shrouds to slow anyone attempting to come over the side. All carronades were double shotted with bags of musket balls and langrage. Cannonballs were stacked along the gunnels, where they could be dropped down on barges to crack holes in their bottoms. Baskets were filled with loaded pistols, cutlasses and marlinspikes. Loaded muskets were stacked every few feet along the deck. Every man had several weapons at his disposal, so that no time would have to be wasted in reloading. Thanks to her many conquests, the privateer had built a vast armory that could now prove essential.

As the last trace of light bled from the still fog-masked sky, all the men took their positions and the *Prince de Neufchatel* was plunged into near total darkness and an uneasy silence. Carefully placed battle lanterns had been lit, but they were now shrouded—to be uncovered again only if needed.

About 9:00 PM, a muffled sound could be heard off to starboard, followed moments later by a clunk. Captain Ordronaux reached out to tap the shoulder of his best marksman, who fired a single shot into the darkness. The flash of return fire confirmed that a barge with at least a dozen men was approaching—and they had revealed their position. Almost instantly, a fusillade of carefully-aimed musket fire from the privateer ripped into the night, and the gasps and screams from the darkness told the men that several enemy targets had been hit. Seconds later, a rocket flare from the *Prince de Neufchatel* lit up the sky—silhouetting against its pale yellow glow a large barge with nearly 30 British marines. Then the full force of two carronade rounds tore into the barge with devastating effect—cutting down its men and splitting open its seams. The barge sank quickly. If there were any survivors in the water, they couldn't be seen.

While most eyes were on the barge, Captain Ordronaux's were searching the outer areas still illuminated by the flare. There could be more barges from the *Endymion* further out in the fog, or they could be approaching from a different direction. But he could see none. Then, just before the light faded, he leaned out to look directly below, and he was the first to see a second British barge already made fast to his hull at midships. Even before he could shout out the alert, the sound of several grapnel hooks biting into the bulwarks and deck told the crew that it was time for hand-to-hand combat to repel boarders.

In fact, there were five barges in all with a total of 146 men. Only the last one had been destroyed. The other four with 117 men had already encircled the *Prince de Neufchatel* and had made fast preparing to board her—one on each side, one at the bow, and one secured to the stern anchor cable. The boarding party still outnumbered the defenders by a better than 3-to-1 margin, but only the Americans knew it.

The next twenty minutes were a blur of fury, suffering and heroics. Knives, cutlasses, pistols, pikes, muskets, fists, teeth were all used as weapons. The deck became slippery with blood, the air choking with the smoke of gunpowder. Kill or be killed in hand-to-hand combat were the only strategic orders. At first, the prisoners below had yelled out encouragement to the attackers. But quickly their voices were drowned out by the sound of pain and rage above decks.

Dozens of Royal marines were cut down as they attempted to break through the nets and climb over the midship gunwales. Those that succeeded were ferociously beaten back and thrown bleeding or dead into the pitch black waters. Boarders fore and aft were slashed, shot, clubbed or beaten into submission—and one-by-one their limp bodies were hurled over the side in case they were playing possum.

Then, from one of the barges below came the appeal, "Quarter. Quarter." The British Lieutenant in charge was surrendering his forces.

Of the four barges taking part in the actual boarding raid, only two were remaining. The Lieutenant reported that a third barge with 16 gravely wounded aboard had been cut loose with orders to return to the *Endymion*. And a fourth barge with 14 injured men that had been pulled from the water had drifted away sometime earlier; its men too weak to continue the fight. Aboard the two barges still tied to the *Prince de Neufchatel*, there were 38 dead, 37 seriously wounded, and 30 exhausted but still functioning. That left 11 men missing and assumed dead—all from the barge sunk by the Americans at the onset of the battle.

Loses aboard the *Prince de Neufchatel* were also heavy—7 men killed, including the pilot Charles Hilburn; 15 were badly wounded; 6 were injured but still able to somewhat function. That left only 8 unhurt, including Captain Jules Ordronaux. It is said that Captain Ordronaux himself had fought like a madman, firing over 80 shots and killing more than 20. If that were true, it would not surprise me.

The British Lieutenant asked that his surrendered forces be taken aboard, so that the wounded could be cared for. Captain Ordronaux refused, explaining that his ship's surgeon had been killed during the battle. He lowered nets and baskets to collect all their weapons, then lowered baskets of food, water and bandages. His refusal, of course, was to conceal the very few defenders he had remaining. The British still had a functioning force more than twice the size of the Americans. Captain Ordronaux told them they would have to ride out the night in their barges, and in the morning they would be issued paroles and allowed to row to the nearby Nantucket shoreline. By accepting a parole, a combatant agreed not to fight again until properly exchanged. The British quickly agreed, knowing that Nantucket was now neutral, and assuming that a British force would soon be there to rescue them.

𝔐 𝔐 𝔐

Hibbard Rae and more than a dozen other armed men had climbed down the sandy cliff to the broad beach below Tom Never's Head. By the time they got there, the gunfire had ended and the fog was beginning to recede, revealing a waxing crescent moon. That's when they saw the large barge being carried in by the tide. At first they thought it was empty, but then they saw movement. Were they British or were they American? How many were they? Silently, Ray and his men dropped to the sand to await these unknown intruders. As the barge beached and swung broadside to the shoreline, its markings gave them the answer—*H.M.S. Endymion*. Then slowly, and with great effort, twelve seemingly half-drowned men struggled out of the barge, carrying two others. These they stretched out on the sand; it appeared they were corpses. Though some of the twelve were armed, all looked far too weak to put up much resistance. Still, the Nantucketers waited, remaining cautious.

When the British huddled together trying to get their bearings and agree on their best option, Hibbard Rae and his men pounced upon them. The Royal Marines were disarmed, their hands tied behind them, and then they were marched single file to the Rae barn—where they were held captive until a rider could bring more men from town. Later, the two bodies were retrieved and buried not far from Tom Never's Pond.

𝔐 𝔐 𝔐

The prize ship *Douglass*—following Captain Ordronaux's signal flag orders—safely passed through the channel between Old Man Shoal and the Nantucket shoreline, somehow eluding the *Endymion*'s search party. The young Nantucket pilot, Tom Hilburn, had learned much from his brother.

At midnight, with the *Prince de Neufchatel* still nowhere in sight, the *Douglass* executed her pre-assigned orders. She rounded the eastern end

of the Island and beached herself near Sankaty Head, about midway between the fishing villages of 'Sconset and Sesachacha. Captain Ordronaux did not want her to be retaken by the British, almost a certainty
if she lost his protection. And it was far better to deliver her as a gift to
the Islanders, rather than to abandon and sink her.

During the night, word quickly spread and more than 250 fishermen
converged on the spot, rigging lines to off-load the *Douglass*'s cargo. The
manifest listed 421 hogsheads of sugar, 190 large casks of rum, 6
hogshead of molasses, 254 bales of cotton, 3 bags of ginger, and 28 ma-
hogany logs. All this—along with the ship's stores, instruments, and best
fittings—were salvaged and stacked on the shore. So large was the haul,
that it took well into the afternoon to off-load it.

By then, virtually every horse cart on the Island had arrived and Captain Jared Gardner took charge of dispersing the goods as fairly as he
could. After first setting aside portions for the pilot and the 6 American
Douglass crew members, he gave out all the rest. That night, laughter and
singing would be heard in most homes. After years of privation, sweets,
rum, and an unexpected gift from the sea have a way of lifting the spirits!

❦   ❦   ❦

Even before daybreak that same morning, hundreds of Nantucketers
lined the south shore and even more peered from the distant roof walks
in town. They knew a battle had been fought, but they had no idea of the
outcome. Then the rising sun revealed the victor. Just 200-yards off the
south shore stood the *Prince de Neufchatel* with all her flags flying. And
the large British frigate they could see on the horizon seemed to be skulk-
ing away. A cheer went up. People hugged their friends and their family.
Joy was in every heart. The Americans had won a great battle over the
British.

As people watched from the shore, Captain Ordronaux freed the two
barges filled with the British dead, wounded, and paroled prisoners-of-
war. During the night, two more men had perished, bringing the total on
board the barges to 40 dead, 35 seriously wounded, and 30 still functioning. They rowed directly toward the beach, letting the rising swells and

low breaking waves carry them up onto the wet sand. There they were confronted by more than 120 armed men.

The British Lieutenant in charge presented a letter from Captain Ordronaux granting paroles for his full party, and requesting that they all be treated with the dignity deserved by men who had fought bravely. The letter was read aloud and inspected. All nodded in agreement. And the British were assisted out of their barges.

The wounded were carried into town in horse carts and brought to a makeshift surgery set up in Dixon's Tavern on the North Wharf—it was called Cross Wharf back then. The uninjured remained behind to bury their dead atop Tom Never's bluff, in a place that overlooked the sea where they fought. Later, they were escorted into Town and taken in by families willing to do so. There they remained until the end of the war, a little over two months later. Neither the *Endymion* nor any other British vessel came to look for them.

Captain Ordronaux kept his wounded aboard and sailed safely to Boston Harbor. There he turned over his prisoners, released his men, sold his cargo, sold his ship, and sold his letter of marque as a privateer. His dead had been buried at sea, and all his wounded recovered. The *Prince de Neufchatel* would sail again, but never with Captain Ordronaux in command. Those knowledgeable in naval lore speak of her still as the most distinguished privateer to carry the American flag. And Ordronaux's name remains a legend. And just as the "Chesapeake Affair" provided us with the patriotic spark to go to war, the *Prince de Neufchatel*'s victory provided us with the patriotic second wind to keep fighting. And recognizing that, the British decided to seek a negotiated peace.

❦   ❦   ❦

Earlier, I mentioned workers fencing in an area named "Plainfield." It's worth commenting on here in more detail, because it marked Nantucket's transition from "land held in common" to rights of private property.

By the time the War of 1812 began, nearly 75 percent of all the land on Nantucket was held in common. And the number of individual Proprietors had grown from the original 27 to 313, due largely to inheritances. In addition, thousands of others on and off the Island had inherited rights to fractional shares that the Proprietors represented for them in their voting. Taken together, these shareholders owned over 20,000 acres of common land, but their rights were in the form of undivided shares—with no *individual* ownership rights to any *specific* piece of the common land.

While common land was fine for sheep grazing, it had proven to be a disaster for farming—crop yields were poor and declining. That's because no one had a personal long-term incentive to work and improve the land. It wasn't theirs, it was everyone's—and in practical terms that meant it was no one's!

Three proprietors—Richard Mitchell, Obed. Macy and Paul Gardner, Jr.—wanted to change that. Combined, they owned nearly 12 percent of the Island's sheep commons shares and they decided to petition the Massachusetts Supreme Judicial Court for the right to break away and convert those shares into private land holdings. The case, officially called "Mitchell vs. Starbuck," was first filed in October 1810, but it was not decided until May 11th 1813.

The Court in its decision ruled that the Petitioners were indeed "tenants in common" and therefore entitled to separate ownership. And the ruling went on to specify that any person owning 100 or more sheep commons shares could convert those shares into private land in one or more designated plots.

As you might expect, given this option, the Mitchell group tried to lay claim to what they considered to be the very best farming land on the Island. The Proprietors objected and filed an appeal with the Courts saying that this was unfair to the other owners because all land was not of the same equal value. A special committee of three commissioners was appointed to work out an equitable way to settle the issue. Despite some serious objections, the Court ruled on December 13th 1813 that while the Petitioners were legally entitled to redeem their shares for 2,520 acres, they would instead receive 2,124 acres in the premium area they preferred. This area, adjacent to the Southeast Quarter, they named "Plainfield." Everyone else called it "The Great Set-Off."

Consider the fact that most of this legal battle was taking place during the War, during the blockades and the embargos, during the time when the Nantucket economy was in shambles, when most of the Islanders were destitute, and the fear of a British invasion was widespread. Land disputes would have seemed to be the least of Nantucket's concerns at that time. But no, then as now, land rights have always been a preoccupation for the people of this Island.

❧   ❧   ❧

10

1846 . . . Exodus

As night fell on July 13th 1846, the people of Nantucket had every reason to feel pride. For more than 25 years, the wealth had poured in and the name "Nantucket" was known and respected around the world. With each year more profitable than the last and no new threats of war, it was hard to believe that the Island's prosperity would ever end.

All that July, the waterfront was alive with activity—a busy shipyard at Brant Point, 5 boat shops, 17 oil factories, 19 candle factories, 10 ropewalks, 22 cooperages, 1 brass foundry, 3 tanneries, 10 blacksmith shops, 4 spar shops, 2 block factories, 2 bakeries, 60 grog shops, numerous clothing stores and food provisioners, several ship chandleries and brickyards, a rum distillery, 4 banks and several insurance companies.

Mansions lined Main Street—renamed from State Street in 1835—and more were being built there and on major streets leading to it. Most of the smaller houses built before 1800 had been torn down, moved or tremendously expanded. New additions included the elegant neoclassical Hadwin House and the stately Wright Mansion—both directly opposite the imposing "Three Bricks" owned by the three Starbuck brothers. And Jared Coffin's massive new brick house now stood proudly at Center and Broad.

Island-wide, the population neared 10,000. And while only 50 people owned 70-percent of all the property, there was work for everybody and good money to be made—most all of it from whaling. With that many people, even the farms did well.

The sheep raising industry was another story. That was just about gone, unable to compete with the higher-quality and lower prices of wool from the western territories and from Australia and New Zealand. From a high of 20,000 sheep in 1826, the flock was now down to about a thousand head and there was talk of closing the sheepshearing yards near Miacomet Pond. This, of course, was seen as no loss to the people of Nantucket Town, who had come to despise the sheep which nightly invaded the Town by the hundreds to bed down—befouling streets, doorways and walkways in the process.

If you've ever heard of the "Nantucket Sheep War of 1845," that incident was not about land rights, it was about the problem of sheep in the Town. The mess was so bad that Town laws were passed to hire field drivers and pound keepers to round-up trespassing animals. These were herded into pens and kept until the owners paid a stiff fine. When they refused, the pound keepers stopped supplying feed and water to the animals, which were pretty much left to die.

As the Sheep Wars escalated, the owners demanded compensation for the loss of their stock. The Town refused, and at that point the sheep owners hired Daniel Webster to help them seek damages from the field drivers and pound keepers. To block this, the townspeople quickly passed a new law indemnifying the Town's employees against all damage claims. After several months of harsh rhetoric and retaliatory legal maneuvers, the whole affair ended when the Nantucket wool market collapsed and the value of sheep fell so low that it made further legal action pointless. After 187 years, Nantucket's sheep raising days were over. And all but the few remaining major sheep owners were very glad to see it ended.

So one could rightly say that July 13th 1846 was a very happy day on Nantucket. Just about everything was going right. And furthest from everyone's mind was the possibility of the terrifying event that would occur that very night.

Historians like to zero in on a major event that marks the beginning or end of an era. And for Nantucket, that pivotal event is usually said to be the Great Fire. After all, in a single night—July 14th 1846—more than one-third of the Town was reduced to ashes and the entire waterfront complex was lost. Over 400 buildings were destroyed—including Trinity Church and the Atheneum Library & Museum. Only one store was left standing, but miraculously all the Island's other churches and all the large mansions were spared.

While certainly devastating, the 1846 Great Fire was *not* the principal reason for Nantucket's decline as the world's whaling capitol. Major fires had also occurred in 1836, 1838 and 1844. Then as now, rebuilding began almost immediately—usually to the betterment of the area. Look to any city of this period in America and you'll almost always find a Great Fire prominent in their history.

Other reasons given for Nantucket's decline include the persistent problems of the sandbar at the harbor's entrance, the lure of the California Gold Rush, and the discovery of petroleum leading to the invention of kerosene for lighting. Even the Civil War is given as a contributing factor. Without doubt, all played some part. But it was an era-changing event—occurring hundreds of miles to the northwest—that more than any other single factor sealed Nantucket's economic fate. That event was the opening of the Erie Canal. This absolutely brilliant engineering feat unleashed America's industrial revolution, transformed the nation's economy, changed the country's centers of power, and shifted the entire focus of the citizenry away from the seas to the continent's interior.

🦋 🦋 🦋

Whaling was truly America's first industry. And from the beginning, Nantucket was the epicenter of whaling. Prior to the American War of Independence, Nantucket whale oil and bone accounted for a full fifth of New England's exports to England. And these commodities were so valuable that Nantucket was considered to be one of the most prized assets in the entire British Empire. Even the disruptions of two wars could not dislodge Nantucket's whaling industry dominance. Other American ports would be used. But the ships and trade were still largely controlled by Nantucket owners and merchants. In fact, the quarter century from 1820 to 1845 was Nantucket's "Golden Age"—a period of unprecedented prosperity for the whaling trade of the Island. But Nantucket was a one-industry economy, and beneath the surface lurked the seminal change that would prove to be the whaling industry's death knell.

When the Erie Canal was completed in 1825, it remapped the future of America by providing 2,000 miles of navigable water from the Atlantic Ocean to the inland ports on the Great Lakes. Within a year, it cut the time and costs to transport goods to and from the nation's interior by 90-percent and provided a direct and efficient link between New York City and the country's resource-rich center.

Before the Erie Canal, most all of the goods flowing to and from the great Midwest centered on the Port of New Orleans—terminus for the mighty Mississippi and the Ohio, Missouri and Illinois Rivers that fed into it. This gave the entire Midwest region strong political, commercial and social ties to the South.

Almost overnight this focus changed. Within just a few years, New York City became the country's leading port and financial center. Manufacturing cities sprung up all across New York State, along the Great Lakes, and throughout the Midwest. Lush lands were cleared and cultivated, producing abundant harvests that found ready markets thanks to fast and low-cost transportation. In increasing numbers, New Englanders migrated west via the Canal, followed by a massive immigration of Northern Europeans. The American Industrial Revolution and the move westward had begun—transforming the country from a vast wilderness with population centers concentrated along its Eastern coastline, into what would become an agricultural, industrial and commercial world power.

Before the Erie Canal, there was a better than even chance that British-controlled Canada would become the dominant economic force in North America. To help block this, the Canal was designed to connect with Lake Erie rather than Lake Ontario. This nearly doubled its length and costs and posed enormous engineering challenges. But it denied a still-hostile Canada much of the Canal's benefits and focused economic growth in the United States rather than Canada.

Many historians even say that the Erie Canal changed the likely outcome of the American Civil War by ending the South's dominant influence on the Midwest. Without this shift to Northern influence, the War and the issue of slavery might have had a far different outcome.

It's also impossible to overstate the psychological impact of the Canal on the American people, so bold and brilliant was its achievement. Predicted by European canal experts to take over 150 years to build, the 363-mile long Erie Canal was completed in just eight years by engineering novices in an age before steam engines and dynamite. The longest canal in the world, it cut through hundreds of miles of primeval forests, across great swamps, over enormous stone aqueducts, through miles of solid rock. With its 83 locks that lifted barges an amazing 565-feet from the Hudson River to Lake Erie, it was and still remains the single most important public work ever built in the United States. And beyond that, it showed Americans that anything was possible if imagination, ingenuity and organization were focused on a problem. New machines were invented almost on the spot to overcome every obstacle. The Canal became the birthplace and first school of American Engineering. The age of a vibrant industrial America had begun!

🎇　🎇　🎇

After the Great Fire, the Town rebuilt quickly with a widened lower Main Street, brick buildings and a new Atheneum. The dock complex was put back into service. The money was there to go even further in redeveloping and modernizing the whaling industry infrastructure, but for the first time in Nantucket's history there seemed to be a reluctance to do so. While still profitable, whaling meant tying up capital for years with high risks on every voyage. Thinking about the potential for bigger profits and faster returns, some of the shipowners and merchants decided to gradually shift more of their assets to mainland industries. Jared Coffin sold his new Broad Street home and moved to Boston. Most others remained, but quietly invested in knitting mills and other mainland enterprises. No investment was made to dredge the harbor entrance and build a jetty. The "camel"—a type of floating dry dock used to lift the bigger ships over the sandbar—remained in use. Better to invest the money elsewhere and to deploy even more of the larger ships to mainland ports with direct railroad links to the markets.

This shift in attitude was not limited to the owners. For the men, the rewards of whaling—while still good—began to seem comparatively less attractive: Three years at sea with hard, dangerous and dirty work, and a payout totally dependent on the voyage's yield . . . *versus* a good job or a good sailing berth with guaranteed payment for one's efforts.

So the real truth is that the Great Fire didn't destroy Nantucket's economy. There was plenty of money to rebuild and they did so quickly. The sandbar didn't destroy Nantucket's economy. The know-how and funds existed to deepen the harbor's entrance. The Gold Rush didn't destroy Nantucket's economy. While it attracted hundreds of men to distant California, it was short-lived and profits for most were non-existent. Even the development of kerosene, which would supplant whale oil and spermaceti candles for lighting, was well off in the future—as was the Civil War's call up to arms. While all are named as the reasons for Nantucket's decline, they were not the root causes. It was personal ambition and the opportunity for faster and greater rewards on the mainland that destroyed Nantucket's single-industry economy. The Island Empire had lost its glitter, and the exodus of money and jobs had begun.

For a time, the exodus progressed slowly. As I mentioned, the 1846 population was just short of 10,000. Four years later in 1850 it had dropped to 8,800. Then the pace of abandonment picked up. In 1860 it was 6,100. In 1865 it was 4,800. In 1870 it was 4,100. And in 1875 it was down to 3,200—a decline of 78-percent in 29 years.

At the time the Erie Canal opened in 1825, Nantucket shipowners held title to 125 whalers—with 83 of them registered in Nantucket and 42 registered in New Bedford. By the time of the Great Fire in 1846, they owned 85 whalers, with 16 registered in Nantucket and 69 registered in New Bedford. By 1857, they owned 99 whalers, with 4 registered in Nantucket and 95 registered in New Bedford. Then fairly quickly, Nantucket shipowners began to sell their fleets to willing buyers in New Bed-

ford, Stonington, New London, Sag Harbor and other ports. They knew
there was still money to be made in whaling, but they also knew that even
more money could be made in other ways in a newly industrializing
America.

When did Nantucket's whaling era really end? If you're looking for a
hard date, you could say 1869 when the bark *Oak*—the last of the Nantucket whalers—sailed away, never to return. But for most here on the Island, it was almost 15 years earlier when it was clear to most everyone that
the 50 men who controlled the Island's wealth had cast their eyes elsewhere. They saw whaling was their past, not their future.

🦋　🦋　🦋

By jumping ahead to the Great Fire of 1846 in telling you the Island's
story, I've skipped over several things that you should really know about
the Southeast Quarter. So let's go back almost thirty years.

When the War of 1812 ended in February 1815, there was considerable joy and great confidence that the whaling industry and the sheep industry would quickly bounce back. But nature decreed that we would
first have another two years of privation. Less than two months after the
war ended, the Tambora Volcano in Indonesia exploded, hurling enormous quantities of ash into the atmosphere. They say that the Tambora
blast was 75-times larger than the Mt. St. Helens explosion that occurred
some years ago in Oregon. Ash from Tambora darkened the sky and
dimmed the sun worldwide. Here on Nantucket, it plunged us into an
18-month-long winter.

During 1815 and 1816, there was frost and snow every month of the
year, with temperatures in February plummeting to 11 below zero. All
crops failed and most of the Island's vegetation was destroyed. Farming
and sheeping became impossible. And to compound the problem, heavy
taxes were levied on property owners to make up for the Island's deferred
federal tax payments during the war. This put a very heavy burden on the
owners of land here in the Southeast Quarter, where private ownership
had become more common. The seafaring men, the shipowners and the
merchants were largely exempted from taxes, because only real estate

holdings were taxed. And the undivided common lands were considered too complex to tax. The original 27 shares had now grown to over 2,000,000—with most of the owners unrecorded or long ago moved away.

In Town there were very few jobs to be had. With half the whaling fleet lost during the war, owners ordered new ships built or refitted *in other ports* to speed their delivery. Assuming that the first new oil to be brought in would command top dollar, ship owners took out major credit loans to finance putting as many ships as possible into service. As a result, every ship they could muster sailed away for a two year, three year or longer voyage. By 1816, Nantucket harbor was again empty of whalers— with no work to be had until they returned. Beggars were back on the streets and the soup kitchens reopened. The women re-sewed old garments to give to the poor. Then in November, the Great Point Lighthouse burned to the ground, extinguishing for many their fading hope of better times to come.

But by the spring of 1817, the Island's fortunes began to turn upward dramatically. The sun's warmth coaxed the crops to sprout and blossom. Ships began to return to the harbor, their holds full of whale oil and bone. And the prices they commanded were exceptional. A two-year failure of the whale fishery in Northern Europe meant that Nantucket merchants had little competition.

Success after success followed. Nantucket's Golden Age had begun— so named not only for the boom times and wealth, but for the conspicuous display of that wealth—no longer constrained as it once was by Quaker reserve and custom.

In 1818, the Pacific National Bank was built; and the first steamboat—*Eagle*—arrived with 60 visitors from the mainland. In 1823, the Methodist Church on Center Street was built. And in the year following, Peter Ewell placed the milestones along the road to 'Sconset. A visit to 'Sconset was considered an outing not to be missed by the Island's gentry and their growing number of guests.

By 1826, more than a dozen small new farms had sprung up in the Southeast Quarter. Vegetables, fruits, grains, milk, butter and meat were produced in abundance. And more than 20,000 sheep now grazed all across the common lands—with most on the eastern end of the island. Wool market quotations were given out daily at afternoon tea and watched as intently as you'd follow the stock market today. Each June a "Shearing" festival was held, giving the entire Island an excuse to frolic. Lasting four or more days and held in two locations, the festival involved the whole community in feasting, dancing and games. Sheep shearing yards were set up near Miacomet Pond and Washing Pond. Crews of shearers were brought in to wash and shear the sheep, while the citizens cheered them on.

Massive new homes were built on Main Street and on the streets leading to it. But the one that I'd especially like to call to your attention is Moor's End on Pleasant Street, between Candle House Lane and Mill Streets. This is the imposing red brick mansion with the high brick wall concealing its garden. Built in 1827 for Jared Coffin, a very successful shipowner, Moor's End allowed him to indulge his passion for magnificent gardens of the type he had seen in Europe. The Moor's End garden was very formal and strictly symmetrical in layout—with twenty-six flower beds bordered in precisely-trimmed boxwood, with connecting walkways leading to a central floral medallion and fountain. It was the most impressive garden to be found on the Island, but it had one limitation—its size. Filled with plantings, it did not allow Jared Coffin and his wife to entertain out-of-doors on the grand scale they would like to. So in 1829, they created Bloomingdale near 'Sconset,

Virtually no one on the Island today has even heard of Bloomingdale, but if you look very carefully at an early 1830 map—hand drawn by Lucy S. Macy when she was a schoolgirl—you'll find it. Also, look at the big 1869 Ewer map in the Atheneum and you'll see it between the 6th and 7th milestones on Milestone Road, beneath Cain's Hill at the northern end of Tom Never's Swamp.

Securing a large tract of land from the owners of Plainfield and another section south of Corn Pond, Jarred Coffin hired a British landscape designer to lay out and construct sweeping gardens of the naturalistic style that had become so popular in England. Gentle hillocks and sloping fields, flowing streams and free-form ponds, meandering walkways and narrow towpaths formed the hardscape. Feathery trees and lush bushes, scattered stands of flowering shrubs and fruit trees, random fields and clumps of brightly-colored wild blossoms, sweeping lawns, and water gardens of reeds and water lilies created the illusion of a perfect Eden untouched by man. To this he added rose and vine arbors, benches, gazebos, arched bridges and a large trellis-covered central pavilion with a raised wooden floor for dinner parties and dancing. Service buildings and kitchens were concealed as greenhouses and potting sheds.

It was here at Bloomingdale that Nantucket's most lavish parties were held throughout the spring, summer and early fall. Gay dinner parties, chowder parties, dances and fancy dress balls at Bloomingdale filled the busy social calendars of the Island's most prominent families. And once each summer, the gates were thrown open to the gentry's young people for an ice cream social.

'Sconset itself was becoming something of a summer resort for the wealthier whaling captains and successful small business owners—even if their visit was just for a day. Two taverns did a thriving business and a few of the fishing stages were converted into comfortable cottages for overnight stays. When not working, even the "common folk" made treks to 'Sconset for picnics, to watch the fishermen, and to enjoy the ocean views and fresh air—free from the pungent smell of the Town's tryworks.

Times were good in the Southeast Quarter. And to everyone's astonishment, in 1834 even the bluefish returned after a 70 year absence.

Bloomingdale held sway as the place to be seen for nearly a dozen years, but for some reason we can only speculate about, Jared Coffin's interest in entertaining began to wane. Fewer and fewer parties were held at Bloomingdale, until in 1844 no invitations were issued. That same year, Jared Coffin ordered construction on his big new house at Center and Broad Streets. It was completed in late 1845, but then put on the market in spring 1846—just two months before the Great Fire. Jared Coffin and his wife had promptly abandoned Nantucket for Boston—with the sale of Moor's End, the new Broad Street house and Bloomingdale left in the hands of his agent. Moor's End sold almost immediately, but the sale of the new house to a steamship company for $7,000 was not completed until after the fire. In 1847, it was reopened as a hotel named "Ocean House." Today you know it as that fine old hotel called the "Jared

FIGURE 4   Jared Coffin—Circa 1855

In 1827, Jared Coffin built his imposing brick mansion "Moor's End," with its magnificent walled formal garden. Then in 1829 he created "Bloomingdale" near 'Sconset—a vast garden landscape of the "naturalistic" style then all the rage in England. Today he is best remembered for the mansion he built but never occupied on Broad Street—that's now called "The Jared Coffin House." *(Photo courtesy of the Nantucket Historical Association, P227.)*

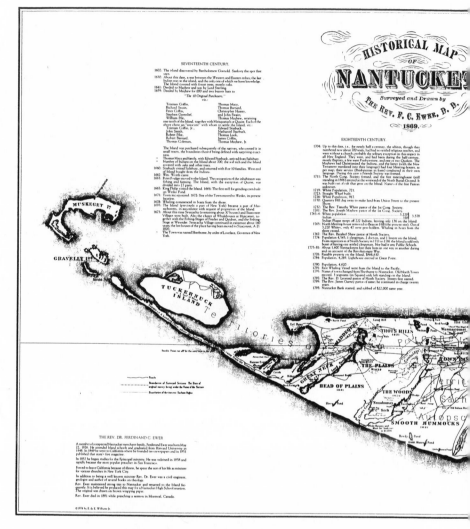

FIGURE 5   Historical Map of Nantucket—Circa 1869

Perhaps the best known Historical Map of the Island is the Rev. F.C.Ewer
Map of 1869. Careful study of the full size original in the Nantucket
Atheneum or at the Nantucket Historical Association will show Jared Coffin's
Bloomingdale Gardens just west of 'Sconset.

(Map reproduced with permission of the Nantucket Atheneum.)

NINETEENTH CENTURY.

...Academy incorporated, and the building erected. It was now a public
...
...weighing 1,000 lbs.) placed in North Tower.
...Methodist Society organized.
...lation, 5,617.
...r Bank and two Insurance Offices established.
...Unitarian Society formed, the Rev. Seth F. Swift, Pastor. The
...s Society languishing on account of losing members to the
...odist and the Unitarian.
...ation, 6,807.
...Library instituted: Josiah Howes, Esq., President.
...Nantucket Gazette issued. It had but a brief existence.
...Rev. Abram Morse pastor at the North. The Mechanics' Associa-
...a literary society, was formed.
...ation, 7,266. 22 ships (21,600 tons) engaged in Whale Fishery.
...dman Library Association formed.
...Public Schools established and the Coffin School opened.
...lation, 7,202.
...new North Meeting-house erected. Athenaeum incorporated. 1836:
...Fire.
...School opened. Great Fire in the town; loss $300,000.
...y Church (Episcopal) erected; the Parish having been organized a
...time before by the Rev. Moses Marcus, B.D.
...lation, 9,712.
...e Fire. July 13 and 14. Whaling declines.
...trees planted by Josiah Sturgis.
...lation, 8,179.
...e Fine groves planted.
...aighed for first time on the Island. 185-. Abram Quary (last man
...ndian blood in him) died.
...lation 6,094.
...ilation, 4,830. Alumni Association (of High School) organized.

Coffin House." Bloomingdale had no takers and the gates remained closed for a generation, as nature slowly reclaimed it. However, 'Sconset grew even more popular as a destination—dubbed the "Newport of Nantucketoise" by some Islanders. And in 1848, it celebrated the opening of its first hotel, "The Atlantic House."

But all that was to fade as the Island settled into its accelerating decline in the late 1850s. One by one, farms in the Southeast Quarter were abandoned. 'Sconset returned to a fishing outpost. And without sheep, the moors grew ever more wild and deserted.

❦   ❦   ❦

By 1875, Nantucket had lost just about everything its people had ever dreamed of. The Wampanoag people and their culture were gone. The communal estates and the baronial aspirations of the original British settlers were gone. The Quakers and their total dominance of the Island's ethics, economics and enterprises were gone. The sheep were gone. Whaling was gone. And 7-out-of–10 inhabitants were gone. Even many of the houses were dismantled and shipped to the mainland.

The Island Empire of Nantucket was all but forgotten.

❦   ❦   ❦

11

1895 ... On The Beach

I 've always thought it particularly ironic that one of the pivotal events leading to Nantucket's decline was the very same force that would later bring it back to life—although in a totally new form.

We've talked about the Erie Canal and the Industrial Revolution that it unleashed. And how that transformed America by opening up the country's interior and creating vast new opportunities in the cities and towns—drawing the population away from the countryside to work in the new factories, plants, mills and offices that were opening everywhere. Commerce, fueled by innovation and invention, was generating unprecedented new wealth and optimism. An expanding network of railroads and steamships was making shipping and personal travel fast and affordable for the first time. As never before in the nation's history, the middle class now had both the means and the ability to travel widely.

Fed by this prosperity and new found freedom to travel, three fresh ideas swept through the popular culture in the late 1880s. The first was *the summer vacation*—a set period of time during the summer each year when all work was suspended, as the mill or factory was closed down during the hottest weeks for maintenance and retooling. The second was *the glorification of nature*. While life in the cities and towns could be quite lively, a growing ache developed in most hearts for the beauties of nature left behind. In popular art, music, literature and oratory, the majesty and beauty of nature was extolled. In science, attention turned to the natural world's profusion of flora and fauna. With little exaggeration, it was said that everyone was becoming a naturalist! This created a compelling desire to "commune with nature" during one's relatively short vacation time. In growing numbers, people flocked to the mountains, to the forests, to the lakes, to the great out of doors—where lodges and resort hotels were being built at a rapid clip to accommodate them. Yes, it was usually cooler there, but it was nature's draw rather than just a lower temperature that attracted them.

The third new idea that swept through the popular culture was *the fashionableness of the seaside.* It may surprise you to learn that prior to 1870, a seaside vacation was considered not at all appealing except to sailing enthusiasts. The idea of sitting on an open beach in full sunshine— or wading into the briny surf—had very little appeal. But all that began to change as naturalists like Thoreau and others introduced their readers to the primal and serene beauty of Cape Cod and other coastal areas. Before long, seaside resorts began to spring up, catering to this growing popular interest. Then the wealthy began to build their huge summer homes in Newport and all along the New England coastline. And before long, wealthy families from as far away as the middle and southern states wanted to spend their summer months at the New England seaside. Young people coined new terms like "taking a bath in the ocean" and "boiling in the surf" to describe their invigorating and daring beach experiences. And it was widely reported in much of the popular press that the combination of fresh sea air, brilliant sunshine, and bracing ocean bathing had restorative properties for both the body and temperament.

Health, beauty and nature—combined with fashionableness—made the seaside vacation an irresistible lure. And that gave a spark of new hope to a once-proud Nantucket, whose industries had fled and whose land had become next to worthless.

❧   ❧   ❧

Tourism began pretty slowly here in Nantucket. At first it was just a trickle of visitors come to see family on the Island. Then more came as the railroads and boat lines began to add little maps and flowery promotional copy to their brochures. Before long, three hotels in Town were doing a fairly good business serving the summer trade. *The Ocean House*—converted from the Jared Coffin mansion by the steamship line just after the Great Fire—was expanded to accommodate 200 guests. *The Springfield House* overlooking the harbor could accommodate about half that many. And *The Sherburne House* on Orange Street advertised it could handle 150 guests. A few summer cottages were built on the bluff near Brant Point, on small plots of land that Captain Charles Moores sold to off-Islanders. He called this area Nantucket Bluffs to give it something of a neighborhood feel.

'Sconset continued to have its own special appeal. As early as 1850—back when the Sankaty Lighthouse was built—a few larger summer homes lined the road stretching from Bloomingdale to the village. That's about the time when they renamed this road Main Street. Gradually, more houses were added, and a few tiny squatter cottages were built in Codfish Park—a new area that had emerged from the sea after the major storms of 1835 and 1841 ate away the cliff to reshape the coastline. But until 1872, 'Sconset still remained a tiny hamlet of little more than 60 summer houses. Even so, its reputation started growing due to the well publicized visits of the famous—notably including, General Ulysses S. Grant.

. As the 1870s began, Nantucket's men of means looked with amazement and great interest at the seaside land boom occurring on the mainland—and even at Oaks Bluff in Martha's Vineyard. They told themselves that surely there was a fortune to be made by creating and selling off vacation lots on the Nantucket shoreline. The land could be acquired very cheaply. Developing an exciting resort concept and laying out the building lots would cost relatively little. Perhaps the largest single investment would be for the promotion and sales efforts needed to bring in the buyers and to close the deals quickly. This told them that their concept had to be big enough and compelling enough to attract large numbers of prospective buyers and to persuade them to make this remote Island, rather than some other coastal place, their summer home site.

The first—and one of the few successful land development plans—occurred in 'Sconset in 1872. Dr. Franklin A. Ellis, a wealthy and very popular physician and dentist, partnered with Charles H. Robinson to buy a large tract of land just south of the gully near post office square in 'Sconset. They named their new development *Sunset Heights*, and to promote it built a footbridge across the gully and constructed an attractive model house that was offered for rentals. Some of the development's lots sold quickly, and Robinson reinvested their proceeds into building a string of tiny cottages modeled after the historic fishstages along the bluff. These too sold quickly, returning a handsome profit to both Ellis and Robinson. A few of these little cottages can still be seen as part of "The Summer House."

Over the next 12 years, Dr. Ellis continued to invest successfully in real estate and other businesses on the Island—including a hotel in 'Sconset, the Pitman & Ellis pharmacy on Main Street (it's now Congdon's), and the Nantucket Railroad. Then in 1884 without warning, he closed his practice and fled the Island, as he had done once before in 1870. One month later he was found dead in a Boston hotel room. Rumors swirled as his large estate remained unsettled for a period of years. There was talk of a long abandoned wife and child, embezzlement of funds from his mother-in-law, and morphine addiction. It was all true.

More than a dozen other land development schemes were launched over the next 20 years. All but one proved financially disastrous. The sole exception was in 1878, again in 'Sconset. This was the famous *Underhill Cottages*.

When Edward F. Underhill first came to 'Sconset in 1878, he was very intrigued with its charm and potential. There were now two successful hotels—the Ocean View House and the Atlantic House—in addition to the tiny Sunset Heights cottages that had been built by Ellis and Robinson, and the old spruced-up fishstage cottages. All were thriving. More than that, every vacationer he spoke with seemed to dearly love 'Sconset, enthusing about its tranquility, beauty and healthy pure air. At that time, the small cottages in Sunset Heights were being sold for $150 to $200 fully furnished, or were available for rental at $30 to $75 for the full season.

Underhill had little experience in real estate. A friend of Horace Greeley, he had been a reporter for the New York Times and later for the New York Herald. Leaving journalism and changing careers, he quickly advanced to become the official stenographer of the New York Surrogate Court. Now at age 48, he became enamored with 'Sconset, a place where he would happily spend the next 20 summers of his life.

Underhill's plan was to build updated and enlarged replicas of the old fishstage houses—warts and all—to rent fully furnished to vacationing families. Investing $20,000 of his savings, he bought land on the south bank—just west of the Sunset Heights complex. Then he hired a retired ships carpenter to start building cottages—complete with three or more tiny bedrooms, cellars and cisterns—to rent for $90 to $175 per season, depending on size and location. He named his own cottage *China Closet* and decorated virtually every inside surface—including the walls and ceilings—with plates, cups, bowls and teapots from his vast chinaware collection.

Tapping into his journalistic skills, Underhill wrote and ran numerous ads, rhapsodizing about the joys of a vacation in what he called—"Sconset by the Sea." His tireless promotional efforts attracted growing numbers of New Yorkers to the hamlet, and word-of-mouth attracted more. In just a few short years, his compound grew to 36 cottages, lining both sides of Pochick, Evelyn and Lily Streets—the later two streets named for his wife and daughter. His cottages proved so popular that they—and even hotel space in the village—had to be booked well in advance.

Underhill's success prompted others like Flagg, Gray and Round to develop and sell house lots in the areas flanking 'Sconset—running north toward Sankaty and west along the Low Beach shoreline. And Underhill's success was pivotal in persuading the Nantucket Railroad to extend its train service from Surfside to 'Sconset in 1884. Up until then, going to 'Sconset required a nearly two-hour, fairly-uncomfortable trek by horse carriage from Town.

To celebrate the train's inaugural, 'Sconset held its first ever Grand Illumination. Oil lamps and candles lit every window and Japanese lanterns lined the streets. Then a dazzling display of pyrotechnics lit up the night sky to the awe and delight of the locals, summer people, and the hundreds more who had crowded into the trains to attend.

With the coming of the train, more and more people vacationed in 'Sconset and increasing numbers of houses were being built—including large summer houses on the bluff. By 1895, more than 2,000 people flocked to 'Sconset each summer and two large hotels—the *Beach House* and the *Ocean View House*—were filled to capacity. 'Sconset seemed to have a special appeal to lawyers, professors, physicians, retired military men, corporate executives and all their families—and notably to people from the theatre.

The famed "Actors' Colony" in 'Sconset really began when the beloved stage character actress Mrs. G.H. "Granny" Gilbert came to vacation at the cottage of producer and actor George Fawcett and his wife Percy Haswell, a renowned Shakespearian actress. When word reached New York that "Granny" Gilbert had decided to make Fawcett her new agent, the press flocked to 'Sconset to interview them both. The first question asked by everyone at the Lamb's Club and in theatrical companies all across the country was—"Where's 'Sconset? What's there?"

The resulting publicity brought more and more theatre people to the hamlet—including "Billy" Thompson the actor and producer, his wife the noted actress Isabel Irving, De Wolf Hopper of Gilbert & Sullivan and "Casey-At-The-Bat" fame, Digby Dell the acclaimed comedian, Harry Woodruff and many more. In today's terms, this was like having Dame Judy Dench, Steven Spielberg, Jack Nicholson, Harrison Ford, Sean Connery, Steve Martin, Jody Foster, Meryl Streep, and Gwyneth Paltrow all choose to vacation with their families in the same tiny village at the same time. And because all the New York and other major theatres were closed during the heat of the summer, they were in residence in 'Sconset for much of the two to three month season—where they could let down their hair and relax.

But being creative theatre people who loved to perform, they delighted in entertaining each other with impromptu shows, musical reviews, costume balls and themed events. Playing tiny instruments and banging homemade drums, they met and cheered each arriving and departing train to welcome and send off one of their friends. And there was always someone new to greet, including the famed actor and matinee idol Robert Hilliard and the legendary "Queen of the Stage" Lillian Russell. In this age of television and movies, it's hard to realize the enormous size and popularity of live theatre in the late 1890s. In New York City alone, there were more than 550 active theatres, with thousands more all across the country. Any city of even modest size had several.

The Actors' Colony made the Underhill Cottages their first home. And as their numbers increased, they also rented or bought houses in the old section. They began to call its tiny main street "Broadway," a name that has now become official. At eleven o'clock each morning they'd convene on the beach beneath the bluff, and then gather in the afternoon on the lawn and porch of the Ocean View hotel for gossip and lively conversation.

It was the Actors' Colony's need for performance space that led to the building of the 'Sconset Casino in 1900. And it was George Fawcett who, along with three friends that same year, sponsored the building of the nine hole golf course next to Milestone Road on what was left of the old Bloomingdale estate. They leased the land from the Coffin family and spent $196 to build the 'Sconset Golf Club.

'Sconset's undeniable charm, its cachet as the choice of the famous, and the availability of fully-furnished cottages to rent or buy made it successful while other Island developments floundered. And perhaps the best evidence of its popularity was the decision to build a new railroad directly from Town to Tom Never's Head and along the shore to 'Sconset. Called the Nantucket Central Railroad, it began service in 1895, four years after the old train to Surfside and 'Sconset was abandoned to bankruptcy. In its first year of operation, the Nantucket Central Railroad ran five roundtrips to 'Sconset each day, with three trips on Sunday. Now getting to 'Sconset took little more than twenty minutes.

I told you that more than a dozen other Nantucket land development schemes had failed in the 1870s and 1880s. Because you showed some interest, let me take a few minutes to tell you a little about them in something of a chronological order.

In 1873—the year after Ellis and Robinson opened *Sunset Heights* in 'Sconset—Henry and Charles Coffin announced *Sherburne Bluffs*, an extraordinarily ambitious development on the north shore just west of Town. Stretching for more than a mile, it offered commanding views of Nantucket Sound and of the private beach 30-feet below. Like Oak Bluffs in Martha's Vineyard, its design featured a broad avenue and promenade fronting the bluff. Two other east-west avenues and twelve cross streets—along with four small parks and a carriage circle—framed 169 sizable vacation home sites.

Henry and Charles Coffin were the sons of Zenas Coffin, the Island's wealthiest shipowner in the period just prior to the Civil War. From their father, they had inherited 326 shares of the "commons" and through their immediate family could vote many more shares. This gave them almost complete control in all decisions made in meetings of the Proprietors. And it assured them automatic approval of any plan to convert their common shares into private "set-offs" in any place of their choosing. All of the land for *Sherburne Bluffs* was acquired in this way, without any cash outlay. A few other partners were brought into the venture—including Charles's son, Matthew Barney, and Charles H. Robinson—the same man who had invested in 'Sconset's *Sunset Heights*.

Even with extensive promotion, the sweeping design concept behind *Sherburne Bluffs* was rejected by the public. No lots were sold for some years. Later, those few who expressed interest in buying land wanted property that fronted directly on the water. To make the sale, the partners agreed to scrap their ideas for a seafront avenue and promenade and to reconfigure the lots into any form preferred by the buyer. One of their first sales was to the famous New York trial lawyer, Charles O'Conner, who in 1881 at age 78 built one of Nantucket's earliest great waterfront homes—a huge Victorian house with a separate brick building to house his 18,000 volume law library.

While not commercially successful, *Sherburne Bluffs* gave the Coffin brothers a lifelong enthusiasm for land development. Over the next dozen years, they would engage in over 430 land transactions.

In 1874, just after the unveiling of *Sherburne Bluffs*, a Worcester speculator named S. B. Tourtelot bought a large tract of land at Madaket and issued a large and beautiful map showing 2,000 house lots, winding roads, parks and other attractions. Though promoted aggressively, the project never attracted buyers.

That same year, New Haven investors Lee & Wooding bought a spread of land at Quaise, and drew up plans for 500 house lots with harbor views. None sold and the planned development was eventually auctioned off for non-payment of taxes.

In 1875, W. & J. Veazie of Boston bought land on the south shore between Hummock Pond and Long Pond and laid out a 1,700 lot development with one section called *Nauticon* and another called *South Hummock*. Only a few lots were sold and after some years the project was abandoned. No houses were built.

In 1876, a 240-lot development near Hinckley Farm was planned. Named *Wannacomet Bluffs*, no sales were made and it too was eventually abandoned.

During all this time, the Coffin brothers and their sons were busy planning a major development on the south shore. Beginning with their own farmland inherited from Zenas, they took in other partners and converted nearly 1,300 sheep commons shares into more land holdings, until they had amassed a beachfront property nearly three miles long and one mile deep. As early as 1873, they had incorporated the venture as *The Nantucket Surfside Land Company*. And they had plans drawn for what they called a "city on the shore"—with sweeping curved avenues, numerous small parks and gardens, a pavilion and bandstand, and a wide promenade overlooking the broad beach where cabanas and changing rooms would be built. Then, to make the project both exciting and accessible, they worked closely with a group of Boston investors led by Philip H. Folger to create Nantucket's first railroad. It would connect the steamboat wharf directly to Surfside. All this took until 1881 to realize.

The concept of a Nantucket Railroad had been discussed for several years, but everything finally came together by the spring of 1881. Work was well underway on the Cape Cod Canal to shorten the sailing time between New York and Boston. And the steamboats *Island Home* and *River Queen* made two trips a day from New Bedford via Woods Hole to Nantucket. Train connections now linked Woods Hole to Boston, New York,

Providence, Newport and other east coast cities. And the planned "city on the shore" at Surfside provided a potentially profitable destination.

On July 4th 1881, with great fanfare, the ribbon was cut and visiting dignitaries and Islanders took the inaugural train trip to Surfside. A festive clambake, concert, speeches and guided strolls along the beach made up for the fact that the site contained only a partially-completed hundred-foot-long depot and a few tents. The formal opening was finally held on July 21st, by which time the depot and permanent kitchen building were completed, a well was dug, and steps were built leading down to the beach. The event featured a lavish spread of food and drink, dancing, and fireworks. Then in August, a reunion of the Coffin clan was staged, built around the 200th anniversary of Tristram Coffin's death. More than 500 Coffins attended thanks to publicity appearing in newspapers across the country. Before the year was over, more than 30,000 passengers had boarded the train to Surfside. However, only a handful of lots were sold.

Over the next several years, large amounts of money were poured into advertising, promotions and site improvements, but to little effect. In 1882, bathhouses were added, a realty office was opened in the depot, and excavation was begun for a resort hotel. To make lots more affordable, the original plan for curved avenues was scrapped in favor of a grid of streets and avenues with hundreds of 50-by-100 foot parcels—only 60 of which sold.

On July 4th of the following year, the new *Surfside Hotel* was opened with great flourish. To make it directly accessible by train, an extra mile of track was laid from the Surfside depot. Located 265-feet back from the shoreline at the far west end of the property and surrounded on three sides by a large piazza, the looming hotel was more than just impressive. Its ground floor was dominated by a spacious dining room and a number of beautifully appointed reception rooms and parlors. The large kitchen, laundry and staff quarters were housed in a separate building reached through an enclose pergola. The hotel's three upper floors provided 54 elegant guest rooms, topped by a mansard roof of the latest style. But beneath its finely decorated exterior was the skeleton and skin of a failed hotel that had been cut up and moved to the site from Riverdale, Rhode Island. At its heart was a legacy of failure!

Over the next few seasons, many came to dine and vacation at the *Surfside Hotel*, but few lots were sold and no cottages were built. Then the Wall Street panic of 1884 made the prospects for success even dimmer.

At this point, all talk of a village plan and promises for future tennis courts and a golf course were dropped. Winter storms repeatedly ravaged the hotel and washed out the rail lines, adding to the cost and discouraging the investors further. Finally in 1887, the once-buoyant *Nantucket Surfside Land Company* couldn't make its mortgage payment. At that point, 900-acres of waterfront land were auctioned off, selling for just $2.80 an acre.

Ownership changed hands several times, but no one could make a go of it. The hotel was refurbished and electrified. Rooms were added. And attractions like bowling alleys, trapeze acts, pigeon shoots and swimming exhibitions were added. Still, next to nothing sold. In desperation, lot sizes were reduced to 20-by-100 feet and advertised at $100 for seaside properties and $20 per lot inland. Still, they didn't sell. As a last resort, lots were offered free if the buyer agreed to let the company build their cottage. There were no takers.

Train service stopped in 1894 and the hotel collapsed in stages, until it was completely gone by the end of the century. The land was sold off for back taxes.

Some say the Surfside project was doomed when the Nantucket Railroad extended its service from Surfside to 'Sconset in 1884. People came to see Surfside and loved its seaside vistas, but when they traveled on to 'Sconset they fell in love with its charm. Even with heavy promotion and beautifully rendered drawings of a future "city on the shore," the fact was that Surfside still offered only a lonely expanse of open oceanfront land—while 'Sconset was already a thriving storybook hamlet with congenial people and lovely cottages to rent or buy. The beachfront rail extension from Surfside to 'Sconset also confirmed the fears of many—that unprotected oceanfront property this far from the mainland could be risky, if not outright dangerous. They heard tales that winter storms frequently washed out the rail lines and even damaged the hotel. And all of that kept them from buying. Increasingly, the Surfside development was seen as a folly.

In 1882, just one year after the development at Surfside began, smaller land schemes were launched at Wauwinet—selling lots near the *Wauwinet House* which was then six years old—and on Tuckernuck Island where the *East End View House* was newly built. One attraction for Tuckernuck was searching for Captain Kidd's treasure, which was said to be buried there. If it was, it was certainly never found.

In 1883, developers bought land on Coatue, where they erected *The Cedar Beach House*—a bathing pavilion with a great toboggan slide, five course shore dinners, and steam launch service to and from Town. Declining sales and a fire ended that venture.

The following year, the 260-foot long *Hotel Nantucket* was built on Brant Point and a number of small cottages were built nearby. Being close to Town, land here began to sell fairly well, giving new—although false—hope to would-be speculators.

The next twelve years saw an ongoing frenzy of investors trying to hit it big with smaller developments all across the Island: In 1884, with a project on the shoreline, southwest of 'Sconset. In 1885, with *Sankaty Heights*. In 1886, with *Sesachacha Pond* and *Lincoln Heights* on the cliff. In 1887, with *Aurora Heights* in 'Sconset. In 1888, with *Dionis City*. In 1889, with *Monomoy Heights*. In 1895, with *Low Beach*, southwest of 'Sconset.

Big hopes and lots of money lost!

All the advertising and promotion for these properties brought increasing numbers of summer tourists to the Island, but the land simply didn't sell. Perhaps the most outrageous story of this era was at *Miacomet Park*, where a New Bedford tea merchant divided 80 acres on the east side of Miacomet Pond into 2,300 lots—each one offered free with the purchase of a pound of his tea. There was a $2 fee to record the deed, but even at this price only 40 people "bought" Nantucket land.

❦   ❦   ❦

It was not for lack of trying that Nantucket avoided the surge of Victorian development that occurred all along the Northeastern U.S. coastline. Speculators grabbed up large blocks of land on Nantucket with all the aggression of an old time Nantucket sea captain pursuing a herd of sperm whales. And like the old time whalers, their sole intent was to slice them up into little pieces and quickly render them into cash. What happened to the remaining carcass was of little to no concern.

But yes, tourism finally did come to Nantucket, and by 1895 a committed new community of summer people was thriving here. The year-round Island population remained about 3,200—but at peak season the population swelled to nearly 10,000. And the influx of new money allowed the Island to recover from its period of sad decline. However, compared to the rest of America, Nantucket was still a place of simple charm, open spaces, peace and beauty.

Here in the Southeast Quarter, 'Sconset had flourished like no other place on the Island. And the Tom Never's area had escaped all attempts at exploitation. It remained a favored place to hike to from 'Sconset—to commune with nature, to picnic, to pick wild berries and wild roses, to gather bayberry and even beans, and to enjoy the glorious sunsets before heading back home. The old farms had overgrown and their structures were long gone, moved to other places or reclaimed by the earth. But standing atop Tom Never's Head was an old Life Saving Station, its derelict tower silhouetted as a welcoming beacon against the brilliant sky. And near it, nestled into a shallow hillside, was a small house and a low horse barn rumored to be the lair of the Hermit of Tom Never's.

Who he was and where he came from remained a mystery for some years. When occasionally he came into Town to purchase flour or other supplies, he spoke with no one other than the shopkeepers. And even then he uttered the fewest of words. People kept their distance, put off by his immense size and fierce appearance. With long matted hair, a flowing black beard, blazing dark eyes, and a rope-cinched black robe that fell to below his knees, he looked to all the world like an old engraving of John the Baptist.

As time passed, stories circulated of his mysterious good deeds. One night when the Sankaty Lighthouse keeper and his wife were too ill to climb the stairs and light the light, some unknown person did it for them. Other nights, doctors were summoned to emergency house calls. A loud rapping on the doctor's door and a voice from the shadows saved many who might otherwise have died. All these were said to be the work of the Hermit.

Who he was and where he came from was finally revealed late one October night. In a letter left at the door of Dr. Harold Williams—dean of Tufts Medical School and a long-time Island summer resident—the Hermit asked the Doctor to visit his home in Tom Never's, bringing with him all four of his distinguished visiting colleagues. These colleagues included the noted scholar Professor Dr. William James, fellow psychologist Dr. Morton Prince, the astronomer Professor Edward Charles Pickering, and the Harvard economist Professor Frank Tausaig. As frequent guests at Dr. Williams' home (which much later would become the Mad Hatter Restaurant), all four had heard stories of the Hermit and were intrigued to have an opportunity to meet with him, to better understand what motivated such a man to live a life of near isolation. And what few facts he included in his letter made them all the more excited to talk with him.

After inviting the five into his small home, the Hermit unfolded his story. He said his name was Matthew Macy, native born but exiled from Nantucket for nearly forty years. Shanghaied as a small lad in New Bedford and then again in Liverpool, he was sold into slavery in Australia and kept manacled and chained, slaving in the mines for a dozen years. Escaping, he eventually made his way to India and to the high Himalayas, almost dying from starvation and exposure during an arduous 18 month long journey. There he was taken in by shepherds and after some indeterminate time was told of holy men high in the mountains who could help him.

Spellbound by his story, the five guests sat in silence as the Hermit poured forth an anguished tale of evil ship captains and land owners, of slave labor and illicit money, of torture and starvation, of burning deserts and freezing cold. And they understood fully his despair when he said that in those days his very soul was rotted out with hatred and bitterness.

After resuming his journey in the Himalayas, Macy eventually found the holy men and was accepted as a disciple to study Hatha Yogi with them. He followed fully their precepts of fasting from food and sleep, special breathing exercises, meditation, and trials of self-discipline—all

designed to build strength of will and deeper moral and intellectual powers. But try as he may, he felt nothing. His heart was as cold as stone.

In the monastery with him, as a fellow student, was a friend of Dr.
James—a young doctor from Frankfurt am Main, where he was affiliated
with a research hospital dealing with the subconscious mind. Befriending
Macy, he took him to Frankfurt and enrolled him in a series of scientific
experiments using hypnotism. During these experiments, Macy revealed
an intense subconscious desire to live free of all people back in his homeland. Dr. James' friend called that the first step in his healing and gave
Macy money for his passage back to Nantucket. The Doctor asked nothing in return, only that Macy tell Dr. James his full story if ever the two
should meet in Nantucket in the future.

Before bidding them "good bye," Macy took the visitors into his
horse barn. There his lantern revealed a freshly painted white wall running the full length of the barn, with the Ten Commandments neatly
printed in large black letters. His final words to them that night were
these—"Here I have been reborn. Here I have found my God."

The Hermit of Tom Never's was seen again many times over the
course of the years. But always in silence, keeping his distance. When and
how he died is not recorded.

In those days, no one other than Matthew Macy lived in Tom
Never's. But the time would soon come when those lands would attract
ambitious men—men with dreams not of God, but of personal profit.
And sadly, I was witness to it all.

FIGURE 6   Underhill's "China Closet" in 'Sconset

More so than anyone before or after, Edward F. Underhill is responsible for the architectural look and atmosphere of 'Sconset as we know it today. First seeing 'Sconset's potential as an upscale summer resort in 1882, he built 36 atmospheric cottages in the style of the old fish stages and advertised their rental availability widely. Underhill aptly named his own cottage "The China Closet," part of which can be seen in this photo.
(Photo courtesy of the Nantucket Historical Association, P9255.)

FIGURE 7   An Actor's Welcome Home

Just back from a triumphant theatrical tour, Harry Woodruff is shown here being heralded by his many "Actors' Colony" friends at the 'Sconset train station. Best known for his portrayal of Ben Hur in a definitive and long-running stage production, Woodruff was also a major musical star and for more than 15 years a mainstay of the "Actors' Colony" shows at the 'Sconset Casino. His 'Sconset home on Morey Lane had the distinction of being the Island's first true "upside down" house.

(Photo courtesy of the Nantucket Historical Association, SC189.)

12

1916 . . . "Going Once . . . "

T he auctioneers charmed the crowds at Tom Nevers Head with souvenir china and trinkets, gifts of gold watches, and their entertaining patter about, "This rare chance to be the first to own a prime building lot overlooking Nantucket Island's most beautiful beach." It was July 18th 1916, and the Nantucket Land Trust was open for business. Free train rides from Town, free refreshments, and the unveiling of what the ads called, "The Most Ideal Cottage Sites on Nantucket," drew several hundred people daily to Tom Nevers throughout the whole summer season. For most, including even life-long Island residents, it was their first visit to Tom Nevers Head. (Notice that by now the apostrophe in Tom Never's had been dropped—another "modern innovation" of the Nantucket Land Trust!)

And when they came, they were mightily impressed. A bunting-draped new railroad station stood at Tom Nevers Square, the central point of the project. Nothing now remains of the station or the Square, but they were located right at the point where Old Tom Nevers Road now branches off to the south.

From Tom Nevers Square it was just a short walk to the imposing Tom Nevers Lodge—with its five-story observation tower, sweeping verandas, handsome dining room, massive stone fireplace, and well-appointed guest rooms. The Lodge boasted all the latest in modern conveniences—electric lights, long distance telephones, baths with hot and cold running water, and even its own sanitary sewage system. In concept, Tom Nevers Lodge was presented as a "club house" for Tom Nevers property owners and their guests—in sharp contrast to the large hotels and resorts that had been built elsewhere on the Island "for the tourist-trade."

To give you some idea of the size and ambition of the Nantucket Land Trust project at Tom Nevers Head, I've brought along some of the original site plans, ads and early photos for you to look through. (NB— I've inserted them as Figures 8–25 at the end of this chapter.)

In all, the Tom Nevers project covered more than 2,000 acres—with two miles of shoreline, stretching west from Tom Nevers Pond. Its northern boundary was an even longer stretch along the Milestone Road, which by then was fully paved. The Nantucket Railroad tracks ran diagonally across the property, creating two sections of nearly equal size. With Tom Nevers Square near the center of the project, all the initial and planned building sites were within convenient walking distance of frequently running trains to both Town and 'Sconset. The entire project covered just about all of the Tom Nevers area as we know it today.

The man behind the Nantucket Land Trust project at Tom Nevers Head was one Franklin E. Smith—a taciturn and canny Boston lawyer/financier who saw opportunity in Nantucket's confused jumble of property ownership and sheep commons rights. Starting in the early 1900s, he formed the Nantucket Cranberry Co. and then quietly began to acquire sheep commons shares from hundreds of small rights holders who thought them near to worthless. In their minds—"a few dollars are better than nothing!"

By 1906, Smith had amassed 613 $^{5/8}$ sheep commons shares out of the total 864 then in existence. This put him in the position to elect his own Proprietors—who would rubber stamp every application he put before them to swap his sheep commons shares for "set-off" deeded land. One of his earliest swaps gave him title to the large swampy area near Gibb's Pond, which he developed for cranberry production. Starting with a 1910 harvest of just 192 quarts, the Nantucket Cranberry Co.'s output climbed to 359,100 quarts by 1920—making the Nantucket cranberry bogs one of the worlds largest.

Initially, Smith surrendered his sheep commons shares at the traditional rate of one share per acre. But as his leverage grew, he acquired larger and larger tracts of land for only token payments. For example, he acquired 400 acres of land at Polpis for just three sheep shares. Later he acquired 1,000 acres in the center of the Island for just eight sheep shares. These tactics made Smith one of the most bitterly resented men on the Island, but what he did was all strictly legal and no one had either the skill or the means to challenge him. And though the Nantucket Land Trust at Tom Nevers would prove to be a financial failure, it was only a minor setback in Franklin E. Smith's growing land ownership empire, which extended to virtually every part of the Island.

For all the massive land set-offs that Smith would acquire through 1927, he had to surrender only 88 $^{8/15}$ sheep commons shares. And by the time of his death in 1952, he still retained privately and through his companies rights to 609 $^{47/120}$ sheep commons shares. The second largest Proprietor—the Town of Nantucket—owned just 37 shares. Understanding the leveraging potential inherent in Nantucket's archaic "common and undivided land ownership" system as established by the Island's founders, Smith—with relatively little capital and a team of low-paid junior law clerks working out of his Boston office—was able to become one of Nantucket's largest land owners.

❦   ❦   ❦

Ask any real estate agent what's important in land values and they'll tell you—"Location, Location, Location." And to Franklin E. Smith, that's exactly what the Tom Nevers area offered—with breathtaking views in every direction, and a commanding presence high above a 2,000-foot wide pristine surf beach bathed by the Atlantic.

But there's another equally determining factor in real estate—"Timing, Timing, Timing." And in this too, Smith thought his timing was perfect. Americans were full of confidence, buoyant enthusiasm, and new found wealth. The national mood was never better. The new Cape Cod

Canal had just opened and tourism was booming. But what Smith didn't—and perhaps couldn't—take into account was that a shark attack would terrify the nation in June of 1916, just days before the Nantucket Land Trust's first land auction at Tom Nevers Head.

To vacationing Americans in 1916, few joys could exceed a sunny day at the seashore, frolicking in the frothy surf. Even those far from the ocean dreamed of one day experiencing it—tempted by glamorous photos in all the magazines and newspapers and by compelling images in the movie shows that had become so wildly popular.

Then tragedy struck on the New Jersey shore, when in a two week period seven bathers were attacked and killed by sharks. Never before had this happened. And even after the first two attacks, scientific experts called it impossible—declaring that coastal sharks never attack people, and that even if they did attack, their jaws were too weak to tear human skin. But the attacks continued. And as fleets of small boats combed the coastline to hunt down these "monsters of the deep" with harpoons, grappling hooks and dynamite—newspapers worldwide horrified readers with graphic headlines and front-page stories, shoving all other national and international news into the background.

When a Great White Shark was finally killed and pulled from the waters, everyone's worst nightmare was confirmed—that giant, man-eating beasts lurked in the water, hungry to devour anyone foolish enough to wade out into the surf. A shark of this size and strength had never been seen before. Follow-up story, after follow-up story commanded the headlines. Scientists were quoted. Fishermen were quoted. Admirals were quoted. The persistent questions—"How many are there?" and "Why have they turned killers?" The speculative answers gave little consolation—"With so many bathers, we've given them a new food source close to shore." and "All the sea deaths in the European war have given them a new taste for blood." Hardly the kind of message that enhanced sales for Franklin E. Smith's new shorefront development, about to be launched that very same year.

Eventually the news media tired of shark stories when no further attacks occurred. But by then, an even bigger fear was developing. This second "timing factor" that Smith didn't, and perhaps couldn't, take into account was war. Little did he realize that the 1914 assassination of Austrian Archduke Francis Ferdinand in far away Sarajevo would plunge Europe into a World War that would eventually impact both Nantucket and Tom Nevers.

On January 29th 1916, the Nantucket *Inquirer and Mirror* broke the news that Germany had secretly constructed "ten submarines of enormous size ... to render ineffective the Allies' blockade ... and to interdict supply shipments sailing from U.S. ports to Europe." The report continued, "In nearing the American coast, they will submerge and run under water until well within the three mile limit." The article ended with this caution, "The arrival of the first of these craft in the Port of New York may be expected any day."

The New York and Boston papers all scoffed at this report, but an unease began to set in among those who realized that Nantucket was very near the main shipping channels to Europe. Was this a time to buy vacation property that jutted far out into the Atlantic—property that could only be reached by a long steamship journey from the mainland? Few thought so. And memories were still vivid about Germany's torpedo sinking of the passenger ship *Lusitania* off the coast of Ireland just eight months before, with a reported death toll of 1,260.

Concern turned to reality when at daybreak on the morning of October 8th 1916, German U-Boat 53 surfaced south of the Island near the Nantucket shoals, to prey upon transatlantic shipping. The American steamer *Kansas* was caught by surprise and then boarded. After an examination of her papers and inspection of her cargo, she was released. But less than an hour later, the British freighter *Strathdene* was not so fortunate. Her crew was ordered to take quickly to the lifeboats, and the ship was riddled by the U-Boat's powerful deck guns and then sunk by torpedoes. At mid-morning, the Norwegian freighter *Christian Knudsen* and the British steamer *West Point* met the same fate. As did the British passenger ship *Stephano* and the British freighter *Kingstonian* a few hours later. Then before sunset, the Dutch freighter *Bloomersdijk* was challenged and sunk. Six ships destroyed within a single day by just one German U-Boat, and all within close proximity to the Nantucket shoals lightship. Alerted by radio messages from the lightship and from the victim ships, American destroyers sped from the United States Naval Station at Newport to pick up survivors. But since America was not yet in the war, they were ordered not to search for or challenge the submarine. This was particularly galling to the men and officers aboard, because all knew that only the day before U-Boat 53 had put into their homeport at Newport to make a formal courtesy call on the Admiral. The smiling German U-Boat commander gave no indication of his deadly mission.

Those who lived in or summered in Nantucket grew understandably very nervous. The far-away European war was now being waged just off the Island's south shore. And rumors spread that Germany planned to seize Nantucket as a submarine refueling and resupply base. News also reached the Island that German saboteurs had blown up a munitions arsenal on Black Tom Island in New Jersey, with an estimated $22-million loss and a set-back in America's defensive artillery capabilities. By January 31st 1917, the Port of New York was officially closed, so great was the hazard posed by the preying German U-Boats.

These concerns grew even greater when the U.S. officially declared war on the Central Powers on April 6th 1917. So seriously did everyone take the threat that in Nantucket's first liberty-bond drive that June, over 3,000 Nantucketers pledged over $411,000—with most of it coming from the summer people. Not long after, to great relief, a large and active Naval Reserve force was stationed on the Island—with over 300 officers and men and a large fleet of boats.

The impact of the war on the Island's summer economy was not as profound as many had feared. But certainly no one was buying land or building new homes. People still came to their summer cottages, but for far shorter stays. And most hotels and eateries had so few guests that they operated with skeleton crews. Still, only a very few closed their doors for good.

One emotional lift came to the Island on September 13th 1917, when President and Mrs. Woodrow Wilson and their daughter Mrs. Francis B. Sayre steamed into the harbor aboard the Presidential yacht *Mayflower*. On a cruise along the New England coast, the President asked that they stop in 'Sconset for a surprise visit to see his two grandchildren who were vacationing there with his daughter's parents-in-law.

With only two hours warning, the whole Town and the Navy contingent turned out at the dock to cheer the President and his family. One hour later, the Presidential party arrived in 'Sconset aboard a horse-drawn coach.

In 'Sconset, the villagers had assembled in a boarding house to host a fancy lobster dinner for the President, but through an embarrassing mix-up it never came off. The Presidential party spent their entire time in 'Sconset inside the Sayre cottage, and then later that night returned to Town and their awaiting launch. Everyone assumed that the President had been invited to the dinner, but they were all so preoccupied with preparations that they had neglected to tell the Presidential party or the Sayres. The Wilsons were left to eat a cold dinner of leftovers from the Sayre's icebox—while much later that night, after the President's departure, the embarrassed villagers ate an enormous lobster meal by themselves.

❦   ❦   ❦

During the initial 1916 summer, the Nantucket Land Trust auctioned off fewer than two dozen lots—almost all in the First Section, which occupied the southeast corner of the property. Winning bids generally ranged from $50 to $100 for building lots sized 50′ × 100′. But a few much larger properties were "sold to important friends"—friends with familiar Nantucket names like Brock, Barney and Coffin—well in advance of the official July opening. Albert G. Brock was deeded a 64-acre parcel at the west end of the property, with nearly a half-mile of railroad frontage. Alanson S. Barney was deeded a larger than 14-acre parcel, also at the west end of the property, but much closer to the ocean. And Agnes S. Coffin was deeded three choice lots totaling a little over 22 acres on the newly named Coffin Road. Of special note was a provision in the deed that gave Mrs. Coffin and her heirs and assignees a guaranteed right of way to the beach and a "right or privilege . . . to erect and maintain fifty bathhouses . . . between the top of the bank and the high water mark." The only limit in the deed was that each bathhouse not exceed 25-feet in height, and 15′ × 15′ in groundcover.

To improve train service to the site, Smith "persuaded" the railroad to expand operations. More cars were added and turntables were installed in both Town and 'Sconset. The trip to Tom Nevers from Town was cut to less than 20-minutes, and from 'Sconset to under 10-minutes. Five scheduled trains ran daily, with more on auction days—which were generally held on Wednesdays through Saturdays during July and August.

At the same time, Smith led the fight to bring automobiles to Nantucket. After more than a dozen years of heavy local restrictions and attempted prohibitions on the use of cars on the Island—attempts that were all declared unconstitutional—the State Legislature in 1914 passed the Nantucket Automobile Exclusion Act, making Nantucket Island the only place in the United States with a total ban on the use of motor cars. This ban made the Tom Nevers Head project conveniently accessible only by train. The only other alternatives—other than horseback or walking—were horse-carts and bicycles.

In 1910—after a 16 year-long effort—the paving of the Milestone Road to 'Sconset had finally been completed. And by 1914, the State had planted fine new pine saplings all along its route. But Tom Nevers Head could only be reached via a deeply rutted sand road that branched south off the Milestone Road near marker # 5. This made the journey from Town by horse coach well over an hour—with the last portion bumpy, swaying and decidedly not modern.

Increasingly, Smith saw repeal of the Nantucket Automobile Exclusion Act as vital to his interests. The war was not only squeezing Tom Nevers land sales to a trickle, it was also proving to be a death knell for the railroad. In 1917, the railroad operated at a $1,500 deficit and owed an extra $3,000 for fuel. Seeing no workable alternative, the directors of the railroad voted on January 3rd 1918 to cease operations and sell the company's property. By March, workmen began to tear out the rails to be barged off-Island. By the way, there's a popular myth that says the iron from the Nantucket railroad was sent to France for the war effort, where it was used in the Marne River Valley to help block the German drive on Paris. That story was spread to help make the railroad's sad end seem somehow a little patriotic. In truth, World War I was over within six months, and that Nantucket scrap iron never left the mainland.

With the prospect of no railroad, Smith desperately needed an end to the ban on autos. Less than a week after learning of the directors' decision to cease operations, he filed a bill in the Massachusetts Legislature to repeal the Automobile Exclusion Act. Then in March at the State House in Boston, he staged a brilliantly documented presentation, arguing that with the impending death of the railroad, motor cars were now essential to the well being of the people of Nantucket. Even with more than 200 vocal Nantucket residents there to oppose him, Smith persuaded the Legislature to hold a special vote among the citizenry. On May 15th 1918, the final vote was tallied—with 366 in favor of ending the ban on autos, and 296 opposed. By a margin of just 70 votes, the decision to allow motor cars on the Island was passed.

Within days, dozens of cars were brought to the Island. By mid-August, nearly a hundred would arrive. Smith had the road to Tom Nevers Head graded and paved. And in June, a new nine-passenger omnibus began to shuttle patrons to and from the site—with five trips per day and three on Sunday. The shuttle also provided service between Tom Nevers and 'Sconset. By July, a scheduled bus line inaugurated roundtrip service from Town to 'Sconset.

Still land sales at the Tom Nevers project remained meager. Some plots were sold, but no one built cottages. Tom Nevers Lodge added surf bathing facilities, tennis, afternoon tea, shore dinners, and promoted private parties with music and dancing. A succession of well qualified managers and cooks were brought in over the next several seasons. This attracted many for day-long outings and overnight stays, but land buyers were virtually non-existent. Eventually the Lodge closed and became forgotten—other than as a secret rendezvous spot for teenage parties. Finally, on August 26th 1938, its derelict remnants went up in flames—overwhelmed by an arsonist torch.

❦   ❦   ❦

World War I, of course, also had an impact on 'Sconset—thinning summer crowds and subduing their high jinks. Also, more and more of the Actors' Colony were lured away to the mushrooming "Moving-Picture

Industry"—with attractive contract offers for year-round work in Fort Lee, New Jersey and later in Hollywood. More than 700 theatrical films were made in 1916 alone. And actors everywhere were dazzled to learn that Charlie Chaplin's salary in 1917 had topped $1,000,000. For a performer, the chance to work in the "movies" became an absolutely irresistible lure.

So each year, fewer and fewer returned—until only a hint of the once colorful and lively Actors' Colony remained. Some still owned homes in 'Sconset, but rented them out. Eventually, most sold them off as the automobile spawned the popularity of summer theatres under tents, and an early form of air conditioning allowed the city theatres to attract crowds even during July and August. The theatre stars and their families now rarely came to 'Sconset. They were too busy working. But writers and artists did come, continuing 'Sconset's reputation for attracting people in the arts. Some were colorful, many were famous, but they were certainly more reserved and more likely to keep to themselves.

In 1919, the Ocean View Hotel—that once famous "club house" for theatre folk was torn down. But a new era for the 'Sconset Casino was about to begin.

❦   ❦   ❦

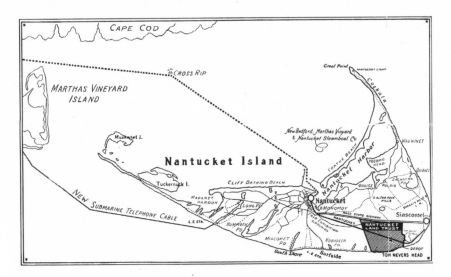

FIGURE 8   Nantucket Land Trust—Circa 1916

A new rail line brought prospective buyers directly from Town to the new
2,000acre development at Tom Nevers Head. The train also linked Tom Nevers to 'Sconset, just a 10-minute ride away.

FIGURE 9   Tom Nevers RR Station—Circa 1916

The "new" Tom Nevers RR Station was, in fact, salvaged from the then abandoned station at Surfside. Free train rides attracted hundreds to the Tom Nevers site, to look if not to buy. Many life-long Island residents had never ventured there before.
(Photo courtesy of the Nantucket Historical Association, P9997.)

FIGURE 10   **Panoramic View at Tom Nevers Head: 1916**

With its broad private bathing beach to the left, and Atlantic Avenue as a promenade stretching west along the shorefront, the Tom Nevers site offered unrivaled views of the ocean, and both the rising and setting sun. Atlantic Boulevard has become Wanoma Road today.

FIGURE 11   **Panoramic View at Tom Nevers Road: 1916**

Looking northwest from Tom Nevers Head to the Railroad Station in the distance at Tom Nevers Square. Today, this road is known as Old Tom Nevers Road. In this photo (and in Figure 10) the intersecting roads of the planned development can be seen.

ABSOLUTE AUCTION SALE

Wednesday, Thursday, Friday and Saturday
Afternoons, at 2.30 Sharp, Rain or Shine.

This is without doubt a most remarkable opportunity to secure valuable locations for summer homes. Large Lots, Wide Streets, Water, Private Beach, Surf Bathing, Reasonable Restrictions. Telephone Service.

Title Perfect, Guaranteed and Registered
by Commonwealth. A Chance to Buy
at Your Price. Easy Terms if Desired. Every Lot Restricted.

N E X T

BIRDS-EYE VIEW OF "TOM NEVERS HEAD" TRACT— NEW "TOM NEVERS LODGE" ON THE HIGHLAND
"Lodge" Now Open. Rooms and Cafe. Moderate Prices. J. Lewis Rice, Mgr. Phone 151-21.

W E E K

FREE! FREE!
Hundreds of Valuable and Attractive
Gifts Distributed During the Sale Just to
Advertise---No Obligation to Purchase or Even Bid.

THE TRAIN LEAVES NANTUCKET AT 1.30.
LIMITED NUMBER OF FREE CAR TICKETS AT 35 MAIN ST.

NANTUCKET LAND TRUST

Office of Trustees   E. MILTON MOSHER, Genrel Manager.   Treasurer—Room 441
1332 Beacon Street, Brookline.   FRANKLIN E. SMITH (TRUSTEES) EDGAR C. LINN.   50 Congress Street, Boston.

BUREAU OF INFORMATION AT "TOM NEVERS." OPEN SUNDAYS.

Open Evenings.   Nantucket Office and Display Window, 35 Main Street.   **Phone 167.**
AUCTION SALE CONDUCTED BY SAM P. WHITCOMB, REAL ESTATE AUCTIONEER, BOSTON.

FIGURE 12   **1916 Ad Announcing Land Sale Auctions**

This half-page newspaper ad announced the new Tom Nevers development and tried to build excitement for its opening. In contrast to earlier developments, all the cottage lots at Tom Nevers were to be sold at Auction. The artist's "birds-eye view" of the site shows the new Tom Nevers Lodge in the upper left at Tom Nevers Head—and Tom Nevers Square with its new RR Station in the lower right. In the logo design for the new development, the apostrophe in "Tom Never's" was dropped for the first time. Since then, the area has been known as "Tom Nevers."

FIGURE 13   **1916 Ad Promoting Site Attractions**   *(opposite)*

Follow-up ads stressed the great opportunity and need to act quickly—"This is without a doubt a most remarkable opportunity to secure valuable locations for summer homes. Large Lots, Wide Streets, Water, Private Beach, Surf Bathing, Reasonable Restrictions, Telephone Service . . . Act Quick And Get In On The Ground Floor." Transportation to and from the Auctions was "FREE." And there would be—"Hundreds of Valuable Souvenirs Given Away Absolutely FREE To Visitors."

ABSOLUTE
AUCTION SALE

No Reserve---No Limit.

SALE BEGINS **EACH DAY AT 2.30 SHARP** RAIN OR SHINE

Wednesday, Thursday, Friday
and Saturday, Next Week

This is without doubt a most remarkable opportunity to secure valuable locations for summer homes.
Large Lots, Wide Streets, Water, Private Beach, Surf Bathing.
Reasonable Restrictions. Telephone Service.

TITLE PERFECT, GUARANTEED, REGISTERED by COMMONWEALTH

This method of selling allows you to buy at your own price.

ACT QUICK AND GET IN ON THE GROUND FLOOR.

We Reserve the Right to Change to Private Sale at Any Future Date.

EASY TERMS IF DESIRED.

OCEAN FRONT LOTS ARE LIMITED.

THE BEST ARE AT

TOM NEVERS

BIRDS-EYE VIEW OF "TOM NEVERS HEAD" TRACT—NEW "TOM NEVERS LODGE" ON THE HEADLAND.

THE MOST IDÉAL COTTAGE SITE
ON NANTUCKET

The Auctioneers Reserve the Right to Reject the Bid of Any Person Not Desired.

Free   Transportation

**LEAVING
NANTUCKET**
on 1.15 train.

Special Car,

**FROM
TOM NEVERS**
on 5.10 train.

Special Car.

IF DRIVING, LEAVE STATE HIGHWAY BEYOND FIFTH MILESTONE, AT TOM NEVERS SIGN.

HUNDREDS OF VALUABLE SOUVENIRS
GIVEN ABSOLUTELY FREE TO VISITORS

SALE CONDUCTED BY DAMMERS & GILLETTE, REAL ESTATE AUCTIONEERS, NEW YORK AND BOSTON.

NANTUCKET LAND TRUST

FRANKLIN E. SMITH AND EDGAR C. LINN, TRUSTEES.

Office of Trustees, Suites 3 and 4, 1352 Beacon St., Brookline, Mass.   Office of Treasurer, Room 441, 50 Congress St., Boston, Mass.
E. MILTON MOSHER, General Manager.

OFFICE AND DISPLAY WINDOW, 35 MAIN STREET.
Phone 167.   Open Evenings.

FIGURE 14   1916 Ad Announcing Free Band Concerts

To build even more excitement, this full-page ad added two more incentives to visit the site—An invitation to inspect the soon to be opened Tom Nevers Lodge—And an invitation to attend a Grand Concert by the Worcester Brass Band. Notice that a sales office had also been opened at 35 Main Street.

FIGURE 15   Tom Nevers Lodge—Circa 1916

The tower in the new Tom Nevers Lodge provided remarkable views in all directions, from both public balconies and private guest rooms. Dining and dancing were held in the public rooms below and refreshments were served on the piazzas.

FIGURE 16   Boardwalk To The Beach—Circa 1916

A stairway gave direct and easy access from the Lodge to the beach. And a boardwalk crossed the sand to the surf.

FIGURE 17   Newspaper Cut of the Lodge

Ads and articles appeared regularly all year long.

FIGURE 18   The Café in Tom Nevers Lodge

The Café featured an inviting stone fireplace, unique to the Island, and served meals "a la carte." A console Victrola with a library of records gave guests a choice of music for dining and dancing.

FIGURE 19   Riding Classes at The Lodge

Horse riding classes were conducted daily all during the summer season as an added amenity.

FIGURE 20   A Band Concert at The Lodge

The very popular Worcester Brass Band performed throughout the whole summer.

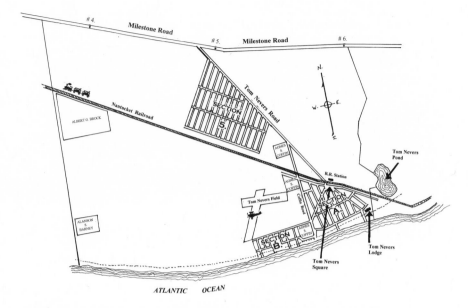

FIGURE 21   **Master Plan of the 1916 Tom Nevers Development**

This master plan shows the overall 2,000-acre Nantucket Land Trust site—
with the three major sections included in the initial real estate sale offering.
(The location of the original Tom Nevers Airfield, which would be built 11
years later, is also shown.) In all, more than 3,400 building lots were offered for
sale. On the pages that follow, each of these three major sections is shown in
more detail.

FIGURE 22   Section "A" Plan Detail

Section "A" included both Tom Nevers Square (with its RR Station) and Tom Nevers Lodge. Waterfront lots averaged 50′ × 170′ in size, and inland lots averaged 50′ × 100′. In all, 489 building lots were offered in Section "A."

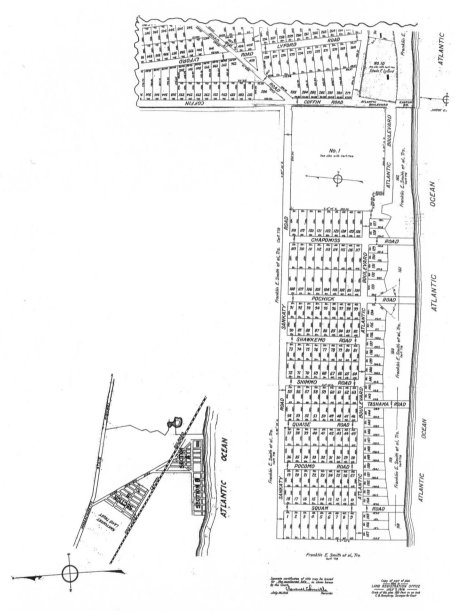

FIGURE 23   Section "B" Plan Detail

Section "B" offered choice building lots with premium waterfront views. Plot sizes ranged from 45′ × 100′—to 50′ × 175′. In all, 162 lots were offered in Section "B."

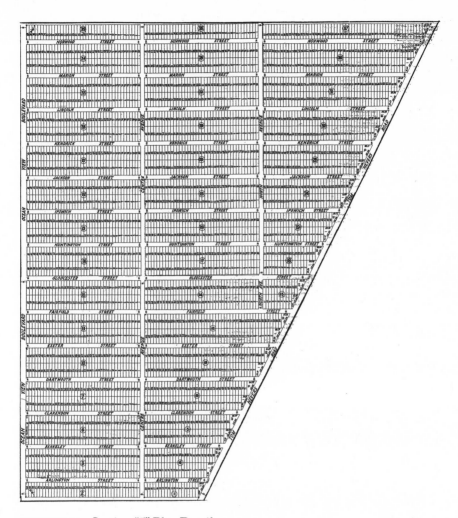

FIGURE 24   Section "5" Plan Detail

The largest of the development's initial three sections, Section "5" boasted 2,751 building lots—laid out in a conventional grid pattern of 14 streets with 3 cross avenues. Very convenient to transportation, Section "5" was bordered on the northeast by Tom Nevers Road and on the southwest by the Nantucket Railroad. All building lots in Section "5" were 25' × 100' in size.

FIGURE 25   View From Tom Nevers Station to The Lodge

Even after 10 years of steady effort, very few lots were sold in the massive Tom Nevers development. Thousands came, but they went home without buying. Empty oceanfront land held little appeal compared to the lively charm of nearby 'Sconset.

(Photo courtesy of the Nantucket Historical Association, P1361.)

13

1927 ... Tom Nevers Field

On May 19th 1927—three days before Charles Lindbergh thrilled the world with his legendary 33^1/$_3$-hour solo flight to Paris—I watched as the first aircraft to land on Nantucket touched down in a field east of Nobadeer Farm. It carried the president of the Boston Airport Corporation and two motion picture cameramen from *Pathe News*—on board to film Nantucket and the Tom Nevers land tract from the air. Within days, this newsreel footage was edited and distributed nationwide, all part of a concerted new plan to revive interest and to promote land sales in the project.

Three weeks earlier, a group of the new investors had flown over the Tom Nevers site to inspect their holdings from the air and to be shown the location picked for the new Tom Nevers Airfield. When cleared and leveled, it would have two intersecting runways—the north-south strip running 2,100-feet long by 335-feet wide, the east-west strip running 1,900-feet long by 300-feet wide—with support facilities constructed on the land adjacent. The investors were told that if work progressed as scheduled, regular passenger service from Boston would begin on June 15th. In actuality, it began on July 4th, using a brand new tri-motor Stinson-Detroiter christened *Miss Nantucket*. The plane could carry four passengers in a comfortable closed compartment and up to 300 pounds of luggage. The *Inquirer and Mirror* declared in its next issue—"(this) air plane service will make Nantucket a suburb of Boston and New York."

So you see, Nantucket's first airport was in Tom Nevers and it was indeed called "Tom Nevers Field." It was located about two-miles east of the current airport—just northeast of today's old Navy Base. Years later, it would be taken over by the Curtiss Flying Service and eventually become known as Curtiss-Wright Field. Today, there's an upscale housing subdivision there that's called "Wright's Landing." If you study the plot maps for this subdivision, you'll still be able to see the original configuration of Nantucket's first airport.

A flurry of real estate transactions masked Franklin E. Smith's true role in this whole undertaking. On a single day—May 22nd 1926—titles to the hundreds of unsold lots in the original Nantucket Land Trust were deeded over to one William E. Beach and his wife Susan, of Weymouth, MA. Later that same day, Beach and his wife transferred ownership of the X-shaped landing field portion to Boston Airport Corporation—and on that very same day, deeded over all the remaining land to the Brier Cliff Land Trust, Inc., a Delaware Corporation with headquarters in Boston. That Smith remained a dominant force is suggested by his central role as head of the welcoming committee for the first plane to land near the site one year later—and again at the official opening of Tom Nevers Field on July 4th 1927.

Then, only seven months later, "official ownership" of the Tom Nevers project changed hands again, this time with the title being transferred from the Brier Cliff Land Trust to a firm called the "Drug Securities Company." Five trustees for the company were listed on the deed— Clarke T. Baldwin, Brenton K. Fisk, Joseph A. Galvin, Leigh B. Liggett and Louis L. Liggett. While Smith's name was not included, many believed he was more than just a silent partner. But even under a succession of "new management," the Tom Nevers land development project never took off, largely because 'Sconset had once again eclipsed it as the favored place to summer on Nantucket.

❦ ❦ ❦

1927 was a time of renewed gaiety in 'Sconset. I say "renewed" because 'Sconset had lost much of its sparkle during the war years and after the departure of the Artists' Colony. The Casino—once the vibrant center of 'Sconset's social life—had slipped into disrepair and debt. While its six tennis courts and two bowling alleys were still open, and its main hall was still used for silent movies and an occasional dance or lecture, the neglected building stood as a sad reminder to many of its past glory days. All that remained of the glittering masquerade balls, the musical reviews, the vaudevilles, and the week-long carnivals were the series of dusty black-and-white photographs that lined the walls of a side alcove.

But the 1920s brought a new generation and their money and talent to 'Sconset. And with them came new life for the Casino. In 1923, shares of stock were sold to pay off the Casino's debt. And one member—David Gray, son of a major backer and first president of Ford Motor Company—personally underwrote the Casino's complete renovation. He brought in the famed New York architectural firm of McKim, Mead and White for structural improvements and to design the great hall's unique latticework interior. This was the same architectural firm that designed New York City's acclaimed Pennsylvania Station, the Boston Public Library, the Newport Casino, the Washington Memorial Arch, the Morgan Library, major campus redesigns for both Columbia and Harvard Universities, and hundreds of other important commissions. The entire renovation cost Gray in excess of $32,500, and that was just the beginning of his generosity. If you look near the base of the flagpole in the center of 'Sconset Square, you'll find a plaque expressing the "perpetual gratitude" of the Casino membership to their fellow member and benefactor—David Gray.

1923 also brought back the tradition of vaudeville shows, follies and dances to the Casino. Robert Benchley—the humorist and charter member of the famed Algonquin Circle . . . was a creative driving force, along with the Broadway and film star Patricia Collinge and the multi-talented Tony Sarg—artist, puppeteer, and creator of the original Macy's Thanksgiving Day Parade with its famous balloons. Semi-weekly dances were held, this time with big orchestras featuring as many as fifteen players.

Throughout the '20s and '30s famous bands like Bobby Hackett, Meyer Davis and Lester Lanin appeared regularly. All the latest dances—from the Camel Walk to the Charleston to the Lindy—were premiered. And masquerade balls, with elaborate hand-crafted costumes, were again held every season. In between, fairs, treasure hunts, frolics, musicals, recitals, fashion shows, tea parties, and bridge tournaments kept the full summer season lively.

During Prohibition—which lasted until 1935—grape punch was the official Casino libation. But unscheduled flights landing near Bean Hill, and private motor launches rendezvousing with Canadian and European steamers outside the three mile limit, kept 'Sconset—and in fact all of Nantucket—well stocked with something far stronger. But for the young people, and for teetotalers, the Chanticleer just across the street was the place to go for both sodas and ice cream.

While members were partying at the Casino, far more sober activities were taking place elsewhere in 'Sconset. In 1922, Professor Frederick C. Howe announced the formation of his *'Sconset School of Opinion*, billed as "a summer gathering place for liberal scholars and intellectuals." Howe was well known and well connected in the socialist movement. He had made his reputation as a lawyer, economist, political reformer, professor, and member of President Wilson's staff at the Versailles Peace Conference. (Later he would prove to be one of the most controversial and criticized members of FDR's New Deal "Brain Trust.") Howe was also a 'Sconset summer resident who had bought the "Tavern on the Moors" restaurant on School Street and a growing number of rental properties. With his *'Sconset School of Opinion*, Howe hoped to make 'Sconset one of America's elite forums for furthering the world socialist movement—while also attracting paying guests to his properties.

In its first year, the *'Sconset School of Opinion* enrolled 125 participants, many bringing along their families for the full season. Featured lecturers included the head of the American Socialist Party, and the director of the ACLU. Lectures and panel discussions were held every morning and evening, with afternoons free for the beach, golf and other relaxations. And all sessions were open to the general public. At first, most of the regular summer people and 'Sconset natives couldn't resist calling those attending the sessions at Howe's "Tavern on the Moors"—where the general sessions were conducted—"The Commies on the Moors." But Professor Howe and the School's attendees were all so pleasant and civil that they soon became widely accepted into the 'Sconset summer community.

In subsequent seasons, the *'Sconset School of Opinion* headlined speakers like Carl VanDoren and Sinclair Lewis and, somewhat later, noted professors from Europe and leftist members of the British Parliament. Still later came Mortimer Adler and Will Durant. And for the youth, Howe added weekly dances and brought in Miss Anita Zahn to conduct her free-spirited "Duncan School of Dancing and Body Development." As many as 250 students registered. The leftist elite had found a new home in 'Sconset!

Today, everyone talks of 'Sconset's colorful Actors' Colony and how it made the tiny hamlet so famous and compelling to summer vacationers at the turn of the century. But few even know of the existence of the *'Sconset School of Opinion* and the role it played in doing the same thing a generation later. Started in 1922, it grew in international reputation and popularity for eight years until quelled by the Great Depression. As the Depression deepened, one-by-one Howe's 'Sconset properties were foreclosed or taken for back taxes. So he packed up his books and his note papers and shifted his energies to the Roosevelt administration, trying to reshape America's farm policies. But his views were considered far too radical and were never adopted. Frederick C. Howe, bristling with "modern ideas" to the very end, died in 1940.

❦   ❦   ❦

FIGURE 26   Map of 'Sconset With Key Locations

1. Old Fish Stage Shacks . . . later converted to tiny cottages
2. Sunset Heights . . . 'Sconset's first real development
3. 'Sconset Railroad Station
4. Underhill Cottages . . . put 'Sconset on the tourism map
5. The 'Sconset Casino . . . joy of the Actors' Community
6. Atlantic House Hotel . . . now long gone
7. Beach House Hotel . . . now long gone
8. Ocean View House . . . now long gone
9. Tavern on the Moors . . . home to the "'Sconset School of Opinion"

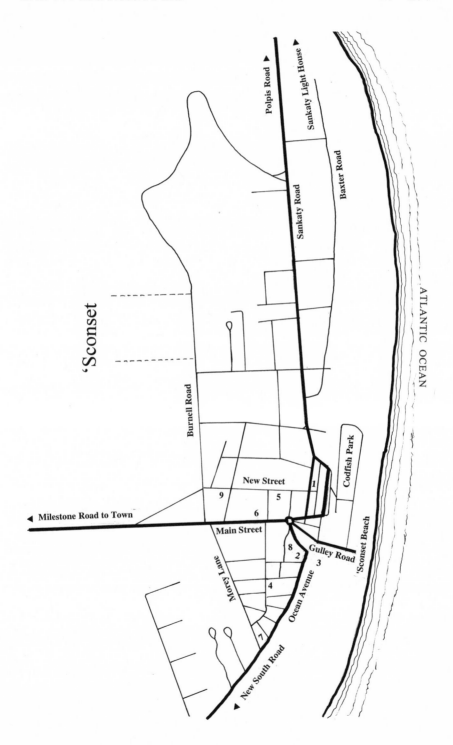

14

1942 . . . "Who Goes There?"

During the Second World War, almost the entire Southeast Quarter was taken over by the Navy and declared strictly off-limits to civilians. As I recall it, five guardhouses blocked road access to Low Beach, Tom Nevers, Madequecham Valley and Nobadeer—while jeeps with mounted machine guns patrolled the Milestone Road and the east and west boundaries of the property. Coast Guardsmen with attack dogs patrolled all the beaches, not only in the Southeast Quarter but around the entire Island. And Coast Guard motor launches and gunboats extended the protective ring seaward.

Like the rest of the Nation, the people of Nantucket were profoundly shocked by the December 7th 1941 sneak attack on Pearl Harbor. Shocked, not so much because America was now at war, but because the attack had come from Japan in the Pacific, rather than from Germany in the Atlantic. For months, bits of shipping wreckage, cargo refuse and oil clumps had been washing up on the east and south shore beaches—grim evidence that Nazi submarines were taking increased control of the Atlantic shipping lanes. And nightly radio broadcasts brought chilling news of the lethal force of Hitler's Germany and its breathtakingly bold advances. For some time before Pearl Harbor, the people of Nantucket believed that war was probably inevitable. Now it was here! A reality!

❀ ❀ ❀

To remind you how quickly things deteriorated in the years leading up to the war, just consider what the people of Nantucket heard as they gathered around their radios each night with growing apprehension. Remember, this was a time before the immediacy of television reporting, and a time when land war was traditionally characterized by long-term, static, dug-in artillery and troop positions—

On August 24th 1939, Germany and Russia sign a non-aggression pact, effectively negating all of Germany's standing peace treaties and agreements with the West. Just eight days later, Hitler invades Poland. And three days after that, Nazi subs torpedo and sink the British liner *Athenia*—with 1,400 passengers aboard, including 292 Americans. Mobilizing against what they call "a clear and certain threat," Great Britain and France declare war against Germany—and the British dispatch an Expeditionary Force of 158,000 troops to France.

On September 17th 1939, Stalin joins Hitler in invading Poland, and nine weeks later marches on Finland. Throughout the winter, Germany consolidates its gains and issues a series of ultimatums to several other countries. Then on April 9th 1940, Germany occupies Denmark and attacks Norway. And on May 10th, Germany invades Holland, Belgium and Luxembourg, all on the same day. Within a week, German forces break through the French lines and seize Brussels—then begin a dash to the English Channel, attempting to trap and destroy retreating allied forces. Leaving their artillery and heavy equipment behind, 220,000 British and 120,000 French soldiers just manage to escape from the piers and beaches of Dunkirk in a makeshift and frenzied flotilla of naval, merchant and small private craft.

On June 11th 1940—in an act which President Roosevelt calls, "A stab in the back," Italy declares war on Great Britain and France. Three days later, Hitler triumphantly enters Paris. And German bombers begin their deadly air strikes against Britain. On August 24th, the day and night bombing blitz of London begins and continues with unrelenting fury.

As Great Britain prepares to resist a Nazi invasion, increasing amounts of munitions and supplies are shipped from America. Merchant ships—many entering the shipping lanes near Nantucket—begin their high-risk voyages, as wolf packs of Nazi submarines converge to sink them. Initial hopes that the U.S. can stay out of the European war are increasingly seen as unrealistic. If Hitler is to be stopped, direct American assistance will be needed.

On September 3rd 1940, the U.S. "lends" Great Britain 50 old destroyers in exchange for a 99 year "lease" on British sea and air bases in the Western Hemisphere. The London blitz continues unabated. But some glimmer of hope returns, when on September 11th British bombers get through to strike back at Berlin.

On March 11th 1941, Congress votes to give Britain massive financial and material assistance under an expanded "Lend-Lease" program. But officially, the U.S. considers itself a non-combatant. Hitler fortifies his positions along the entire English Channel and North Sea coastlines and continues the brutal aerial attacks on London, readying for a multi-pronged invasion to come. At the same time, he turns eastward to open a second front. On April 6th, he invades Yugoslavia and Greece. On June 22nd, Damascus falls and Hitler begins a massive frontal assault against Russia.

To most all the world, it appears that Hitler will be victorious—conquering all of Europe, the British Isles, North Africa, the Middle East, and much of Russia. Can the United States stand aside and let that happen? Americans are divided on this question. Some saying it's not our fight, others saying that unless America acts now, we will be the next target of Hitler's ambition.

Then comes December 7th 1941 and Pearl Harbor. Within hours, Hitler and Italy join Japan in declaring war on America. And with much of the American fleet now crippled in the Pacific, Hitler immediately orders the Luftwaffe and the German Navy to seize control of the Atlantic, to keep America bottled up.

✵　✵　✵

The people of Nantucket were certain that a German attack would come soon from both the air and the sea. On December 9th, radio news alerts reported that enemy bombers were seen heading for the New England coastline. Throughout the week, State officials cautioned that bombing could be expected before the first of the year. Immediately, Nantucket organized a Public Safety Committee to prepare for the worst. As in World War I, the Island seemed a logical—indeed ideal—place for Germany to secure a U.S. foothold; a base from which bomber and submarine attacks could be launched against the mainland.

In December of 1941, the total population of Nantucket was just short of 3,000. (During the war to come, more than 400 would leave to serve in uniform.) But even a group of Islanders this small could resolve to mount a determined resistance. Within two days, air raid wardens were appointed and trained. Coast Guard teams were dispatched to patrol the beaches against Nazi saboteurs or landing parties. A watch tower was constructed near the Old Mill and staffed around the clock. New telephone lines were run to connect the lookout posts to both Civil Defense Headquarters and to the Coast Guard stations. Sand bags were filled and stacked at key locations throughout the Town, and citizens were advised to layer their attics with sand and to keep sand buckets in their homes to extinguish incendiary bombs. The sand was dug by volunteers and delivered by truck to each location to speed compliance. Citizens were warned that a single enemy bomber could release over 200 incendiary bombs, and that fighting the fires would be a personal responsibility because the entire Island had only five pieces of fire fighting equipment.

Fortunately, the air and sea attacks never came. But frequent reports of lights seen at sea—especially near 'Sconset—kept everyone alert and tense. Families gathered around their radios each night, chilled by reports of Hitler's and Japan's seemingly unstoppable advance. But the Pearl Harbor sneak attack had unleashed an anger and resolve among Americans to defeat this evil at any price.

By February 1942, regular dim-outs and frequent blackout tests were begun. Street lights and all exterior lights on buildings were masked or extinguished completely. Windows were hung with heavy draperies or blankets. The top halves of vehicle headlights were painted black. Boats sailed dark, save for their small green and red running lights. Nantucket would not let itself be an easy target.

From the beginning, the U.S. Navy recognized Nantucket's strategic importance. But it would take some time before it could achieve a major presence on the Island. Yet even as factories and plants across America started to gear up to build warplanes, efforts were begun to establish a Navy airfield on Nantucket.

Until early 1941, the Island's airport was still small and privately owned—little more than two grass-covered strips and a few support buildings. Now located at Nobadeer—because of its closer access to Town—the property had been offered for sale several times to the Town, but always turned down. Then as now, excessive noise made the airport unpopular with most voters. But on June 13th 1941, the Town finally agreed to purchase the airfield, counting on a federal grant of $274,000 from the Civil Aeronautics Authority to pave and improve the property. This federal program, designed to upgrade all the country's airports, required at minimum two hard-surfaced runways and compliance with strict cost-control guidelines.

But when the CAA and Army engineers surveyed the Nantucket property early that autumn, they calculated that improvements to meet federal standards would cost in excess of $500,000—largely because Nantucket's remote location would require that materials and work crews be brought in from off-Island. By November 15th, it appeared likely to everyone that plans to improve the airport would have to be abandoned. Without hard-surfaced runways, no federal monies could be appropriated—and available federal funding would fall far short of the cost to hard-surface them. Then came the attack on Pearl Harbor and new priorities for the nation.

After drawing up plans for a much-enlarged Nantucket Airport, the federal government issued construction contracts in the spring of 1942. By summer, heavy equipment was barged in and work begun. On October 29th 1942, the site was officially leased to the federal government and then subsequently assigned to the Navy Department. Construction work continued, but a particularly severe winter delayed completion until late the following year. (From December through February, temperatures hit record lows—ranging from 2° to 8° below zero.)

While airport construction was underway, most all of the Southeast Quarter was secured and cordoned off by the Navy. Under wartime leases with several property owners, all the land south of Milestone Road . . . from the east side of the airport to the western end of 'Sconset—was declared a military reservation. The Navy planned several uses for this property.

On Low Beach, near 'Sconset, a series of radio towers and low-lying buildings were erected. The true purpose of this installation was masked by disinformation. Generally thought to be high-powered ship-to-shore radio transmitters and receivers, only after the war ended was it revealed that the site was in fact an early and secret Loran Station—a vital new long-range aid to navigation.

The central portion of the compound—the Tom Nevers area—was used to train Navy combat pilots. Bombing and machine gun targets were erected in several locations—including one on a floating raft moored in Tom Nevers Pond. Planes dispatched from Quonset Naval Air Station in Rhode Island would make their bombing and machine gun runs to Nantucket, encountering wind and weather conditions not unlike those expected along the English Channel. Many of our new young Navy pilots had come from the heartland and had never before flown in thick fog and heavy coastal weather. The Southeast Quarter on Nantucket became their training ground for Europe.

We still hear stories about World War II bombs being unearthed in Tom Nevers. But in almost all cases they're duds. Live bombs were rarely used in the training because the goal was hitting—but not destroying—the targets. Live bombs would require the constant rebuilding of the target ranges and prove very dangerous to the ground personnel servicing the area. If you hear an explosion today, it's most likely the sound of the bomb squad's demolition charges and not the bomb itself exploding. But be careful, just in case that old round is indeed a live one!

Once Nantucket Airport was completed, it too became a Navy training facility. Pilots from Quonset Naval Air Station could practice their navigation, landing and take off skills here in all kinds of weather. After flying their assigned anti-submarine warfare patrols, they'd land at Nantucket Airport to refuel and re-arm with duds—then bomb and strafe beach and inland targets at Tom Nevers—then land again at the Airport to re-arm with live ammo before heading back to Quonset. The Airport also served as part of a broader Coastal Defense network. Strategically located 30 miles out to sea, it extended the protective coverage of the sea lanes leading to both Boston and New York Harbors.

As the young men and women of Nantucket left to join the Armed Forces, hundreds of other military personnel came to the Island. First came the Coast Guard, then a company of Army MPs, then the Navy. But from the start of the war, summer tourism effectively ended. Gasoline was rationed, and private cars were difficult if not impossible to buy or replace. Ads and posters asked patriotic Americans, "Is This Trip Necessary?" And in the case of Nantucket, it wasn't.

In the summer of 1942, two of the three ferries serving the Island were requisitioned by the government. The *Naushon* became a hospital ship and the *New Bedford* became a freighter. Both were sent to Europe. With food rationing and a decline in visitors, the Sea Cliff Hotel and many of the Inns and restaurants closed down for the 1942 and 1943 seasons. And the Sankaty Head Golf Club reduced its playable course to nine holes.

Are you old enough to remember the World War II food shortages and the ration books and stamps designed to make food distribution equitable? They covered just about everything from meats and canned goods . . . to butter, cheese, fats and oils . . . to sugar, coffee and chocolate. Shortages and rationing made for some inventive cuisine, but no one on Nantucket went hungry, as they had in wars past. And victory gardens supplemented each family's diet. Found in most every yard, they were seen as both practical and patriotic.

By late 1944, the tide against Germany and Japan had turned, and Nantucket was no longer seen to be in jeopardy. Weary from three hard years of war and yearning for a simpler time and place, many in New York and Boston and elsewhere found Nantucket's newspaper and magazine ads particularly compelling. They described the Island as, "An Oasis of Peace in a World at War." These ads persuaded many to come back to Nantucket for the 1945 summer season. This revitalized the tourism trade and swelled the number of celebrants taking to the streets when church bells and boat horns heralded VE-Day on May 8th . . . and VJ-Day on August 14th 1945. At long last, the war was over!

❦   ❦   ❦

Throughout all of World War II, Nantucket saw no direct enemy action. No bombs fell, no shots were fired, no Nazi saboteurs landed. The one brief direct contact with the enemy came after the war, when on July 24th 1946 an escaped German POW was apprehended in 'Sconset. Living under the assumed name of Robert LaForge, and passing himself off as a Swiss-French refugee from Alsace, the 24-year old Fred Kammerdiner had been working in 'Sconset for five months as a painter and handyman. He was living quietly there with a woman who helped him escape—a 40-year old American using the alias Anna Hamilton.

Not many Americans realize that during the war thousands of captured German troops were brought to the U.S. and interred in POW camps here. One of these camps was at Fort Devens, Massachusetts—and it was here that the Austrian-born German Army sergeant, Fred Kammerdiner, was imprisoned after his capture by U.S. troops in August 1943 at Messina in Sicily. By and large, the German POWs in America were treated very well, and in time many were even given daytime work passes to hold jobs on the farms and in the towns near their bases. After the war ended and they were returned home, a number of these former POWs applied for permission to emigrate back to America—where they eventually married, raised families and became citizens.

But sergeant Kammerdiner was not so patient. In December 1944—nineteen months before his recapture in 'Sconset—he charmed Anna Hamilton, a civilian base worker, to smuggle him out of the POW camp in a laundry truck she was driving. For more than a year he avoided detection in New York City and elsewhere. Then, six months after the war officially ended, he traveled to 'Sconset to join Hamilton in a house she had recently purchased.

As one of 43 escaped POWs, Kammerdiner was still a wanted man. And so it was that the FBI came to 'Sconset on July 24th 1946 to arrest him and to also arrest Anna Hamilton for her role in "aiding the enemy during wartime and harboring an escaped POW." On Nantucket, the word spread like wild fire that the FBI had arrested two German agents hiding in 'Sconset. But to those in 'Sconset who had come to know them both, they were just two unassuming and hard working people—not at all like those Nazi spies shown in the movies. Their arrest came as a complete surprise. Both Kammerdiner and Hamilton were tried and convicted. She received a suspended sentence, with the judge calling her offense a "crime of the heart." He was deported, never to return to America—or to Anna—again.

❦ ❦ ❦

1946 was a year of dramatic change in Nantucket, as hundreds of young men and women returned from military service. Anxious to start families, they bought homes and started new businesses. Inns, restaurants, retail shops, service businesses, and entertainment spots sprouted up everywhere. Many vets learned new trades by apprenticing with the Island's aging contractors. Others took advantage of the GI Bill, studying off-Island to bring new skills back to Nantucket.

On June 20th 1946, the Navy turned the airport back to the Town of Nantucket. That same day, Northeast Airlines began daily passenger and airmail service from New York and Boston. Using DC-3s with a capacity for 24 passengers, Northeast made eight trips daily throughout the entire summer season. That same summer, the Steamship line carried more than 10,000 cars to the Island and promised to add an extra boat the following season. After four years of wearing battleship gray, the steamships were repainted once again to sport their original gleaming white color.

Old time Nantucket residents were, of course, thrilled to have their loved ones return safely—only 11 had died in the war—but all the change and the influx of so many vacationers in a booming economy seemed a bit overwhelming. As early as July 27th 1946, prominent citizens began protesting what they called "semi-nude parades" in the streets and "growing vandalism." They demanded "an ordinance prohibiting the wearing of bathing costumes on the streets"—and strict new laws to arrest and punish "roving hoodlums who exceed accepted standards of order and good taste." Increasingly, the code name used to describe the island's newcomers was, "That cheap New York crowd!"

The Nantucket Civic League in its 1946 annual report captured the concern of the island's establishment in these words—

"The victorious ending of America's supreme war struggle just a year ago has witnessed changes in the Island's peace-time economy. Hundreds of men and women in the country's services have returned to their homes and pursuits; new business enterprises have been undertaken; a unprecedented number of transfers of ownership of properties effected; civilian transportation by air inaugurated; additional boat service given. An influx of summer visitors such has never been known has required larger accommodations of hotels, restaurants, rooming houses, markets and places of entertainment and recreation.

"This rapid expansion of our economy imposes a heavy strain upon our civic services, creating fresh problems in traffic control, health and protection of life and property.

"It will take wisdom, courage and foresight to plan for the future. It would be a calamity to allow our Island to deteriorate into a cheap seaside resort . . . Let us work to the end that the peculiar charm of old tradition and the beauty that is distinctive of our life here may not suffer through misdirected efforts towards a sound prosperity."

Sounds kind of familiar, doesn't it? The last part of that 60 year old quote might have been written today. You hear it at meetings, hear it from neighbors, read it in letters to the editor. I've included this quote here *not* to imply that things haven't changed all that much in Nantucket, but rather to make the exact opposite point. On Nantucket, change is *always* occurring. That change is hated by those who love the Island for what it *was*. They grow upset and then grow bitter, as they find themselves inevitably displaced by the newcomers—those who love the Island not for what it was, but for what *it's becoming*. It's a cycle that has been repeated again and again from the time humans first came to this Island.

❦   ❦   ❦

In 1946, the Navy also gave up most of its leases in the Southeast Quarter—particularly in the greater Tom Nevers area. (Only its site on Low Beach with the Loran station was retained.) But as you might expect, after years of use as an aerial target range, the property's market appeal for housing was non-existent. It was said that you couldn't give land away in Tom Nevers. And so most of the Southeast Quarter sat fallow, escaping the topsy-turvy development occurring elsewhere on the Island during the late 1940s and '50s.

'Sconset again proved the exception. Once more it became the darling spot of the old summer community, and original musical reviews and theatrical repertory companies played to capacity crowds at the Casino. But increasingly, after the war people came for shorter vacations. Full summer rentals were replaced by "July people" and "August people," and many husbands just flew in and out to join their families for long weekends. The big houses on the bluff were still owned by the same families, although now they were shared between the siblings who had inherited them. The net result of all this was a dramatic increase in the *total number* of different individuals deciding to vacation each summer in 'Sconset. Yet the character of 'Sconset remained much the same.

While the post war years had brought significant change to Nantucket, the Southeast Quarter had largely escaped its full impact. That change would come, but it would take two men of vision to shape it.

15

1946 . . . The Cunningham Purchase

Shortly after World War II ended, John P. Cunningham and his wife Patricia came to 'Sconset for a brief vacation. As he explored around the Island, Cunningham became more and more intrigued with that vast expanse of open land in the Southeast Quarter that the Navy had just turned back to its owners. Everyone kept telling Cunningham that this land was now next to worthless, which intrigued him with the idea that he might be able "to pick up the whole thing for a song." Unlike most of the others who came before him, Cunningham was not a real estate developer or a land speculator. He was an extremely successful New York advertising executive who simply thought it would be great fun to own a huge spread of ocean front land on Nantucket. And who knew, maybe one day he'd build a big estate there or maybe sell or gift it away if its value climbed in the future.

I won't tell you what the Cunninghams paid for the entire area we now know as Tom Nevers. But it was as Cunningham described it, "Little more than a good day's pay." The final deed transfer papers were signed on November 27th 1946 and then pretty much just filed away. In the fullest sense, the Cunninghams became absentee owners. John Cunningham was simply too busy to even think much about Tom Nevers. But that 1946 impulse of his to buy up "worthless land" kept the entire parcel together for the next eight years, and that proved pivotal to Tom Nevers' future. Without Cunningham, the area would likely have been carved up into a patch quilt of tiny low value lots.

❧   ❧   ❧

John Cunningham was one of the most creative and popular men in the advertising business, during a long career that began in 1920 and ended with his retirement in 1961. His many innovations reshaped the entire advertising business, won him a room full of awards, and earned him election to the Advertising Hall of Fame. And along the way, he served a chairman of the Advertising Federation of America and chairman of the American Association of Advertising Agencies.

Fresh out of Harvard College in 1919, John Cunningham joined the art department of Newell-Emmett—a very prominent New York City ad agency that would one day change its name to Cunningham & Walsh. Impressed by the imagination of his college drawings for the Harvard Lampoon, N-E's creative directors felt that he had great potential. But even they were surprised by his fast progress and huge impact on their business.

Within a year of his joining the agency, Cunningham enlarged his focus to also become a copywriter. Almost immediately, he began to create visually powerful ads that communicated with few words. This was considered a true advertising breakthrough. Back then, the words were considered to be far more important than the visuals, and copywriters and artists almost never collaborated. The writers authored all the ads on their typewriters and then sent them off to another floor "to be prettied-up" by an artist. But because Cunningham was both an artist and a writer, he opened the industry's eyes to the power of visual/verbal communications and led the way to integrating writers and artists into collaborative teams.

Perhaps John Cunningham's most famous ad campaign was launched in 1926, when he was still only 28 years old. Almost overnight it created a nationwide furor—prompting newspaper and magazine editorials pro and con, and leading to heated debates in homes, offices and social clubs all across the country. And within weeks, it sent Chesterfield cigarette sales soaring.

Cunningham's campaign was the first to break the taboo against showing a woman in cigarette advertising. But intriguingly, in Cunningham's ads, the man was the only one smoking. And there were just four words in the entire ad—spoken by a somewhat coy young woman as she looked a bit mischievously to her male companion—*"Blow Some My Way."* Ad historians have called these—"The most important four words of advertising copy ever written." Important, because they changed an entire culture and led the way to an entirely new form of advertising.

Clearly, during the heart of the Roaring Twenties, many women were already smoking—seeing cigarettes as a statement of their independence. But to many others, women who smoked were considered "bold." Cunningham's campaign worked spectacularly because it gave voice to the undercurrent desires of the modern woman—seeking equality but without compromising a ladylike persona. As a result of the campaign, cigarette smoking soon became socially acceptable for women of all social classes and ages. And remarkably, it increased Chesterfield sales to men just as strongly. It seemed to capture perfectly a man's self-image as the acknowledged experienced one in any male/female relationship.

Some also saw Cunningham's campaign as a classic role-reversal of the story of Adam and Eve in the Garden—with the forbidden fruit now a cigarette instead of an apple, and with Adam now portrayed as the tempter.

Today, of course, we have a fuller understanding of the health consequences of smoking. And we've largely succeeded in making cigarettes socially unacceptable, if not illegal. So to us, a headline like—*"Blow Some My Way."*—may seem repulsive. But 1926 was another time. Back then it was compellingly seductive.

Success after success followed. Constantly innovating, Cunningham next added market research to the creative process—insisting that his copywriters, art directors and account executives get out into the field to better understand consumers. Later, he would require them all to work a week or more each year in their clients' retail locations. This led to a series of astonishingly successful campaigns like the one Cunningham did for Texaco—stressing clean restrooms at Texaco's service stations, rather than the superiority of the company's petroleum products. Due to Cunningham, the era of modern advertising had begun!

It's an understatement to say that John Cunningham was a dominant force in the world of advertising. And an overstatement to say that he played any direct role other than financial in Tom Nevers' future. But without him, it's very unlikely that things in Tom Nevers would be as they are today.

❧   ❧   ❧

During the summer of 1954, John Cunningham was approached by the U.S. Department of Defense, who wanted to buy a 30-acre parcel of his land where today's old Navy Base is located. (In 1958 and 1960, the Navy would add more land, for a total of 47 acres.)

FIGURE 27   **John Cunningham's Breakthrough Ad Campaign**
Cunningham's startling ad campaign for Chesterfield Cigarettes transformed the popular culture almost overnight—and revolutionized the field of advertising. This and other Cunningham campaigns won him election into the Advertising Hall of Fame.

At age 56, Cunningham had just been elected president of Cunningham & Walsh and was now busier than ever. The government's interest prompted him to rethink his Tom Nevers holdings. Realizing that he would probably never use any of his Nantucket property, he decided to sell it all.

On November 16th 1954, Cunningham sold the 30 acres to the federal government for a nominal fee and sold all the balance to Bill Lawrence's newly-formed Nantucket Beach Properties. The price to Lawrence was $50,000—astonishingly low when one considers the value of that same land today.

Seven years later, at age 63, John Cunningham retired from his chairmanship of Cunningham & Walsh. Though suffering from severe diabetes, he lived another 24 years, making his home in the Riverdale section of the Bronx. He died in 1985 at age 87, while vacationing in St. Croix, V.I. His heirs included his wife Patricia and four sisters, but he left no children.

John Cunningham never returned to Nantucket's Southeast Quarter. But if he had, he would hardly have recognized it. The Navy Base had come and then gone. And Nantucket Beach properties had transformed much of the Tom Nevers area. But all this did not happen without some intriguing incidents, some colorful characters, and no small amount of controversy.

✵   ✵   ✵

16

1955 . . . An Ear To The Sea

The U.S. Navy returned to the Island again in force on January 27th 1955, when a massive LST steamed into Nantucket Harbor, swung open its huge bow doors and lowered its ramp onto Steamboat Wharf. At 327-feet, it was the largest vessel to every visit the Island and its arrival came as a complete surprise to all but the Coast Guard, the harbor master, and the Island police. Of course, we all knew that the Navy had bought some waterfront land in Tom Nevers, but we were totally surprised to see the size and scope of their "invasion." Aboard the LST was a full battalion of Seabees, with their heavy construction equipment and tons of materials—all destined for their newly-acquired 30-acre Navy Base at Tom Nevers.

As word of the Navy's arrival spread, hundreds of Nantucketers converged on the waterfront. But they were held back as unloading continued for hours. Down the ramp came earthmovers, caterpillar tractors, cranes, generators, drilling rigs, jeeps, and trucks stacked high with building materials. Then the LST pulled in its bow ramp, eased off the dock, and edged into the slip at the south side of the wharf, where hundreds of tarp-covered pallets were offloaded by crane.

Curious Nantucketers lined the Town's narrow streets as a seemingly unending procession of vehicles threaded its way from the docks to the Rotary, then out the 'Sconset Road, and on to Tom Nevers. The question everyone asked—"What are they building out there?" And the answer, repeated again and again, was—"That's 100 percent classified, under strict orders from Washington." But clearly, something big was happening. And its precise nature would not be revealed for another 36 years, when in 1991 the true mission of the Navy Base at Tom Nevers was finally declassified. In the meantime, a plausible cover story was developed and leaked to satisfy growing public curiosity.

Initially, the Navy Base covered the 30 acres acquired from John Cunningham. (Within three years, 15 acres more would be added, putting its northern boundary next to the old Tom Nevers/Curtiss-Wright Airfield.) But most importantly, from the beginning the Base controlled nearly 1,100 feet of beachfront—running east from Pebble Beach. Back in 1955, that beach was still more than 600 feet wide. Between 1887 and 1950, accretion had broadened the entire Tom Nevers' beach to nearly 2,000 feet wide, before erosion began to reclaim it. But it was the sea—and not the beach—that the U.S. Government was interested in.

After securing the area, the Seabees immediately erected a perimeter fence with guard houses. Then they constructed a complex of Quonset huts, roadways, radio towers, and concrete pads and emplacements. Living in tents during that winter and spring, the Navy construction personnel kept pretty much to themselves and had only limited contact with the Islanders. After that initial unloading at Steamboat Wharf, all further shipments of construction materials, supplies and equipment were landed directly on the beach at Tom Nevers—brought in by sea using LSTs and smaller beach landing craft.

On May 17th 1955—under Secretary of the Navy Notice #5450— "U.S. Naval Facility Nantucket" was officially established. In Navy lingo, it was dubbed "NAVFAC Nantucket." Immediately, orders were cut to transfer more than 100 officers and enlisted men to the facility—relieving the remaining small contingent of Seabees. And on August 1st 1955, in a special ceremony attended by Island dignitaries, the facility was formally commissioned. In the generalized statement read by the new CO at the commissioning ceremony, NAVFAC Nantucket was described as "an oceanographic research station." And informally, word began to spread that its mission was to measure and chart the currents, temperatures and salinity of the waters in the Cape and Islands area—as part of a broader effort to map and monitor the shifting shoals along the New England coastline, for more effective anti-submarine defenses. This "cover story" remained in place until the facility was finally decommissioned 21 years later. And it was underscored and institutionalized by the official base motto that was widely posted and promoted in 1963—"First in Research."

But in truth, NAVFAC Nantucket was a top secret "SOSUS" facility—with a mission so important that it required a top security clearance to even know what the term "SOSUS" stood for. (Fewer than ten of the NAVFAC Nantucket personnel had this level of clearance.) And to mask any speculation over what SOSUS signified, the unclassified mission name "Caesar" was established for use during the facility's construction, equipment installation and operation. So to the world at large—including all but a very few U.S. Navy personnel, Government officials, and scientists—NAVFAC Nantucket was just some sort of tiny and fairly dull "Caesar oceanographic research installation."

The name "SOSUS" stood for SOund SUrveillance System—a technologically-advanced, undersea, long-range detection system to locate and track all submarine movements—not only along the U.S. coastline, but worldwide. Thousands of highly-sensitive hydrophones were deployed in fixed arrays at key locations across both the Atlantic and Pacific sea beds—with each regional sector linked by cable to land-based "listening" facilities. (In 1955, NAVFAC Nantucket was one of the initial eleven operational SOSUS facilities—with three covering the Atlantic and six covering the Pacific. Later, many more SOSUS listening facilities would be added—including posts in the Mediterranean and elsewhere around the globe.)

All the sailors at NAVFAC Nantucket were well aware that the base collected oceanographic data via a thick undersea cable that ran through a conduit beneath the sand and up into a high-security building where "the techies did their stuff." But ninety-percent of them had no idea of the enormous size and scope of the operation. A few claimed the cable was fifty-miles long; but most argued that they knew it was no more than ten.

It's a surprising fact that the NAVFAC Nantucket cable spanned the entire Atlantic Ocean! From Tom Nevers it ran north to Nova Scotia, then northeast past Greenland and Iceland, and then east to the Norwegian Sea. Specially-outfitted U.S. Navy and British Royal Navy workships laid the cable and placed and tested the hydrophone arrays. All this work took place in top secret, with cable supply ships and workships dispatched from a number of different ports. The massive size of this undertaking was further concealed by the total lack of fanfare in connecting the cable to its terminus point at NAVFAC Nantucket in Tom Nevers. In making the hook-up, a single small workship was used to run an obviously short length of cable to the shoreline.

The technology behind the SOSUS project took more than five years to develop. And it began with a very probing evaluation of the lethal impact of enemy submarine warfare on Allied forces and supply lines during World War II. The irrefutable conclusion of this study was that in future conflicts, effective anti-submarine warfare would depend on the constant monitoring of all undersea threats long before they got close enough to be "lit-up" by seaboard Sonar. Clearly, a shore-based monitoring system was the only practical way to do this. The ocean was simply too vast, and the weather too variable, to make the use of surface ships or aircraft feasible in a permanent monitoring system.

But the engineering challenges in a land-based system were formidable. New types of underwater listening devices would have to be developed to detect faint acoustical signals at far greater distances—with enough precision to identify the specific nature of any threat by matching its acoustical signature to known standards. A deployment technique for the precision placement of these devices at great depths in fixed array patterns would have to be perfected, to permit the accurate targeting and tracking of each threat through triangulation. The data generated by these devices would have to be transmitted without degradation or distortion over vast lengths of cable. Each shore-based monitoring station would have to manage and analyze enormous amounts of data on a real-time basis—with the ability to isolate, differentiate and track the movements of a large number of targets at the same time. A secure communications network would have to be developed to relay this threat information instantly to SOSUS Command—where it could be combined with data from other SOSUS regional sectors and analyzed for threat action. In today's hi-tech world, all this may seem pretty straight-forward and commonplace. But in the early '50s, it was all new and daunting.

To overcome these challenges and perfect the SOSUS system, the U.S. Navy brought in the best scientific and engineering minds in the country. A team at MIT was charged with conceptualizing and designing the system architecture. Bell Labs and a team at Columbia University focused on exploiting long-range acoustics in the ocean. Western Electric Company and the Office of Naval Research designed and built specialized hydrophones and relay and data collection systems. To further enhance security, code names like "Project Jezebel" and "Project Colossus" were used to cover various parts of the program. By 1955—after extensive testing off Eleuthera Island in the Bahamas—SOSUS was at last ready for full deployment.

Throughout the 21 years of its existence, NAVFAC Nantucket was continually upgraded to harness leading-edge computer capabilities and advanced acoustic imaging technology. At sea, a series of technology upgrades were also made to increase threat detection performance. And cable maintenance was ongoing. All this was necessary to keep up with the threat of quieter submarines and enemy counter-tactics to evade SOSUS detection. The Soviets knew we were monitoring their submarine sound signatures. They just didn't know how we were doing it, or where, or how much we knew.

The base infrastructure was also continually upgraded. By 1960, NAVFAC Nantucket had 4 permanent cement block buildings, 16 Quonset huts, and a separate wood-framed barracks. In 1962, work commenced on T-Building—a greatly expanded high-security technical center packed with the latest electronic equipment. T-Building was strictly off-limits to all except a handful of command and operational personnel. Armed guards made sure of it. That same year, a cement block administration building, an impressive array of radio transmission antennas, and a water storage tower were built. In Nantucket Town, on Vesper Lane, a Navy Housing Project called Gouin Village was built to provide family housing. It was named in honor of the recently-deceased Vice Admiral Marcel E. A. Gouin, a Nantucket native whose very name was synonymous with the history of naval aviation. Known as "the jet-flying Admiral," the much-decorated Gouin saw heavy combat action in the Pacific during World War II, and held major air commands from 1929 until his retirement in 1954.

In 1963 at the base, a new barracks building and a new mess hall were constructed to replace the old ones. And later that same year, a brick rec center and club for enlisted men was completed. (Much, much later—in 1981 in fact—this building would become the VFW Club House, which was finally abandoned and torn down in 2002, when erosion rendered it unsafe.) Swim cabanas were also built on the beach for the recreational enjoyment of the men and their families. By 1965, the last of the Quonset huts were replaced with new cement block buildings. In all, the Federal Government spent over $6-million in facility upgrades.

One NAVFAC Nantucket improvement that still sparks debate is the bunker that many say was built as a Cold War fallout shelter for President John F. Kennedy and his family. The argument goes that the Tom Nevers base was chosen because it could be reached by helicopter in just minutes from the Summer White House in Hyannis Port—a location that would most certainly be targeted by Soviet missiles if a "first strike" attack was launched, as would the military airfields in the area. But others say that this JFK Bunker claim is just folk legend. They say that one need only to take a critical look inside the Tom Nevers bunker to know that its potential use as a Presidential fallout shelter is pure fantasy.

Built by Mobile Construction Battalion Six from Rhode Island and completed in June 1962, the NAVFAC Nantucket bunker does appear to be nothing more than a typical ammunition bunker—a mound of earth 15-feet high, 48-feet long, and 25-feet wide—with a few protruding vent pipes on top and a heavy steel entrance hatch at ground level. But the fact that the base facility had no heavy artillery emplacements—and thus required no large caliber ammunition storage—lends some credence to the claim that the bunker is more than it at first seems.

During construction, base personnel were told that the bunker was being built for the safe storage of JATO bottles—those pressurized gas cylinders that hold highly-flammable jet-assist-takeoff fuel. And it is true that sector patrol planes occasionally landed at the old Tom Nevers/Curtiss-Wright field adjacent to the base. But at the same time, base personnel with a SOSUS security clearance were told that the bunker was being built as an air raid shelter to protect top secret SOSUS data in the event of an enemy air or missile attack. However, T-Building was already equipped with heavy-duty fireproof safes, and there were never any training drills to transfer secret materials quickly to the bunker.

If indeed, the bunker was designed to protect the President in the case of nuclear attack, clearly it was intended only for very short-term use—perhaps a matter of hours until he could be safely moved to a more secure and well-equipped site. While the bunker did contain cots and a few pieces of standard military-issue metal furniture—plus storage shelves stocked with C-rations, bottled water, blankets and survival gear—there was no communications equipment of any kind. And contrary to the rumors circulating after the base closure, the bunker was not handsomely appointed. Spartan more accurately described it.

The main bunker chamber resembled the interior of a large Quonset hut—with a corrugated metal roof of 12-foot radius. Atop it was a protective layer of tar, poured concrete and several feet of sand and earth backfill. Inside the chamber, ventilation tubes with air filters ran the full length of the roof, as did electrical conduit pipes with bare bulb lighting. At the far end of the bunker, a series of small open-topped stalls screened off tiny sink, shower, toilet and dressing areas. Water and electric power lines ran into the bunker underground from primary base utility sources. It was certainly not power and water self-sufficient.

A horizontal 12-foot-long corrugated metal tube of 7-foot diameter connected the bunker to the outside world. It served as an air interlock chamber, with secured doors at each end. If the main entrance door malfunctioned or was blocked by debris, two escape hatches allowed another way to exit or enter the bunker.

So, was this a fallout shelter for President Kennedy if he needed to be evacuated from Hyannis Port? Yes, it was built for that purpose. But almost from the very beginning it was considered to be a fifth-ranked option. The Secret Service had it in their playbook, but it was well down the list of alternatives.

The problem with the Tom Nevers site was that the high water table in the area prevented building a completely underground fortified bunker and command center. The CO of Mobile Construction Battalion Six reported this up the line, and the decision was made to go with the next best alternative—a partially-buried berm-covered bunker in the form of a classic ammunition dump. While the bunker would never be adequate for any prolonged use by the President, it could still be used as a stepping stone site to evacuation through Nantucket Airport, if that proved necessary. Obviously, it made more sense to helicopter the President directly from Hyannis Port to Nantucket Airport if Air Force One or a military aircraft could be brought in fast enough. But if there was any delay, the bunker at NAVFAC Nantucket could be used as a "wait" point. However, a far better alternative was to fly the President directly to the even closer Otis Air Force Base in Falmouth on Cape Cod, or directly to any other nearby airfield where an already refueled Air Force One was likely standing by for his return to Washington.

During his term in office, President Kennedy came to Nantucket only once—and even then, he never left his presidential yacht, *Honey Fitz*. That was in 1963, when he paid a very brief visit to the Island during a Labor Day cruise across Nantucket Sound. Less than three months later, he would be assassinated in Dallas.

Eventually, the Tom Nevers presidential fallout shelter became a storage space. Not for JATO bottles or SOSUS data, but for spare fire extinguishers, maintenance equipment, and old cots. It still exists today on the old Navy Base property, but its entrance door has long since been welded shut. This bunker is the only remaining sign of NAVFAC Nantucket's long and important presence in Tom Nevers.

❦   ❦   ❦

The SOSUS system proved itself a tremendous success during the Cold War, effectively checkmating the aggressive play of the Soviet submarine force. Again and again, the Soviets tried to foray into our waters—almost always to be met by waiting U.S. subs, surface ships or anti-submarine-warfare aircraft. They ran maneuvers to test the vulnerability of our fleet and our convoy protection, again without much success. And as they expended ever growing sums to develop quieter propulsion systems for their nuclear missile-equipped submarine fleet, we always proved capable of detecting their positions and deployment. Starting with the conventional Soviet snorkeling diesel subs in the 1950s, through the ever larger and deadlier nuclear subs of the 1960s, '70s, and '80s—the Foxtrot Class. The Victor Class, the Charlie Class, the Gulf Class, the Delta Class, and more—SOSUS checkmated them all.

It was SOSUS that detected the position and support role of Soviet nuclear submarines during the Cuban Missile Crisis in late October of 1962. One reason that Khrushchev aborted his final placement of nuclear missiles in Cuba was that the U.S. made it clear that his missile delivery ship and its support subs had been precisely targeted and would be "taken out" unless they turned back.

It was SOSUS that played the lead role in pinpointing the exact location of the *U.S.S. Thresher* when it sank in 1963, and the *U.S.S. Scorpion* when it sank southwest of the Azores in 1968—and the Soviet Gulf Class SSB when it sank north of Hawaii also in 1968.

Based on its success and a changing military threat environment, the SOSUS mission was expanded over the years. In the 1960s, it added a missile-impact location capability to monitor the range and performance of test-fired missiles—both U.S. and foreign. In the 1970s, it added a deployable undersea surveillance capability—using a towed array of sensors that could extend SOSUS precision to almost any hot spot around the world. The 1980s brought further modernization—including a more advanced deployable system with far greater tactical capabilities. And along the way, there was much more.

Over the years, many new SOSUS listening posts were added and some older ones were deactivated—including NAVFAC Nantucket in 1976, after 21 years of service. But this closing did not signify the end of the SOSUS project. It still continues today.

When the Iron Curtain fell in 1989, the threat of nuclear submarine attack on America or its allies lessened considerably. So when the USSR finally ceased to exist in 1991, the SOSUS system mission was officially declassified. Then a program of SOSUS base consolidations began. Now complete, this reconfigured network puts SOSUS on full standby status—which means that all the SOSUS data is still real-time generated, but only selectively monitored based on potential threat level and location. Should an enemy or rogue submarine threat reemerge, the full system can be fully re-activated quickly to protect U.S. interests worldwide. And currently, an advanced Phase II deepwater, undersea surveillance system is being developed that can be reconfigured as needed for multiple mission applications.

One item of special interest, considering Nantucket's whaling heritage. SOSUS is currently being used in the North Pacific to study and analyze the low-frequency vocalizations of marine mammals in the open ocean. This SOSUS mission is adding tremendously to our understanding of how, and more importantly, *what* these truly amazing creatures communicate.

❄   ❄   ❄

On December 18th 1975, the U.S. Navy announced that NAVFAC Nantucket would be officially closed down on June 30th 1976, and that many of its 123 enlisted men and 13 officers would be transferred out starting immediately. Most all the rest and all movable equipment would be shipped off-Island before March. The base commander, Lt. Commander John Dooley, had orders to board up the buildings, drain the pipes, and leave the base in a secured condition before turning it over to the General Services Administration, which would be in charge of its final disposition.

As you might expect, the closing of NAVFAC Nantucket had a fairly large impact on the Island. Of the 136 men stationed there, many had their families with them. Off the base, 33 Navy families lived in Gouin Village and 30 more rented private houses. And 38 Navy kids attended Nantucket public schools. Also, a good number of single Navy men had fiancées or sweethearts on the Island. Marriage would take some local girls away from their families and their lifelong friends; while others would be left behind mending broken hearts. (In time, many couples and some single men would return to Nantucket once their service tours were completed, to settle down and raise families. But for the moment, their leaving was traumatic.)

Those who lived on the Island back in those days will probably always remember the high-spirited exhibition football games between "Navy" and the Nantucket High School "Whalers." Without question, the men of NAVFAC Nantucket had become an integral part of the Island community and would be greatly missed. Remember, Nantucket had a much smaller population in those days.

And then there was the economic impact. NAVFAC Nantucket was the second largest consumer of electricity on the Island (the Coast Guard was first)—and the biggest telephone user by far. And with a base payroll and operations budget of nearly $1,300,000—it had become an important contributor to the year-round economy.

Beyond that was the question of the 45-acre Navy Base site at Tom Nevers. What would become of it? The Town wanted it for recreational uses, others wanted it for development, and still others had educational uses in mind.

Hoping to receive the property as a gift—or at least for a nominal fee—the Town made application to the Department of the Interior's Bureau of Outdoor Recreation. And there their application sat for nearly two years. Then the General Services Administration announced that it would be in charge of the property's final liquidation, because no Federal or State agency had declared an interest in acquiring it. The GSA invited bids, along with an application detailing the property's intended use. As a guideline for the bids, the GSA revealed that the 45.68 acres up for sale had an appraised fair market value of $500,000. Clearly, the Town would have to compete for the property, but it did have an edge—the GSA assured it that any other potential buyer's "use plan" would require the approval of Nantucket officials before being accepted.

One strong bid came from a Mr. Timken of the Timken Roller Bearings family. But because the Town refused to grant him development rights, his bid was rejected. Nantucket Beach Properties also wanted the property, but felt the price was far too high. That left three bidders competing with the Town of Nantucket—and all three were educational institutions with a single vision.

Working through the U.S. Department of Health, Education and Welfare, Boston University announced that they hoped to transform about 60-percent of the old Navy Base facility into a year-round campus. Another 33-percent would become part of the University of Massachusetts system, and the remaining small parcel would become a creative arts center run by the Nantucket Island School of Design & the Arts (NISDA). This proposal created much excitement, but drew major opposition from the general public—which prompted the Nantucket Board of Selectmen to unanimously reject the BU/UMass/NISDA proposal. Their official objection was the permanent loss of 1,600-feet of beachfront to the people of Nantucket—even though BU in its proposal offered to "provide irrevocable public access to the beach for its present uses." But the larger reason for the public outcry was the belief that the influx of thousands of college kids would drastically change the whole character of Nantucket. And to block that, Nantucket was suddenly very willing to pay full market price for the property.

At a Town Meeting on April 3rd 1979—nearly three years after the Navy vacated the property—the people of Nantucket voted overwhelmingly to purchase the entire 45.68 acre former U.S. Navy Base at Tom Nevers for $525,000. In submitting the Island's bid to the GSA, elaborate recreational-use plans were also submitted, as required in the bidding process. The bid was accepted by the Federal Government and the property was transferred to the Town. The detailed—and very ambitious—recreational-use plans were filed away and never implemented.

But eventually, the old Navy Base was cleared of its derelict buildings and increasingly used as a family recreational area. And now 25 years later, it's officially called "Tom Nevers Field."

❧   ❧   ❧

But let's go back to the Cold War era, when NAVFAC Nantucket was first established. It was 1955 and these were scary times, with the threat of nuclear attack foremost in everyone's mind. Virtually every school in the country held "duck and cover" drills, training kids to hide beneath their desks each and every time the emergency siren blew. Civil Defense teams were organized in every city and village, including Nantucket.

Stalin was dead and a succession of would-be premiers were vying for power. The Rosenbergs had been tried, convicted and executed for giving America's atomic secrets to Russia. And the McCarthy TV hearings convinced most Americans that the Soviets had many more agents in our midst.

The USSR was embarked on a massive build-up of their nuclear arsenal and far surpassed the U.S. in long-range missile technology. And they were beginning to build a formidable submarine fleet, capable of launching nuclear weapons from beneath the sea. All of Eastern Europe was under Soviet domination, and their designs for the rest of the world were well known. In our own hemisphere, Castro had seized power in Cuba and then declared his alignment with Russia.

To help protect the U.S. mainland from a "first strike" airborne attack, America deployed a ring of radar-based systems—including the Distant Early Warning System (or DEW Line) to monitor the Arctic approaches. And to help protect against a "first strike" submarine-borne attack, America deployed SOSUS—with the base at Tom Nevers as one of its key elements. Also, in this time before "eye-in-the-sky" satellite monitoring, America had to rely on high-altitude spy planes and fixed location seismic systems to detect Soviet land-base missile deployments and launches.

Of course, none of these systems could actually defend America against nuclear attack. They would simply provide an early enough warning to let us retaliate with a nuclear counter-attack of our own, in a kind of Dr. Strangelove stand-off. Thus, for more than a generation, our total nuclear defense strategy was based on the concept of "mutually assured annihilation." And the scary part was that everyone knew it and lived with it daily.

Because this strategy worked, today it all seems so matter-of-fact analytical that it has almost been forgotten. But back then, believe me, it was forefront in everyone's mind and very upsetting.

For example, in the 1960 presidential campaign, the debate centered on the fear that the U.S. had fallen dangerously behind the Soviets in both the production and deployment of nuclear missiles. And the cover story in the September 15th 1961 issue *Life Magazine* was—"How You Can Survive Fallout." Across the country, towns and cities were preparing community fallout shelters for the general public. And many people were building fallout shelters in their homes or yards.

In November 1962—about a month after the Cuban Missile Crisis and the same year that the Kennedy bunker was built at NAVFAC Nantucket—the first two public fallout shelters were opened on the Island. One was in the basement of "Our Island Home," then on Lower Orange Street. The second was in the basement of St. Mary's Church on Federal Street. Work was also well underway for fallout shelters in the basements of both banks—the Pacific National Bank and the Nantucket Institute for Savings. Later, shelters would be opened in the Cyrus Pierce School and in the Academy Hill School. To equip emergency rescue workers, the Town secured five radiation outfits and 24 fallout protection suits. And more were on order.

While all this was happening, the Navy Base at Tom Nevers seemed somehow far removed from the action. After all, it was just an oceanographic research facility and not part of our national defenses. At least that's what the people of Nantucket thought. But if they could have looked into the data files at T-Building in NAVFAC Nantucket, they would have seen first hand the boldness and frequency with which the Soviets tried to invade our waters and airspace—not yet to attack, but to probe how close they could get before detection and to gauge the fullness of our response. Seeing all that, the people of Nantucket would have had even more reason to be alarmed. A Cold War cat-and-mouse game with potential life-or-death consequences was being played out right on our doorstep.

Meanwhile, in the open fields next to NAVFAC Nantucket, a new phase in the Southeast Quarter's development was just beginning. And there, it was not fear but unbridled optimism that reigned.

❧   ❧   ❧

17

1955 ... Tom Nevers Becomes a Community

W hile the U.S. Navy was secretly developing a SOSUS facility at NAVFAC Nantucket, it was equally exciting to watch Bill Lawrence drawing up his initial plans for a new kind of Nantucket community in the Tom Nevers area. Lawrence was an engaging, accomplished and highly successful real estate investor with a keen understanding of what appealed to affluent middle class home buyers. He knew they were turned off by the monotonous rows of look-alike, closely-packed houses in the "modern developments" being built in the post-war housing boom. They wanted space, they wanted charm, they wanted houses with character surrounded by lush foliage. And he knew he could make money by giving it to them.

During World War II, Bill Lawrence had served under General "Wild Bill" Donovan in the OSS—The Office of Strategic Services—the forerunner of today's CIA. "Wild Bill"—who had received his nickname and the Congressional Medal of Honor for heroism while commanding the Fighting 69th infantry regiment in France during World War I, and who in peacetime had led several international commissions while also running a successful New York City law practice—was a personal friend of President Franklin Delano Roosevelt. The two shared concerns that a new European war was brewing that would again draw American forces into the fight. So Donovan agreed when FDR asked him to become his personal eyes and ears in Europe. From 1935 to 1941, Donovan made frequent trips to Italy, Spain, England, the Balkans and elsewhere on FDR's behalf as an unofficial observer for the U.S. government. Then once it seemed that America's involvement in the war was becoming inevitable, FDR asked Donovan to draw up plans for a new military intelligence agency to operate around the world. In 1942, the OSS was officially commissioned by Presidential Order and "Wild Bill" Donovan was appointed to run it. And Bill Lawrence was one of the men selected by Donovan to staff it.

In every way, Donovan served as an inspirational leader to his OSS team, especially to Bill Lawrence. Always charming and always positive, the stocky, white-haired Donovan exuded the supreme confidence, fearlessness and intensity of purpose that brought out the very best in his men and women—many of whom were assigned to seemingly impossible secret missions. In all this, he became a powerful role model to Bill Lawrence.

After the War, Lawrence returned home to his family's business in Bronxville, New York—Lawrence Investing Company—a third-generation real estate development firm that had made its mark in New York's Westchester County. Under Lawrence's leadership, the firm planned and built several communities near Bronxville and other historic villages. These developments shared three common elements—meandering roads that emulated old country lanes, this in sharp contrast to the rigid grid layouts found in most new developments—underground power and telephone lines, again to add the sense of old time simplicity—and a building code that assured both variation and architectural harmony in the community. All this would serve as the model for Lawrence's Tom Nevers development project; and all this would be new to Nantucket.

For his Tom Nevers development, Lawrence chose the name—Nantucket Beach Properties—and then set about refining his master plan for the area. Building lots would be at least 1½-acres, some larger. All the roads would be private and follow the natural contours of the land. The scrub oak foliage would be kept dense and wild—not clear cut like Franklin Smith had done for his 1916 development. Nantucket Beach Properties would do no construction, that was to be left to the individual property owners—but all deeds would include strict building guidelines and require design approval from the company. The height limitation would be set at 1½ stories, with no upper decks allowed. Nantucket Beach Properties would provide all road maintenance for a modest fee, this to include roadside plantings and grass cutting, and wintertime snow plowing. But once 60-percent of the lots were sold, owners would be required to form their own property owners association to take over the maintenance of their private roads. To that end, each lot ran right to the center of the road to assure that even the roads were private and not community property. All this was clearly spelled out in each deed.

Nantucket Beach Properties reserved a large tract at Tom Nevers Head for possible future enhancements, including a club house and hotel. Other areas were set aside for possible use as tennis courts and a golf course. But none of these were ever promoted or promised as inducements to purchase land. The one exception was Pebble Beach—the area just west of NAVFAC Nantucket. Here a 500' × 500' beachfront parcel of land was set aside for the exclusive use of Tom Nevers residents. For many years, every land parcel purchased from Nantucket Beach Properties included deeded rights to the use of this beachfront property.

Once the master plan was drawn up and financing secured, Lawrence made application to the Town for all the necessary variances and special permits. No development of this type had been seen in Nantucket and there was some reluctance to approve it. The area's old 1916 grid pattern of roads—though most were never built—still appeared as "paper roads" in the Town's Registry of Deeds. These would have to be cancelled out before a new pattern of roads could be approved. Also, there was also some question about clear titles to several small lots in the area west of Tom Nevers Road. Sold at auction back in the 1910s and 1920s, these lots were long ago taken for back taxes; but some worried that Nantucket Beach Properties' ownership could one day be legally challenged. And if so, that would put the Town in the middle, because it was the Town that seized these properties and sold them to John Cunningham, who in turn

sold them to Lawrence. Unwilling to deal with an issue that might require the Town to indemnify Nantucket Beach Properties against potential title claims, the Town made a split decision. It gave Lawrence
permission to fully reconfigure all his property to the east and south of
Tom Nevers Road, but it withheld permission to reconfigure the large
area west of Tom Nevers Road. Approval there would be considered
later. In the meanwhile, the original grid pattern of 14 closely spaced
"paper roads" and 3 "paper cross avenues" recorded in 1916 would remain
fixed.

Over a period of several years, Nantucket Beach Properties gradually
developed its east and south property—laying out roads and installing underground utilities. The first section to be offered ran from Flintlock
Road to the ocean. The selling price was $4,000 per acre. Several fami-
lies bought land and began to build summer houses, snuggled deep into
the surrounding scrub oak. A number of these buyers were life-long
'Sconset summer people, who had tired of juggling the use of their inherited 'Sconset homes with their siblings and growing flocks of energetic
nephews and nieces. Tom Nevers gave them a peaceful place of their
own, still close to their friends and social life in 'Sconset. Summer people
from other parts of the Island also bought property, as did some builders
hoping to one day build spec houses for resale.

Based on this initial success, Nantucket Beach Properties opened a
second section—running from Lyons Lane to Flintlock. And they hired
as a resident manager a genial man named Harry Reid—who had relocated to the Island after selling his very high-end florist and silk flower
shop in midtown Manhattan. A community in Tom Nevers was beginning to take shape and others on the Island began to take notice.

❧   ❧   ❧

During the 1950s and early 1960s, Nantucket was seen as a pretty much
depressed and decaying location. Some young people who took summer
jobs in the Hamptons at the tonier resorts wouldn't even admit to their
co-workers that they hailed from Nantucket. It was considered too much

a poor backwater to confess to. But that began to change in 1963, when Walter Beinecke at age 45 returned to the Island.

As a boy and young man, Beinecke had been a seasonal resident of 'Sconset and dearly loved the Island's natural beauty and historic heritage. Now, as a wealthy retired businessman, he envisioned a renewed and revitalized downtown Nantucket that would act as a magnet to attract upscale summer vacationers. And as heir to the S&H Green Stamp fortune, he had the means and the connections to make it happen.

Beinecke set up Sherburne Associates as his redevelopment vehicle and formed the Nantucket Historical Trust to bring in craftsmen skilled in historic preservation and adaptive reuse. He also brought in artists, weavers, furniture makers, landscape gardeners, painters, and others with skills in the decorative arts—the only requirements being their talent and love of things traditional and historic. Together, they all worked on Sherburne Associate's first showcase project—the Jared Coffin House (the old Ocean House Hotel), which Beinecke bought, renamed and completely restored. Then came a rapid succession of acquisitions and restorations—most of the important buildings on Main Street, Center Street, Federal Street and Easton Street—including both the White Elephant and Harbor House Hotels. And crowning it all was the total revitalization of the Nantucket Boat Basin. The entire deteriorating and partly-abandoned waterfront area was rebuilt with new piers, new and restored fishing shacks, new galleries and retail locations, and an impressive and well-equipped marina to attract the moneyed yachting set. Straight Wharf, Old South Wharf and Commercial Wharf were all recreated by Sherburne Associates.

Many old time Nantucketers were horrified by Beinecke's charge-ahead efforts, and he quickly became the most hated and most loved man on the Island—depending, of course, on whether you shared his vision (and could potentially make money off his developments) or abhorred the whole idea of turning Nantucket into an upscale resort attracting "all those snooty and pushy off-Island people." Once again, Nantucket was changing, with a new wave of Paradise-seekers about to displace the old ways that many thought would last forever on Nantucket.

While Sherburne Associates' business ventures were confined to the historic Town Center, Walter Beinecke also played a big role in protecting the outlying areas from what he called the wrong kind of development. His actions here greatly benefited the Southeast Quarter, especially Tom Nevers.

With several others—including a man named Roy Larsen, who was then president of Time, Inc.—Beinecke helped to establish the Nantucket Conservation Foundation. This gave the Island a non-profit vehicle to protect large tracts of land from commercial development. Back in 1959, Beinecke, Larsen, Arthur Dean and others had purchased the old Nantucket Cranberry Co. This property included 331-acres of producing bogs north of the Milestone Road and 810-acres of undeveloped bog land to the south of the road—running from Tom Nevers Pond almost to 'Sconset. All of this land they donated to the Nantucket Conservation Foundation. Bill Lawrence of Nantucket Beach Properties then donated the land adjoining Tom Nevers Pond. And the Larsen family donated an additional 513-acres between Madequecham Valley and Tom Nevers. This put a large percentage of the Southeast Quarter under conservation, and ringed Nantucket Beach Properties' holdings with a "forever wild" greenbelt.

All these redevelopment and conservation efforts did not escape media attention across the country. And growing numbers came to see the "new" old Nantucket. Falling in love with its charms, they found a place unlike all others—historic uniqueness, natural beauty, pristine beaches, cool breezes, first-class services, and a total escape from the hurly-burly of most resort communities. And just as the original British settlers had seen the Island's remoteness as a great asset—because the sea provided a protective "fence" for their sheep raising—these newcomers saw Nantucket's remoteness as the natural equivalent of a gated community, protecting them from the cares and intrusions of mainland life. Little wonder that many chose to buy land.

❧   ❧   ❧

As on much of the Island, more and more summer houses began to sprout up in the Tom Nevers area. And by the 1970s, for the first time in

Nantucket's history, people began to worry about unchecked development. They feared that without some controls, the growing number of small housing developments and random placement of individual buildings would change the whole character of the Island.

At a Town Meeting in March of 1970, the Historic District was expanded to cover the entire Island. In 1971, Nantucket's first master plan was developed. And in September of 1972, the first zoning laws were enacted. In 1973, a professional was brought in to direct the Nantucket Planning Board's efforts full-time.

In October 1976, Tom Nevers became the center of some controversy. Nantucket Beach Properties applied for a special zoning variance to create the Island's first "cluster subdivision" on a 42-acre plot off Flintlock Road, to be called "Lighthouse Lane." The idea was to cluster houses close together as a sort of mini-village—with pathways, picket fences, a shared tennis court area, and a large surrounding greenbelt. Rather than to have 13 houses—with each built on a 3-acre lot as required by zoning—the cluster subdivision would have 13 small houses spaced much closer together on 1-acre lots. A little over 5-acres would be set aside for 4 tennis courts and a pro house, and the remaining 24-acres would become conservation land kept "forever wild."

This was exactly the type of land use plan that the Nantucket Planning Board had been advocating. They hailed it as more consistent with the Island's historical character—tiny settlements rather than a big spread out mainland-style suburban development. But negative reaction to the plan was fast and vocal—especially from the people who already owned property in Tom Nevers. In fact, the cluster subdivision proposal gave them the impetus to form the Nantucket Civic Association—whose first president was Dr. Margaret Kilkoyne, a medical researcher at Columbia University College of Physicians and Surgeons, and whose mysterious disappearance three years later would draw national media attention.

The Tom Nevers Civic Association said that they were not opposed to the cluster development concept in principle, but that they were opposed to both how and where Nantucket Beach Properties planned to implement it. They emphasized that the original Tom Nevers lot purchasers valued their isolation and did not welcome a high-density "town" in their midst.

In hearing after hearing before the Zoning Board of Appeals and at the Planning Board, the arguments and counter-arguments continued for nearly a year. But finally, Nantucket Beach Properties' appeal for a cluster subdivision was denied.

This setback in no way slowed down development in Tom Nevers. Many lots were sold and construction crews could be seen and heard almost everywhere in the area. Individual builders were putting up spec houses with period charm and particular appeal to "tax shelter" investors. This was a time when a tax loss on a rental vacation property could be used to offset the very high taxes on ordinary personal income. You could buy a fine summer home, use it yourself for a two week vacation, and rent it out for the rest of the season—with almost all of your operating costs, and even depreciation, subsidized in large part by personal tax savings. And all the while, if the economy held and the location you picked was a good one, the value of your property would keep rising. Ultimately, you could sell the place at a big profit, or stop renting and have a delightful second home for retirement. All this proved to be a tremendous catalyst for real estate development—everywhere, including Tom Nevers.

By this time, Bill Lawrence had retired and the new management team leading Nantucket Beach Properties decided to drop their old building restrictions in favor of the recently published building guidelines issued by the Historic District Commission. Because of their great appeal to buyers, "upside-down houses"—with second-story decks to provide sweeping views—became the new building design standard, both in Tom Nevers and across much of the Island.

In 1979, Nantucket Beach Properties paved Longwood Drive and three cul-de-sacs off it to open a new section that they called "Sankaty View." This subdivision added 50 more 3-acre building lots and one 15-acre parcel at the junction of Tom Nevers and Milestone Roads. It was thought that this larger lot might one day be used for a food market and small shops. But as you know, that never happened. (Three friends eventually bought it and carved it up into five more building lots.) Elsewhere in Tom Nevers, speculators purchased multiple parcels to build their own small subdivisions. All this activity prompted the Nantucket Land Council to run ads in the Inquirer and Mirror expressing alarm over the many new houses being planned for Tom Nevers. Under the headline—"Slow It Down"—they implored Nantucket voters to turn out in force to express their opposition to the Planning Board and Selectmen. But development charged ahead anyway.

❧   ❧   ❧

An amazing backdrop to all this real estate development activity in the 1970s was a concerted effort by the Federal Government to put sweeping new controls on all the land and all the beaches of Nantucket. If enacted into law, almost all of Tom Nevers would be re-zoned as "Lands Forever Wild." No further building would be permitted, all undeveloped properties would be taken immediately by eminent domain, and all existing houses would have to be either moved or torn down within 25 years. All this was the brainchild of Senator Edward M. Kennedy.

❧   ❧   ❧

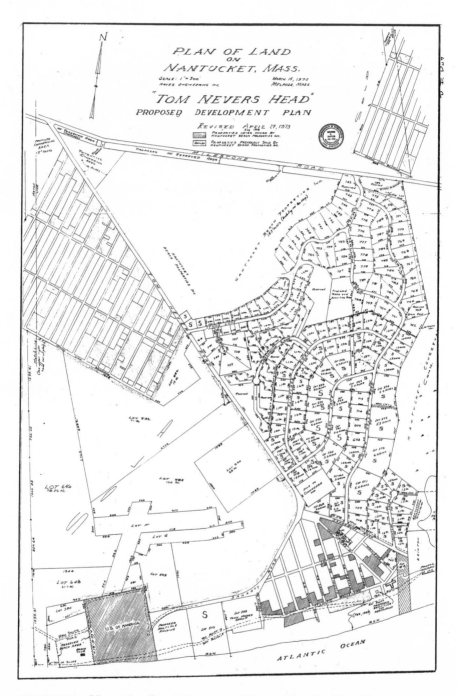

FIGURE 28   Nantucket Beach Properties' Master Plan For Tom Nevers—
Circa 1973

18

1972 . . . Big Brother

On April 11th 1972, without the slightest warning to those of us living on Nantucket, a bill was introduced into the U.S. Senate that would put the entire Island of Nantucket under Federal control. Introduced by Senator Edward M. Kennedy of Massachusetts, the bill authorized the creation of the Nantucket Sound Islands Trust. Kennedy characterized the Trust as—"a practical and enlightened way to freeze the current disastrous course of development and redirect it along planned, sensible avenues."

Under Kennedy's plan, both Nantucket and Martha's Vineyard—and the smaller islands of Nantucket Sound—would fall under the jurisdiction of a 21 member Commission to be appointed by the Secretary of the Interior. Nantucket would have five seats on this Commission, Martha's Vineyard would have eight, and Barnstable would have one. The Secretary of the Interior, the Governor of Massachusetts, and the EPA would each nominate one more. And the final four Commission members would be nominated by the U.S. Senate and House Members from Massachusetts—selected by them to represent the more important conservation and preservation groups on the Islands.

Along with the bill came a map that carved up Nantucket into three general land use classifications. "Class A: Lands Forever Wild"—"Class

B: Scenic Preservation Lands"—and "Class D: Town Planned Lands."
(There was also a "Class C: County Planned Lands" classification, but
that applied to Martha's Vineyard only, since on Nantucket the Town
and County covered the same area.)

Let me describe the rules for each of these land use classifications—

"Class A: Lands Forever Wild" would be returned to their natural and
wild state. If you owned any undeveloped land in this area, it would be
taken by eminent domain unless you made arrangements first to gift it to
an approved non-profit conservation foundation. If you owned developed land, you would be allowed the use of your buildings and other already existing improvements for up to 25 years, but then they would have
to be torn down or relocated. In the meantime, the general public would
have free open access to all your property.

"Class B: Scenic Preservation Lands" would be frozen in their current
state of development, with no further construction or improvements beyond that which already existed. If you owned any undeveloped land, you
could never build on it. (You could sell it or gift it, but without development potential, it would become essentially worthless.) If you owned developed land, you would be limited to making modest repairs and
replacements to your structures. (But even so, market demand would
make these properties far more valuable.) All land in the Scenic Preservation areas would remain private property, with no access for the general
public. And as such, the Federal government would provide no funding
for eminent domain property takings.

The Kennedy bill did provide one exception to the total ban on new
development in the Scenic Preservation areas. Public buildings like
schools and hospitals could be built if a need was demonstrated and the
"Class D: Town Planned Lands" could not accommodate them. But here
the normal approval process was reversed—with the burden of proof
falling on those requesting permission to build, rather than on those seeking to limit development. And the prior approval of both the Island's
Planning Commission and Board of Selectmen would be required before
permission could be requested from the Secretary of the Interior's 21
member Commission.

"Class D: Town Planned Lands" would be the locus of all future development on the Island, and here the Board of Selectmen would have full responsibility for all planning and zoning controls. Approval from the Secretary of the Interior's Commission was not needed. But all further construction and improvements in the Class D areas would require both a demonstrated need and the specific approval of the Town's governing body.

Now you may be wondering exactly what land fell into each of these three land use areas—

The *"Class D: Town Planned Lands"* included seven locations—about half of the current Town of Nantucket—about half of the current 'Sconset—about 25 acres in Quidnet—about 60 acres in Wauwinet—about 250 acres in Surfside—about 325 acres in Madaket—and Nantucket Airport, including a narrow strip of land connecting it to Town. Taken all together, this represented only about 10 percent of the Island's total acreage.

The *"Class A: Lands Forever Wild"* included five large areas—most all of the land running west from Sesachacha Pond to Shimmo, and running south to New South Road—most all of the land between Hummock Pond and Long Pond, and running south from Eel Point Road to the Atlantic Ocean—all of Great Point and Coatue—all of Eel Point running east to North Head Long Pond, and running south from Nantucket Sound to the Madaket Road—and all of the Island's beach lands from the mean low water mark up to the start of upland vegetation. Taken all together, this represented about 40 percent of the Island's total acreage.

One special comment about the Island's beaches. Under the Kennedy bill, all beach land would be taken by eminent domain for free public access, whether in private, public or foundation hands. And in addition, the Secretary of the Interior and the Commission could establish rights of public passage by eminent domain at key points all along the shoreline.

The *"Class B: Scenic Preservation Lands"* included everything else on the Island not part of the Class A and Class D areas. Taken all together, this represented about 50 percent of the Island's total acreage.

As a point of comparison, you might find it interesting to know that on Martha's Vineyard the proposed restrictions were far less severe. Only about 10 percent of the Vineyard was classified as *Lands Forever Wild* and only 30 percent was classified as *Scenic Preservation Lands.* This left over 60 percent of Martha's Vineyard open to *Town and County Planned* new development. But even so, Massachusetts other U.S. Senator—Edward Brooke—who owned property on Martha's Vineyard, voiced his early strong opposition. This persuaded Senator Kennedy to drop Martha's Vineyard from his final bill.

Anticipating local objections on Nantucket, the Kennedy bill included two special provisions—

1. To blunt concerns about reduced employment opportunities, the bill specified that monies be set aside to provide financial assistance and retraining for those individuals whose livelihoods were seriously jeopardized. This obligation would run for a period of up to 4 years; and the Secretary of the Interior and Secretary of Labor would select the retraining projects. Specifically mentioned in the bill as likely options were aquaculture (fish and shellfish farming) and viticulture (growing grapes for wine.)

2. To blunt concerns about a major influx of back-packing vacationers—such as was occurring at the National Parks—the Secretary of the Interior would be directed to study ways to restrict access to the Island by both boat and plane. Additionally, he would be directed to study ways to reduce the number of cars allowed on the Island. (But the bill held out little real hope that any of these study recommendations would be enacted, by acknowledging that it was "strongly repugnant to the American system to limit freedom of travel.") And in fact, a little publicized provision in the bill empowered the Secretary of the Interior "to develop any portion of the Trust Lands he deemed especially adaptable for public use areas . . . including camping, swimming, boating, sailing, etc." While not a National Park, public funding would require that Nantucket's *"Forever Wild Lands"* be freely open for the recreational enjoyment of all comers.

And what about compensation? Total Federal funding for all the land and property to be taken by eminent domain was to be capped at

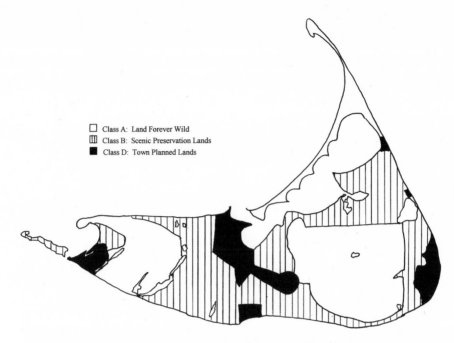

☐ Class A: Land Forever Wild
▥ Class B: Scenic Preservation Lands
■ Class D: Town Planned Lands

FIGURE 29　**1972 Federal Plan To Take Over Nantucket**

In 1972, without any prior warning, Senator Edward Kennedy introduced Federal legislation that would have put all of Nantucket Island under the jurisdiction of the Federal Government—subject to stringent new land-use regulations. Class A areas (shown in white above) would be declared public lands and would have to be returned to their natural and wild state—with all existing buildings torn down or moved off-site within 25 years. Class B areas (shown in stripes above) would be frozen in their current state of development, with no further construction allowed. Only in Class D areas (shown in black) would any new construction be allowed—but only with a demonstrated need and the specific prior approval of Town Government. If enacted, only 10-percent of the Island's total acreage would be available for all future development. And a large percentage of the Southeast Quarter would be purged of all development.

$20-million, with a maximum of $5-million more to cover all development, operating and retraining expenses. And this budget included all the islands of Nantucket Sound, including Martha's Vineyard. Considering the amount of land to be taken by eminent domain, it seemed apparent that property owners would receive only a tiny fraction of their land's fair market value.

❦   ❦   ❦

Reaction to the Kennedy bill was swift and vocal. On April 25th 1972, more than 1,200 Nantucket residents jammed into the Nantucket High School auditorium to hear a special presentation by K. Dunn Gifford and to pepper him with questions. During the 3½-hour session, Gifford denied that he had personally masterminded the bill and denied that he was on Senator Kennedy's staff. But he did acknowledge that several year-round and seasonal residents had played a key role in drawing up the bill. When asked for their names, he declined, saying that they didn't want to be identified "because they would be called traitors and other names." He announced that a special assistant to Senator Kennedy was in the hall to take notes that they would be carried back to the Senator to help him finalize the bill's provisions.

In trying to sell the bill, Gifford painted an alarming picture of the Island's future without Federal intervention. He predicted that without the bill, 2000 new homes would be built on the Island within the next year alone—more than 13-times the current annual rate today. He claimed that these were not his figures, but that they came directly from the Nantucket Planning Board.

He argued that the bill was not a Federal takeover, but rather a legislative assist from Washington in thwarting a land rush fueled by greedy mainland developers—a land rush that would destroy the Island if left unchecked.

But clearly, the citizens of Nantucket weren't buying it. Question after question revealed the downside of the Kennedy bill and its harsh realities. Words like "creeping socialism" and "Big Brother" raced around the hall. One person rose to implore—"We have no desire to become a stale, lifeless, federal campground." Another exclaimed, to great applause—"I feel like an Indian about to be sentenced to a reservation."

At the end of the meeting, Gifford asked for a voice vote on how many wanted to see development slowed down on the Island. There was a roar of "ayes" and no one said "nay." Then he asked how many were in favor of the Kennedy bill, and nearly 7-out-of-10 shouted "nay." But still, the bill's supporters felt encouraged. This was the public's first exposure to the bill, and already they had secured a 30-percent base to build upon. And their efforts to pass it were only just beginning.

Over the next 15 months, supporters of the Kennedy bill worked quietly behind the scenes to enlist the support of the Island's non-profit groups, and they formed the Committee To Preserve Nantucket to study public opinion. Senator Kennedy visited the Island to speak to these groups and to hold a public hearing.

As you might expect, during this whole time building on Nantucket was thrown into turmoil. Many banks refused to lend money or write mortgages even on already-approved projects due to the uncertainty over their future market values. Others, with independent financing, rushed ahead to build—gambling that the bill's April 11th 1972 "new building freeze date" would be extended to the date of the bill's actual signing into law. If they were right, they would have a property with enormously increased resale value. But if wrong, they'd have to tear down the buildings at their own expense—losing even more than their initial investment. Ironically, the bill prompted an increase in building on the Island—with over 300 homes built, compared to fewer than 150 built the year before.

During this period, important changes in the Town's bylaws were also voted in and enacted. For the first time zoning became law on Nantucket—reversing several years of rejection by voters. Sweeping land use restrictions were also enacted. Nantucket somehow wanted to prove that it could solve its own problems without surrendering to the Federal government.

❀   ❀   ❀

On July 16th 1973, over 800 people showed up for a special U.S. Senate subcommittee hearing that was held in the Nantucket High School gymnasium. Presiding was Senator Alan Bible of Nevada, Chairman of the Senate Interior Subcommittee on Parks and Recreation. Also on the dais were Senator Kennedy and Senator Bennett Johnston of Louisiana.

One by one, witnesses representing the Island's major organizations rose in support of the bill—heads of the Board of Selectmen, the County Commissioners, the Planning Board, the Nantucket Conservation Foundation, the Nantucket Historical Trust, the Nantucket Civic League, the Preservation Institute, and the Madaket Conservation Association. Witnesses also supporting the bill included a prominent realtor, a general contractor, a land surveyor, and two large property owners. Almost alone in opposition to the bill as written was Nantucket's State Representative, Arthur Desrocher, who spoke as a private citizen. He argued that the bill went too far and was too restrictive, citing ten specific and detailed objections. He characterized the Kennedy bill as "Federal Snob Zoning" and pleaded that it not be passed into law.

Before ending the hearing, Senator Bible asked the general audience at the hearing for a show of hands in support or opposition to the bill. At least several hundred hands rose in support, and only about 20 hands registered opposition. He then asked all those in the hall who were year-round residents to stand, and then in-turn non-residents. Only about 20-percent were year-round residents, all the rest were seasonal property owners. This prompted a question by Senator Bible. He asked if the Town government had ever polled the people living in Nantucket about their feelings on this bill. Senator Kennedy said that an unofficial vote had been taken at a January meeting that he chaired—with 600 people in attendance, mostly Islanders. He reported that in that voice vote about 80-percent were in favor of the bill, 15-percent were in favor with some reservations, and just 5-percent were opposed. But, he added, he would welcome any effort to ascertain current opinion. Speaking from the floor, a recommendation was made to put that question to voters in the November election. There were no objections, so certain were the bill's supporters of its positive endorsement. But that ballot issue would be delayed for another three years, giving the opposition time to rally its forces.

As the debate continued, Nantucket became more and more polarized. Retirees, summer residents and the elite were strongly in favor of the bill's passage, seeing it as essential to the Island's future. Working families and most long-time residents saw it as a socialistic infringement on their rights to home rule and private property. Yes, everyone wanted to slow down development. But to the bill's opponents, allowing the Island to become a ward of the Federal government was not only chilling, it was down-right un-American! And constant use of the words—"for the common good"—by the bill's supporters only added to that perception. Remember, in those days, Nantucket was still strongly conservative and strongly Republican. It wasn't until the late '70s when the influx of young activists and New Deal-era retirees began to change that.

Ignoring growing local opposition, the U.S. Senate approved an amended Kennedy bill in 1975 and a companion bill was introduced into the U.S. House of Representatives. Alerted to dwindling public support for the measure, the House Subcommittee on Parks and Recreation recommended an 18-month study before taking a position. This setback for the Kennedy initiative would extend the swirling debate into its fourth year.

Finally, the issue was brought before Nantucket voters in a special Town Meeting in 1976, where the Kennedy proposal was resoundingly defeated. Faced with this reality, Senator Kennedy and U.S. Representative Gerry Studds announced on January 6th 1977 that they would reintroduce a version of the bill that would provide more local control. But these efforts faded away as Kennedy's and Studds' attention had to be refocused on Nantucket's attempt to secede from the State of Massachusetts. In the April 4th 1977 annual election, a nonbinding referendum to secede was favored by a margin of four-to-one by Nantucket voters. This secession movement came as a protest to the Island's redistricting loss of its own representative in the State Legislature, but it also reflected some unhappiness with both Kennedy's and Studds' intrusion into Island affairs.

❧   ❧   ❧

If the Kennedy bill had passed, there would not be a single building left standing today in Tom Nevers and across virtually all of the Southeast Quarter. Only the oldest part of 'Sconset and a few older houses on its fringes and along the southern shoreline would remain. But there is a fairly good chance that campers and back-packers from all across the country would be roaming the Southeast Quarter's landscape and congregating on the beaches and atop Tom Nevers Head. Choice public land with free and open access is like that!

But even in losing, the Kennedy bill did many great things for Nantucket. Without it, zoning laws might never have been passed, and an Island-wide commitment to land conservation through gifting and market-priced purchase might never have materialized to the impressive level that exists today. Also, many local initiatives and bylaws to moderate unchecked development might never have been voted in and enacted. All this under local control, without the intervention of the Federal or State government.

On the downside, the Kennedy bill brought Nantucket to the attention of the national media—informing millions who had never heard of the Island that it was indeed a rare jewel just off the New England coastline. This prompted even more high-end vacation home buyers to come to the Island, fueling a rapid rise in property values. And in no small way, it assured the success of Nantucket Beach Properties' expanding development of Tom Nevers.

❧   ❧   ❧

I can't move ahead with the rest of my story, without first reflecting on what the fight over the Kennedy bill tells us about basic human nature. In fact, it's a microcosm of all we've seen throughout Nantucket's long history.

In every special place, the land is precious to those of us who own it. We've worked and saved, and often sacrificed and even fought to secure it. It's more than just our piece of private property. It's our home—and as

I've said several times before, our earth-bound substitute for Eden. And we're resolved to never again have it taken from us. Not by bankers, not by government, and certainly not by neighbors.

Yet at the same time, we crave to stop the encroachment of others on land near to ours. And we'll willingly conspire to limit, or even take away, our neighbor's private property rights if we feel our own quality of life is affected. We use the law, if it applies. And that is proper. But if no laws exist, we'll often try to invent new ones or go even further. And we assuage our guilt by calling our actions—"for the common good." But unless our neighbor agrees that it is to his "good" too—or unless he is fully and justly compensated—our intransigence is little more than that old sin called covetousness.

Sadly, we all share these human urges and human failings when it comes to our land and to private property. Would that it were otherwise.

❁   ❁   ❁

19

1985 . . . The Smell of Money

I t was in the air, it was in the bloodstream. Everyone knew that the price of Nantucket land was soaring. Anyone who could afford it wanted to get in on the action. And with as little as 10-percent down you could do it. Buy a property—not to hold or use—but to flip in a year or two, or hopefully far less. Use that money to buy more or bigger properties at 10-percent down and repeat the whole process. That's the art and science of leveraging wealth in real estate. And for most of the 1980s, that formula seemed to work like magic on Nantucket.

Why and how did this happen in the 1980s? Three economic factors converged to create Nantucket's own "perfect storm" of real estate speculation—much as three large Atlantic storms unexpectedly converged nearly 10 years later to create the cataclysmic "No Name Storm" we still talk of on the Island.

The first economic factor was a State-mandated requirement that all cities and towns in the Commonwealth use the full fair market value of each property in assessing their local real estate taxes. This prompted Nantucket to hire a professional real estate appraisal firm to update property values that hadn't much changed in a generation or more. Almost overnight, a person who thought he owned a $6,250 property now learned that it was really worth $125,000. At that price, he might very well be willing to sell. Or better yet, he could pull out most of that equity with a new mortgage and have lots of new-found wealth to invest.

The second economic factor was an enormous increase in public funding and new legislation to keep prime land free of development. Here in the Southeast Quarter, the Nantucket Conservation Foundation paid $925,000 to acquire 242-acres in the Madequecham Valley—resulting in a tidy $911,000 capital gain for the seller. And the Town paid $525,000 to buy the old Navy Base in Tom Nevers. Elsewhere, the Nantucket Land Bank was quickly buying up land—flush with new funding from the Island's recently enacted 2-percent real estate transaction tax. And to let them buy even faster, bonds were floated—secured by future transaction tax income. Just one example of the Land Bank's impact is their purchase for $2,500,000 of 64-acres near Long Pond from one Walter C. Cairnes. Remember that name. A bit later, you'll see how Cairnes leveraged that money in Tom Nevers and elsewhere.

Year after year these conservation acquisitions continued, with bigger and bigger cash outlays. In 1985 for example, the Nantucket Conservation Foundation bought the old 300-acre Sanford Farm for $4,400,000. All these were enlightened and well negotiated purchases. But when added together with the dramatic increase in private gifting of land to the Island's conservation groups and foundations—gifting made increasingly tax-smart because of the enormous size of the tax deduction that could be taken as a charitable contribution—this wholesale removal of land from the commercial market had a profound effect on Nantucket's real estate price inflation. As you surely learned in Economics 101—if you reduce the supply of an item in great demand, you can expect selling prices to shoot way up. And that's precisely what happened on Nantucket in the 1980s. Successful conservation efforts steadily decreased the amount of land available for purchase, fueling an even faster rise in the market price of the land remaining.

The third economic factor—and the thing that really whipped Nantucket real estate speculation into the feeding frenzy it became—was the surging new demand for Nantucket property by affluent off-Islanders. National media coverage flowing from the failed Kennedy bill had convinced many that the Island's natural beauty was both rare and precious.

National media coverage surrounding Walter Beinecke's successful restoration of the old Town had also convinced them that the Island's charm was authentic and its lifestyle compelling. And national media coverage reporting on the Island's conservation movement and rapidly escalating real estate prices had convinced them that Nantucket property was a great investment and that they should buy now, before missing out.

And so we have Nantucket's "perfect storm" in real estate—

- An overnight twenty-fold increase in fair-market property values.
- A significant reduction in the amount of land available for purchase, driving up prices.
- A strong increase in buyer demand—by people with the money and the motivation to buy now, creating a feeding frenzy of price escalation.

Those are the dynamics. And here's what happened in practice, as Town government tried measure after measure to cope with the relentless force of big and easy money.

In 1981, Nantucket tried to slow down development with a building cap. But the cap actually sped up the pace of new construction, as many rushed to get in under the wire or to take advantage of the bylaw's few mandated exceptions. The cap had been set at 80 new building permits per year. But in its first two years as law, 461 permits were actually issued—and the backlog of new applications kept growing. By the end of 1986, the building cap was allowed to expire, considered pretty much a failure by all.

Nantucket also tried to block large scale developments with new bylaws that required a hurdle of public hearings and a battery of individual approvals. While a few projects were successfully blocked, the cost to the Town in manpower and legal fees proved daunting. And the disapproved properties had a way of springing back to life in a new form, often in an even less desirable form. Take for example a 1982 project off Old South Road that included a 250-room hotel, a conference center, a restaurant and 25 houses. When approval was finally denied, the developer filed a $20-million lawsuit against the Town. And when that failed, the property was ultimately bought by another developer who built nearly 200 homes on the site. Or take the 1985 Woodbury Lane 25-lot subdivision. This project won approval, but not before requiring 45 public hearings. And during that same year, the Town had to defend itself against more than 25 major lawsuits filed by resolute property owners and developers. As the dollars at risk rose dramatically, the number of appeals, hearings, and the resultant suits against the Town became almost overwhelming. Yet despite all efforts to reverse it, the development pace accelerated. In 1984 alone, more than 500 lots were approved for development.

To the growth planners and conservation organizations, all this was discouraging, if not depressing. But to many Nantucket property owners it was thrilling. Land you once considered almost worthless could now bring you a King's ransom. Tired old houses you couldn't afford to maintain could now net you a fortune—either by selling or, better yet, by pulling out your equity with a second mortgage. And if you were smart and moved fast, you could buy more land and more houses—and sell them quickly at twice what you paid, netting at least a five-fold return on your cash outlay.

A look around Nantucket told you that the sky was the limit—and that the risks of loss were virtually non-existent. In 1979, the average house on Nantucket was valued at less than $10,000. In 1980, that average rose to $125,000. In 1985, it rose again to exceed $200,000. And before the decade was over, it would climb again to approach $300,000.

Of course, those were only the averages. Choice properties rose in value even faster. 1983 saw the first Nantucket house sell for more than $1,000,000. Then it became fairly common. In 1985, Moors End—the old Jared Coffin red brick house on Pleasant Street that we talked of earlier—sold for $3,500,000, setting a new record. In 1986, Walter Beinecke sold all 160 of his Sherburne Associates properties for $55,000,000. And in 1987, a group of five Island friends bought the aging Beachside Motel for $7,700,000—with plans to inject millions more to covert it into condos.

I just seven short years, Nantucket had transformed itself yet again—this time to become what locals called "a rich man's Island." And it was that "perfect storm" in real estate that empowered it.

❦ ❦ ❦

The frenzy to buy and build extended all across the Island. But the impact was slightly gentler in the Southeast Quarter, where a large percentage of the land was already in use or under conservation. In 'Sconset, several new houses were being built—but at a fairly leisurely pace—along the bluff to Sankaty Light and radiating out from the old village center. In Tom Nevers, where nearly 150 homes had already been built to the east and south of Tom Nevers Road, only about six or seven new houses were being added each season. This section of the Tom Nevers area was settling in to become a real community.

But the large Nantucket Beach Properties' holdings west of Tom Nevers Road were still largely undeveloped—with only 6 homes on its hundreds of acres. You'll recall that back in the 1960s this was the area that the Town had refused to let Nantucket Beach Properties reconfigure. And in the 1980s, the Town was still reluctant to do so. Weighing its only other options, Nantucket Beach Properties approached the Land Conservation Council in 1985 with an offer to sell all of its remaining property in the Tom Nevers area for $3,000,000. When that failed to materialize, Nantucket Beach Properties accepted an offer from an Island attorney and two of his associates for that portion of the land that we today call Tom Nevers West—which was in fact the very same parcel that Franklin E. Smith called "Section 5" in his 1916 Nantucket Land Trust development. And it was here in the 1980s that land speculation in the Southeast Quarter was concentrated.

Earlier, I mentioned Walter C. Cairnes, who had collected $2,500,000 from the Land Bank for one of his properties. He used part of that money as his down payment to buy Tom Nevers West from the lawyer and his partners—just nine months after they had acquired it—at a very handsome profit to them, I might add. Cairnes used the rest of his money to buy large tracts of land in Surfside and elsewhere around the Island. And the lawyer's group—with two additional partners—used their Tom Nevers West profits to buy the Beachside Motel, a property which I had also mentioned earlier.

Cairnes was a flamboyant little man who lived on a yacht near Cambridge, where he was reported to be a well-connected professor at Harvard—or at MIT, in some of his tellings. He could be spotted regularly in Town with a clutch of leashed dogs and surrounded by tall, young beauties. With panache and charm, he'd describe his exciting plans for Tom Nevers—a village green encircled by cottages, a petting zoo of miniature animals, lush English gardens, perhaps waterways and gondolas. And yes, he'd be willing to accept a few investors for this marvelous venture! Who knew just how many went for it? None that I know of.

❧   ❧   ❧

But then came Black Monday—October 16th 1987—when the Dow dropped 500 points. Coming on top of the 1986 tax law change that severely limited tax deductions for real estate, this downturn took much of the wind out of Nantucket's real estate sails. Buying slowed, and then stopped. Asking prices fell, but there were few buyers. Over-leveraged speculators juggled assets to meet their loan obligations, but then defaulted. Banks threatened foreclosure, and then acted. Almost overnight on Nantucket, the smell of money was replaced with the smell of fear!

When two separate Boston banks went looking for Walter Cairnes in Cambridge to collect the several million dollars he owed them, they ran into a little surprise. The night before, he had hauled in his mooring lines and sailed away in his yacht to points unknown. No one ever found him, although there were reports from time to time about a yacht of similar configuration being seen in the West Indies, in the Mediterranean, or in the Pacific—but each time sporting different paint colors and different names. Ongoing investigations into Cairnes finances revealed that his entire multimillion dollar Nantucket real estate empire was built from leveraging his student loans.

Clearly, the real estate bubble on Nantucket was bursting. The one-year-old Beachside Motel project folded—but not before wiping out the total lifetime assets of its five Island investors. Some older couples on fixed incomes—who had used their homes as collateral for real estate speculation—lost absolutely everything. Hundreds of others saw their real estate gains melt away. The difference between those who could survive and those who could not, rested solely on their ability to meet their loan payment obligations until the good times returned.

A few people actually gained during this period. One was the owner of a Tom Nevers oceanfront property with a big old house. The year before the Nantucket real estate collapse, he sold at a very high price to two young New Yorkers who were already so leveraged that they couldn't get bank financing. So the seller himself acted as the mortgage lender, with installment payment terms that let the buyers use what cash they could squeeze out of their other deals to knock down the old house and replace it with a handsome new beachfront showplace. Then the market collapsed. The buyers defaulted. The seller foreclosed—recovering his original property, but this time with a beautiful $500,000 improvement.

Others successfully negotiated with banks to buy foreclosed property at bargain prices. Faced with a big list of non-performing loans and a growing inventory of foreclosed properties, the banks reluctantly accepted some very low offers. The alternative was a public auction, with even bigger losses likely. Several property owners in Tom Nevers West bought their land directly from the banks in this way.

But inevitably, a public auction of Tom Nevers West land did occur—with 58 of the lots remaining from the Cairnes foreclosure put on the block on April 17th 1990. (Three weeks later, another bank would auction off the rest of Cairnes foreclosed Nantucket property.)

The only serious bidder for the Tom Nevers West property was the Orange & Black Realty Trust, headed by two Princeton grads who bought the entire area for $750,000. At that low price, they believed they could profitably make the land affordable to many Nantucket buyers who had been priced out of the market in the 1980s. Pursuing that objective, Orange & Black would be among the first to succeed in reversing the Nantucket real estate market's decline.

By 1990, the nation's Savings & Loan Institutions were facing a crisis. Loose lending policies and papered-over underperforming loans had brought many S&Ls to the point of insolvency. Only a massive government bailout could stabilize the industry and restore public confidence.

And only lowered prices for devalued properties could jump start the stalled Nantucket real estate market.

In 1990, the number of properties sold on Nantucket dropped 38-percent—and that included properties sold by auction. Tourism was also way down. Virtually all of the highly leveraged speculators had been flushed from the market, and the prices were starting to tumble. In 1991, the average price paid for a Nantucket home dropped to $281,000. Just one year earlier, the average price paid had been $412,000. Not surprisingly, lower prices did their trick—and the number of properties sold by the end of 1991 showed a 44-percent increase.

But there was a marked difference in buyers. Now it was a true desire to become part of the Nantucket community that fueled the market—not a desire to cash in quick and flip properties. People bought to make Nantucket their home away from home, not just a tax-favored, high-return investment. And that would reshape the Island's priorities again in the late 1990s and 2000s.

❦   ❦   ❦

Not everything was about money and land speculation in the 1980s. Three other events had particular importance to those living in the Southeast Quarter. The first was the return of erosion and the changing shape of our shoreline. The second was the demise of the Madequecham Jam, which had attracted thousands each year to our beaches to party. The third was the strange and sad disappearance of Dr. Margaret Kilcoyne, which many still call Nantucket's greatest mystery. I'd be remiss if I didn't tell you a bit about all three.

❦   ❦   ❦

Islands exist at the pleasure of the sea, so we should be grateful for Nantucket's very existence. And we should accept as only fair the fact that our shoreline is ever changing. Some beaches widen, others disappear, some channels open, others close shut, and shoals shift to protect or expose our coastlines. All this is to be expected on an Island like ours, far out into the sea.

For more than 300 years, the sea had treated the Southeast Quarter with generosity—adding white sand to our beaches for most of that time. As late as 1950, the beach at Tom Nevers was still more than 1,000-feet wide. Then it began to recede—at first slowly, then in 1982 with increasing speed. Until today, as you know, the beach is very narrow—and 10- to 15-feet more of the bluff is being consumed by the sea each winter.

At our easternmost point, the Sankaty Light is now just feet away from toppling over the bluff. (In 1953, it had stood more than 250-feet back.) And the erosion from there to 'Sconset—and from 'Sconset to Madequecham—has claimed several cottages and forced homes and other structures to be moved back.

Some say that the Southeast Quarter's erosion problems are the direct result of misguided State environmental regulations, which put a ban on opening Sesachacha Pond to the sea. Twice each year for over 350-years, Sesachacha's opening had been done with great success—first by we Wampanoags, then by the early English settlers, and then by every generation until 1981. By digging a channel across the narrow barrier beach, the Pond's spring-fed waters were allowed to rush out into the sea—and the Pond was refreshed with a surge of returning ocean brine, creating a habitat were shellfish and saltwater fish species flourished. The force of the exiting waters also shaped the offshore sandbars, which were said to protect the coastline from erosion. But with the ban on opening the Pond in 1981, these sandbars began to melt away.

The impact on the Pond itself was equally concerning. Soon it became unable to support significant marine life—being too low in salinity for most ocean species, and too brackish for most fresh water species. And as the Pond's spring-fed waters continued to rise, the surrounding lowlands were flooded and nearby wells were fouled. But still, the EPA refused to budge, insisting that Sesachacha Pond remain closed until a series of costly long-term environmental impact studies were completed.

Finally, in November 1990—after 9 years of asking—the Massachusetts EPA gave Nantucket permission to once again open Sesachacha

Pond to the sea. But this final decision was more political than scientific—prompted by the Governor's unilateral decree that the early British land grants had given the Island of Nantucket total jurisdiction over its own Great Ponds. To avoid being minimalized and to avoid setting a precedent that might undercut its authority, the Massachusetts EPA rushed through its pond opening approval.

Did the opening make a difference in the Southeast Quarter's erosion? It will take a very long time to tell. A series of massive storms pounded our coastline in the early 1990s and ate away huge chunks of the bluffs. And since then, winter storms have eaten away even more. Perhaps the impact would have been less if the Sesachacha-produced sandbars had remained. But perhaps not. The sandbars are rebuilding, and one day that may help. Also, the people of 'Sconset are funding a series of engineering solutions to protect and rebuild their beaches. Some are optimistic. Others say that it's folly to do battle with the sea.

Will the erosion continue? Will it reverse itself? Are we starting to see a turning point? Those are questions I wish I could answer. I know only the past, not the future.

The ocean keeps its secrets, and it alone knows when and if the beaches of the Southeast Quarter will rebuild.

❧ ❧ ❧

People visit the Madequecham Valley today for private enjoyment and spiritual enrichment. They go there to better understand the Island's glacial origins and to experience the Valley's unique landscape and rare plant life. And if they know the old Indian legends, they'll even begin to understand why this place was chosen as the "Death To Cross" dividing line between warring sachems in the far distant past.

Most of the Madequecham Valley is conservation land today. But that protected status is only recent. In the 1980s, it was Ground Zero for one of the biggest unauthorized Party Blowouts in the country—The Madequecham Jam—held every year for many years on or about the first weekend in August.

The Madequecham Jam started as a beach concert and beer party for the few hundred college kids who came each summer to work on the Island. The cops stayed away because "after all, kids will be kids; and they've been working hard and deserve a little break." It was noisy, and yes, there was too much drinking. But it was just one weekend in a very remote place, so the authorities pretty much looked the other way.

But as the word spread, thousands of young people from all over New England and beyond wanted in on the party. More came, year after year. To the point where more than 3,000 converged on Nobadeer Beach on August 2nd 1986—trashing the Madequecham Valley's fragile landscape and befouling many of the homes ringing the area. Outdoor showers were used as latrines, and some homes were broken into for other biological urgencies. The music was blasting, the beer was nonstop, Animal House antics were the rules of the day. And this time the police and the Islanders said—"Enough!" The Madequecham Jam's organizers were called in and ordered to cease and desist in the future. And they agreed, but by this time the Jam had taken on a life of its own.

The parties went underground—with secret dates and sham locations. Boom boxes replaced bands, and coolers and backpacks full of beer replaced kegs and cash bars. Yet even more young people came every year.

All this finally came to an abrupt halt in 1990, when area residents banded together to block all the access roads and physically guard their properties—having received information that this year's Jam would be held on June 28th. But that date proved to be a diversion by the event's organizers. Suspecting resistance, they had secretly spread the word that this year's real date would be August 4th. And this time they expected the partying crowd to exceed 5,000. Tipped off by an informant, the authorities were ready. State troopers on horseback prevented all beach access, and police on the ground confiscated mountains of beer cans before sending everyone home. There were no arrests, but the word was out. There would never be a Madequecham Jam again.

ℋ ℋ ℋ

On January 26th 1980, the well-known and well-liked Dr. Margaret Kilcoyne vanished from her Tom Nevers home. Rumors swirled that she had committed suicide, was murdered, was in hiding or in a sanitarium somewhere off-Island and even that she had been abducted to gain access to her valuable medical research secrets.

Reporters from across the country kept the mystery alive for months. Feature articles appeared in Life magazine, The New York Times, New York Magazine, and dozens of other magazines and newspapers. Radio and TV coverage was even more extensive—with one station going so far as to hire a well known psychic. Intensive investigations by local authorities continued for months. But no answer to her disappearance could ever be found.

Margaret Kilcoyne was no ordinary woman. She was a brilliant medical researcher at Columbia University's College of Physicians and Surgeons in New York City. She was a sparkling conversationalist, with a lively sense of humor. Her kind nature and unaffected manner had earned her a wide circle of friends in New York and Nantucket. And her Island neighbors held her in such esteem that they elected her the first president of the Tom Nevers Civic Association.

The thing that made Margaret Kilcoyne's disappearance so puzzling was the reason she gave for coming up to her Nantucket home that January. She had told everyone that she had just achieved a critical medical breakthrough in her research on hypertension—a breakthrough so important that she planned to announce it at a special press party she'd be hosting on Nantucket in early February. And to that end, upon her arrival two days before, she purchased over $640 worth of groceries and paid $200 more for wine and spirits to equip three houses for the press. She called her findings so significant that they just couldn't wait for her presentation in New Orleans at the International Symposium on Hypertension already scheduled for mid-May. And she hinted that her findings were so important that they might win her a Nobel Prize.

The evening of her disappearance, Margaret Kilcoyne had a very cheerful dinner with her brother Lawrence—a VP with IBM Canada— and two close Island friends. Lawrence reported that Margaret went off to bed sometime around 11:00 PM. When he knocked on her door the next morning, there was no answer and the room was empty. Seeing that her winter coat was still on its hook and that the car was still in the driveway, he searched the rest of the house, then the grounds and surrounding roadways. Growing alarmed, he called the police.

Lawrence Kilcoyne told the authorities that he had become increasingly worried about his sister's mental health, which is why he had come to Nantucket to meet with her. He felt that she was becoming unstable, and now feared the worst.

Over the next two days, the police, fire department, state police, Coast Guard and other rescue personnel combed the Southeast Quarter and south shore beaches. Tom Nevers Pond was dragged and then searched by divers. All passenger departures by boat and plane were checked and double checked. The offshore search extended well beyond the shoals. Increasingly, it seemed like a suicide by ocean drowning.

Then new evidence turned up one week later. Hikers found Margaret Kilcoyne's passport, bankbook, wallet with a single $100 bill, and a pair of sandals—all neatly stacked in a little pile. These were found near Phillip's Run, about 1½-miles northeast of Kilcoyne's Parson Lane home—in a direction opposite from the closest shoreline. Had these been missed in the initial search, or were they recently placed there? Opinion was sharply divided.

Another two days of searching turned up nothing. But then the media-driven leads started to come in. Several sightings of Margaret Kilcoyne in Boston, a sighting on Cape Cod—extensive follow-up showed them both to be cases of mistaken identity. Reports from strangers who had spent an evening with her on the way up to Nantucket—these proved to be genuine but inconclusive.

An investigative team was sent to New York to interview Dr. Kilcoyne's colleagues at Columbia and to search her apartment. Her unclaimed car at the ferry parking lot in Hyannis was recovered. Daily searches of the shoreline were conducted. Search dogs were brought in, along with a low-flying search plane. No solid evidence of suicide, of foul play, or deception could be found. The only solid fact was that she had vanished.

246 Tom Never's Ghost

Normally, the sea gives up its dead. And without a body, other suspicions were voiced. Some theorized that Margaret Kilcoyne had staged her own disappearance as a hoax to publicize her medical breakthrough. And that she would emerge in May in New Orleans with a story of abduction and being held as a hostage. This theory collapsed when she never appeared at the Symposium.

Others argued that she had suffered a mental breakdown and that her brother had placed her in a private institution. His increasing lack of cooperation with the authorities added to this suspicion. But a comprehensive check of public and private facilities in both the U.S. and Canada turned up nothing. And Lawrence Kilcoyne was not reticent about his anger that the press had turned his family's tragedy into a circus—and his suspicion that some of the local authorities were using this sad affair to gain political notoriety.

The majority, however, still believed that Margaret Kilcoyne had committed suicide. But no suicide note was found. And tape recordings of her last phone conversations with her brother were ambiguous. A local psychologist said she sounded agitated and "possibly suicidal." But people who knew her said the recordings were "vintage Margaret"—effusive and chatty.

So what did happen to Margaret Kilcoyne?

After returning to her room that night, she was too energized to sleep and decided to take a long walk to think through her press conference presentation. She left through the slider door in her room, wearing only slacks and a sweater. The night was bitterly cold, but to her it felt bracing.

She walked aimlessly along the roads in Tom Nevers for about an hour, until she realized that she was nearing 'Sconset. And the idea of a midnight swim seemed suddenly appealing. She took her wallet and papers out of her pants pocket and placed them with her sandals in the tall grass where she could later retrieve them—feeling that they were safer here, out of sight, than on the open beach in 'Sconset.

She felt on top of the world and truly elated. In only a few days, people everywhere would celebrate her discovery. Euphoric, she waded into the surf just west of the town beach in 'Sconset. The icy water actually felt warming. And as hypothermia set in, she slipped silently beneath the waves.

The very talented Margaret Kilcoyne had suffered from a mental condition—probably the mania phase of bipolar disorder—that had gone largely undetected by her close friends and co-workers. Her brother suspected that something was wrong, but because she was a flamboyant, fascinating and energetic person, others saw little to alarm them. Only in the final days did the classic symptoms of bipolar mania become apparent—hyperactivity, pressure of speech, flight of ideas, inflated self-esteem, decreased need for sleep, distractibility, and excessive involvement in activities with a high potential for painful consequences. Because she never consulted a psychiatrist, no professional diagnosis exists. But an investigative journalist—who interviewed everyone who had spent time with Margaret Kilcoyne during that January—reported that "her final days were like a living illustration of the definition of Mania" . . . with non-stop chatter, delusions of grandeur, no need for sleep, and hyperactivity.

While Dr. Kilcoyne's research on hypertension was significant, there was no medical breakthrough. And even if there was, why hold a press conference on Nantucket in February, when New York City would be a far more successful location? And if a press conference in Nantucket was truly planned, why had no one from the press been invited?

Margaret Kilcoyne died from hypothermia and accidental drowning. Her decision to wade into the freezing surf that night was not a willful, suicidal act of despair. It was a delusional act of joy—the sad consequence of a manic condition that is highly treatable today.

Margaret Kilcoyne was 50. Nine years after her disappearance, she was declared legally dead by the courts. RIP.

❧   ❧   ❧

20

2000 . . . The Rich & The Super-Rich

N antucket transformed itself yet again in the mid-1990s—a transformation that has continued unabated until today. Simply put, the Island has become the darling of those with serious money—not just the rich, but the super-rich. And with that serious money has come new expectations and lifestyles.

Our historic buildings and streets are still pretty much the same, our beaches and conservation areas are all just as beautiful, our neighbors are as delightful and cordial as ever. But the difference can be seen in soaring property values, in the huge homes being built, in the menus at our restaurants, in the items being sold at our shops, in the art and antiques shown in our galleries, in the seemingly endless whirl of fund-raising benefits, in the high prices of just about everything on the Island, and in the array of "adult toys" that have become necessities of everyday living.

Of course, Nantucket is not alone in this transformation—and in many ways it has assimilated it all with greater ease and less dislocation than many other resort communities. The prevailing fact is that an enormous amount of wealth was created in America during the mid-1990s. And with all this wealth came the need to find new and better ways to spend it.

Pretend for a minute that you're a corporate CEO and that you earn $30,000,000 or more each year. Beyond supporting your favorite charities, what choices do you have to enjoy all that money? Homes in great places probably top your list. And when it comes to great places, Nantucket ranks very high indeed.

Or pretend for a moment that you're a young bond trader with a $4,000,000 bonus each of the last two or three years. Celebrating your success with a wonderful vacation home that is also a smart investment may seem very compelling. And by those criteria, Nantucket could well be at the top of your short list.

Or pretend that you run your own successful consulting, financial or intellectual property company and that telecommunications and computers now let you work from home—a home that can be almost anywhere with an airport. If your favorite vacation spot has always been Nantucket, you might well decide to make the Island your new year-round home.

And on, and on, and on. In a series of hundreds of personal and individual decisions, people of considerable wealth have chosen Nantucket. In 2004, The Inquirer and Mirror reported that between 80 and 100 *billionaires* now have homes on Nantucket. And the millionaires probably number well into the thousands.

Of course, the rich and the super-rich value the same Nantucket qualities that attracted those who bought here before them—the small town charm, the natural beauty, and the historical look and feel of the Island. It's their escape to a time and place lost elsewhere in America. But the rich and the super-rich also prize something else—they place an extraordinarily high value on Nantucket's social cachet and aura of exclusivity—factors that their very presence in such numbers have given to the Island. And it is this "snob factor" more than anything else that irks the Island's "regular folks."

They bemoan Nantucket's loss of quiet simplicity—pointing with nostalgia to the total lack of pretension that once characterized even the wealthiest and most powerful summer residents. They bemoan the loss of down-to-earth "authenticity" and the rise of "celebrity chic"—passing along with derision those "Don't you know who I am?" stories about the Island's self-appointed new elite. And they bemoan what they call trophy homes and McMansions—making a folk legend out of that "without a clue" remark made by a wealthy woman when her plans for an 8,000-square foot summer house were rejected by the Historic District Commission—"But 8,000-square feet is really pretty small; it's less than half the size of my place back home!"

Many Islanders complain that Nantucket isn't what it was. But what is? Change has occurred everywhere, and it has occurred constantly on this Island. Again, as before, we're seeing a new wave of settlers displacing the old—a new wave that enthusiastically declares Nantucket their "Paradise found"—as some of those who came before grieve that their own Nantucket Paradise is slipping away.

One ironic twist is that in Nantucket's latest transformation the Island is on an upward, rather than downward, economic spiral. When new people move in elsewhere, the most common complaint is that they are destroying the neighborhood and driving property values downward. Here, the complaint is that people with too much money are destroying the neighborhood and driving our property values up through the roof. With a complaint like that, it's hard to win much sympathy from others who don't live here.

Certainly, the surge of wealth on Nantucket has shot property values skyward. The average house on the Island now sells for more than $1,900,000. And multi-million dollar sales are so very common that only purchases above $15,000,000 seem to earn headlines. Building costs are also soaring, as buyers want larger custom homes with more amenities. Today's rule-of-thumb for new construction on the Island is a minimum of $350 per square foot. For a 3,000-square foot house, that puts construction costs at over $1,050,000 . . . and that's not counting land.

Basic living costs are also dramatically higher than on the mainland—with groceries about 12-percent higher, energy and gasoline about 30-percent higher, rental housing about 50-percent higher, and single family houses about 300-percent higher. This has forced many to leave the Island, being priced out of the market. And it has created a whole new cadre of Island workers who commute by plane or boat daily from the mainland.

Yet even most lower-income people somehow manage—often working multiple jobs and long hours. Indeed, Nantucket's booming economy has created opportunity for a growing number of eager immigrant workers. Nantucket's year-round Hispanic population now stands at several thousand—with the majority from Brazil, El Salvador, Costa Rica, The Dominican Republic and Guatemala. And their numbers are swelled during the summer season with guest workers from Jamaica and Eastern Europe.

Also thanks to Nantucket's booming economy, many in the construction, real estate and service industries truly prosper. Hundreds of small business owners and self-proprietors working in these fields have joined Nantucket's millionaire class, too.

As always, there's a continuing debate about overdevelopment. But the trend is away from large subdivisions—with most of the growth now occurring in large homes on large lots. And even in the absence of building caps, Island officials and approval authorities have found ways to use environmental and conservation laws to restrict or slow development. The Island's wealthy population has also contributed heavily to the purchase of conservation restrictions on large tracts of prime land—land that might otherwise have to be sold to developers to pay off estate taxes.

To some, these efforts are too limited. They favor far more aggressive ways to limit growth. But on balance, these efforts seem to be working— at least in the judgment of Nantucket's more than 7,500 registered voters.

Today, the "official" year-round population on Nantucket is just over 10,000—back to its previous high-point in the 1840s, a time before Nantucket entered its long decline. But that count doesn't include several thousand foreign nationals, and tens of thousands of seasonal residents and vacationers who swell the summer population to over 60,000—and put considerable stress on the Island's resources during July and August. The good news is that over the past five years, the number of summer people has remained fairly stable. Almost all the recent growth has come from additional year-round residents. Most assume that these are retirees. But the vast majority are in their 30s and 40s—adding to Nantucket's new class of work-from-home millionaires.

❦   ❦   ❦

The Southeast Quarter too has matured and prospered. Once only 'Sconset was a thriving community. Now, the Greater Tom Nevers Area—stretching from the airport to Tom Nevers Pond—has more than 500 property owners, with nearly one-third of them year-round residents. Oceanfront properties valued at $4,000,000 or more line the south shore, and even undeveloped building lots near the Milestone Road sell for more than $850,000. Not since the time of Sachem Wanackmamack has the area been as fully settled and thriving.

But growth in the Southeast Quarter has stabilized because very little land is still available for development. More than 80-percent of the land here is now under conservation or is government owned—making the Southeast Quarter the Island's most protected area.

The old Navy Base is now called Tom Nevers Field—with two baseball diamonds, a roller hockey rink, a playground, and open space for events and recreation. Under the supervision of the Parks & Recreation Department, it's home to the Island Fair, an occasional Country Market, an annual carnival and touring circus, and Nantucket's Demolition Derby. Why the Derby exists at all is an interesting question. It goes back to 1985 when more than 1,200 derelict cars littered the moors. In desperation, the Town brought in tow trucks and a crusher to collect and compact wrecks to ship them off-Island. At great expense, that cleared up the mess but didn't stop new additions. Big fines were considered, but someone came up with the Derby idea—giving adventurous young men all across the Island a real incentive to collect junker cars before they were abandoned. The Demolition Derby was conceived as a fun way to solve a bigger problem—bringing together all those old cars for efficient post-event crushing and shipping off-Island. And it has worked amazingly well.

Gradually, over the years, all the old Navy structures have been removed from Tom Nevers Field. Last to go in 2003 was the enlisted men's recreation center, which had been used for many decades as the VFW Club and Meeting Hall. Erosion forced its removal, and along with it went the relic anti-aircraft gun that once guarded the Southeast Quarters' skies. All that remains now of the Navy presence at Tom Nevers Field is the "Kennedy Bunker" standing tall and grass covered as a strange topographic anomaly. No one wants to be the first to recommend that it go.

I probably should also mention the fictional Tom Nevers Field—that made-up Nantucket airport featured in the NBC sitcom called "Wings." From 1990 to 1997, in 172 episodes, the show entertained millions with the antics of two brothers running a shoestring airline named Sandpiper Air. As the show's popularity grew, more and more Nantucket tourists would ask their tour guides to take them to Tom Nevers Field. They were told that it didn't really exist—that it was just a fiction for the show. But of course, now you know better. You know that back in the early 1900s, Nantucket's first airfield was indeed called Tom Nevers Field. But virtually no one on the Island is aware of that today.

✸   ✸   ✸

What does the future hold for Nantucket and the Southeast Quarter? If you're a student of history, you already know the answer. Good times, followed by bad, followed by good times, followed by bad. Then the cycle repeats. What we don't know is how long each segment of the cycle will last.

Will Nantucket's real estate values continue to soar? For a time, yes. Will the real estate bubble burst and prices fall steeply? One day, yes. Will they later rebound and start a new upward climb? Yes. But again, we don't know when and for how long.

Will the rich and the super-rich start to tire of Nantucket and move on? Yes, many will. Will they be replaced by a new wave of settlers who are even more enthusiastic about the Island? Yes, but for reasons we might not expect. Will the Island continue to change—becoming more like the rest of America? Yes. Will it still retain enough of a difference to make it compellingly attractive? Perhaps not to you, but most certainly to those who will come after.

What I'm saying is that no place on this earth satisfies forever. That it delights us only for a time and then changes. What I'm saying is that the Nantucket you love today differs greatly from the Nantucket that others loved before you came. And that the Nantucket yet to come will

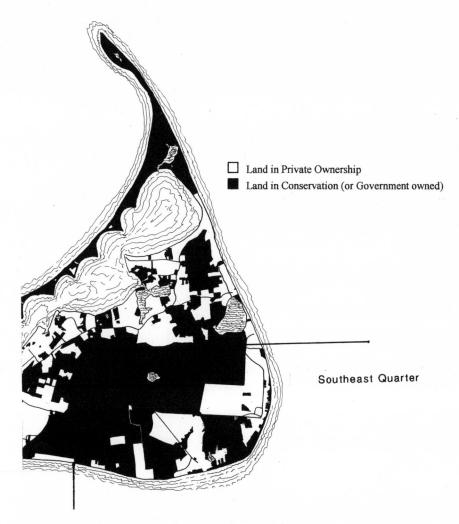

Land in Private Ownership

Land in Conservation (or Government owned)

Southeast Quarter

FIGURE 30   The Southeast Quarter—Circa 2005

Thanks to private contributions and the efforts of several non-profit organizations, more than 80-percent of the Southeast Quarter is now under conservation or government ownership. No other part of the Island has such a high percentage of its land under conservation protection.

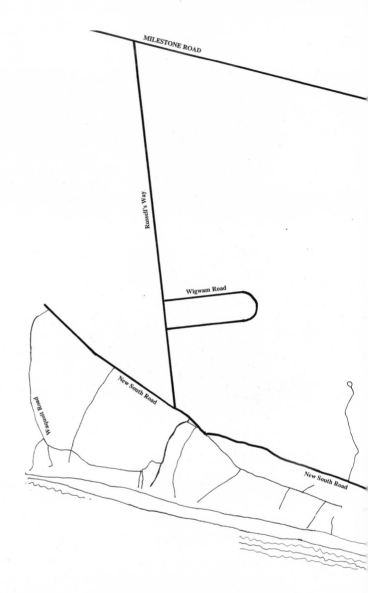

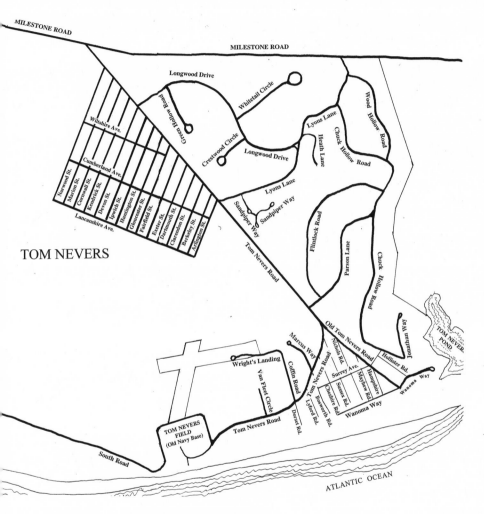

FIGURE 31   Tom Nevers—Circa 2005

The Greater Tom Nevers Area is now home to over 500 families—with more than one-third year-round residents.

without doubt disappoint you—while being seen by others as their new found Eden.

Yes, I'm saying all that and more. If there is any message in all that I've told you this morning, it's this—Our search for an "earthly Eden" is necessarily elusive because we live in an ever changing world. Every time we think we've found our permanent home, it begins to change. We try to block that change to preserve our happiness, but blocking it is beyond our reach. Someone new and younger and more engaged is always there to claim our Eden and reshape it into theirs.

Enjoy all that you have, while you have it. Be grateful, and then let go. This place was lent to you for a brief time only. You are only one of many passing through these parts.

❦   ❦   ❦

Goodbye.

Epilog . . .

With that, Tom rose and left my house.
He did not look back.
The fog engulfed him and he would not come my way again.
How fortunate I feel to have been there when he was passing through
these parts.

Jack Warner

❦   ❦   ❦

FIGURE 32　**The Southeast Quarter As It Exists Today**

Now home to thousands of year-round and seasonal residents, the Southeast
Quarter still remains largely open protected space.
(Reproduced from a Town of Nantucket GIS Zoning Map Sheet.)

APPENDIX

Some Things to Know about Whales

(As told to me by old Tom Never on that June day in the fog.)

The Sperm Whale—

The largest of the Odontoceta or tooth-head whales . . . and the animal that created Nantucket's wealth and world reputation.

- Prized for the spermaceti oil in its huge head.
- Sperm whale oil and candles lit the finest homes. They burned far brighter and cleaner, and as such, commanded the highest prices.
- As a lubricant for precision instruments, spermaceti oil is without equal. Its viscosity and other performance characteristics remain stable across a wide range of temperatures.
- *Average size*—55-feet long and 63-tons (males). Half that size for females.
- *Average yield*—Up to 1890-gallons per animal.
- *Profusion*—Seemingly unlimited in number to Nantucket whalers. Over 1.5-million worldwide in the early 1800s.

The Bowhead Whale—

The largest of the Mysticeta or baleen whales . . . with the longest baleen of any cetacean. Called "whalebone," baleen is a horny, elastic material that hangs in fringed parallel, platelike sheets from the whale's upper jaw or palate . . . allowing the whale to strain out the plankton and other small sealife on which it feeds.

- Prized mainly for its baleen which was used to make corset stays, buggy whips and other implements requiring a strong, flexible core.
- The Arctic Bowhead Whale was especially valuable. Not only did it have the longest baleen . . . up to 14-feet long . . . but also had blubber up to 2-feet thick.
- *Average size*—50-feet long and 42-tons.
- *Average yield*—Up to 3000-pounds of whalebone . . . which could be sold for over $3 per pound in the late 1800s. So lucrative, that whalers sometimes ignored the Bowhead's carcass without processing the blubber.

The Right Whale—

Called the Right Whale because it was considered the "right whale" to harvest by Nantucket whalers before their discovery of the Sperm Whale.

- Similar in appearance to the Arctic Bowhead . . . except for a large, unusually barnacle-encrusted bonnet or callus on its head that served no known purpose.
- Inhabited the more temperate waters of the Northern and Southern Hemispheres.
- A lethargic swimmer that floated when killed, making harvesting easier.
- *Average size*—50-feet long and 42-tons.
- *Average yield*—Less bone and blubber than the Arctic Bowhead. Baleen grew up to 8-feet long. Blubber averaged 16-inches thick.

The Gray Whale—

A relatively slender whale of the baleen species, most common to the Pacific Coast.

- The only baleen whale to feed on bottom-dwelling creatures like clams, crabs and marine worms. Often surfaces after feeding, with bottom mud covering its head and mouth.
- *Average size*—47-feet long and 40-tons.
- *Average yield*—Amount of whalebone and blubber can vary greatly. Less productive than the Right Whale.

The Humpback Whale—

Although plentiful in coastal waters and possessing both thick blubber and 27-inch-long baleen, the Humpback Whale was the least favored species by Nantucket whalers because of its tendency to sink after being killed.

- Fascinating to watch. Performs high backflips and somersaults. Gives loud "love pats" to its companions, using its especially-long flippers.
- *Average size*—45-feet long and 35-tons.
- *Average yield*—Very low because of losses due to the carcass sinking.

The Pilot Whale—

A very small whale harvested in large numbers on Nantucket by drift-whaling, in the days before "in the deep" whaling.

The Killer Whale—

Not a whale but a very large, mostly black dolphin that hunts in large packs and preys on large fish, seals and whales. Of the Orcinus Orca species.

❦   ❦   ❦

Ship Wrecks & Marine Disasters
Off Tom Nevers Head

(As also told to me by old Tom Never on that June day.)

Wrecked Off Tom Nevers . . .

1793	*Sally*	Ship
1813	*Queen*	Ship
1825	*Clio*	Brigantine
1844	*Harriet*	Schooner
1844	*Litchfield*	Schooner
1846	*Earl of Eglington*	Ship
1852	*Shanunga*	Ship
1865	*Newton*	Steamship
1866	*Guilford*	Sloop
1870	*Poinsett*	Brigantine
1879	*William D. Cargill*	Schooner
1903	*Progress*	Schooner
1922	*Doris*	Gas Powered Vessel
1924	*Inez*	Gas Powered Fishing Vessel
1924	*Evelyn & Ralph*	Gas Powered Fishing Vessel

Wrecked On Old Man Shoals . . .

1841	*Fairplay*	Schooner
1861	*Jaffa*	Brigantine
1878	*Guilia D.*	Barque
1881	*Hazard*	Barque

Reference Sources

Sources consulted in an attempt to verify facts—

"Abram's Eyes—The Native American Legacy of Nantucket Island" by Nathaniel Philbrick. © 1998 Mill Hill Press.

"America's First Lady Boss" by Curtiss S. Johnson. © 1965 Silvermine Publishers Incorporated. Reprinted 1985 Macys of Ellinwood.

"Away Off Shore—Nantucket Island and Its People, 1602–1890" by Nathaniel Philbrick. © 1994 Mill Hill Press.

"Bloomingdale Diary—Summer 1896" by Ruth Burleigh Dame and Olive Arnold Dame, as copied from an original manuscript of Olive C. Butman in 1944. Nantucket Historical Association.

"Building with Nantucket in Mind" by Christopher Lang and Kate Stout © 1992 Nantucket Historic District Commission.

"The Coffin Saga" by Will Gardner. © 1949 The Riverside Press.

"Digging for Nantucket's Merrimack Routes" by Nathaniel Philbrick. © 1996 Nantucket Magazine.

"The Discoverers—A History of Man's Search To Know His World And Himself" by Daniel Boorstin. © 1983 Random House.

"A Doomsday Shelter in the Sand" by Lawrence J. Whelan © 1996 Nantucket Magazine—Fall/Holiday 1996 Issue.

"Early Nantucket And Its Whale Houses" by Henry Chandlee Forman. © 1966 Hastings House, NY

"Early Settlers of Nantucket" by Lydia Hinchman. © 1901 Ferris & Leach.

"Edward F. Underhill" by John Lacouture. © January, 1988 Historic Nantucket, Nantucket Historical Association.

"Erie Canal Legacy" by Andy Olenick and Richard O. Reisem. © 2000 The Landmark Society of Western New York.

"Eunice Hussey" by Rev. Louise S. Baker. Written in 1895. © 1938 The Inquirer and Mirror Press.

"Family Housing Manual—Gouin Village" © Naval Facility, Nantucket, Mass.

"The Far-Off Island Railroad—Nantucket's Old Summer Narrow-Gauge" by Clay Lancaster. © 1972 Pleasant Publications.

"From Dawn To Decadence" by Jacques Barzun. © 2000 Harper Collins.

"Guide to Historical Records and Genealogical Resources of Nantucket, Massachusetts" compiled by Betsy Lowenstein and Dual Macintyre. © 1999 Nantucket Historical Association.

"Historic Indian Houses Of Nantucket" by Elizabeth A. Little. (Nantucket Algonquians Studies # 4) © 1981 Nantucket Historical Association.

"A History of Commerce on Nantucket" by Michael Manville. © 2000 The Official Guide to Nantucket, Nantucket Chamber of Commerce.

"The History of Nantucket" by Obed Macy, with additions by William C. Macy. © 1880 Mansfield: Macy & Pratt.

"The History of Nantucket" by Alexander Starbuck. © 1924 C.E. Goodspeed & Co. Reprinted © 1969 Charles E. Tuttle Company.

"Holiday Island" by Clay Lancaster. © 1993 Nantucket Historical Association.

"Horse Commons At Nantucket Island, 1660–1760" by Elizabeth A. Little. (Nantucket Algonquians Studies # 9) © 1986 Elizabeth A. Little.

"In the Talons of an Eagle" by Nathaniel Philbrick. © 1996 Nantucket Magazine.

"An Incident During The War of 1812" by Edouard A. Stackpole. © January, 1989 Historic Nantucket, Nantucket Historical Association.

"The Indian Contribution To Along Shore Whaling at Nantucket" by Elizabeth A. Little. (Nantucket Algonquians Studies # 8) © 1981 Nantucket Historical Association.

"The Indomitable R.H. Macy" by Curtiss S. Johnson. © 1964 Vantage Press. Reprinted 1985 Macys of Ellinwood.

"An Introduction to the Prehistory of Nantucket" by Bernard H. Stockley. © January, 1968 Historic Nantucket, Nantucket Historical Association.

"The Inquirer and Mirror" various articles from microfilm. © The Inquirer and Mirror.

"An Island Patchwork" by Eleanor Early. © 1944 The Riverside Press/Houghton Mifflin Company.

"Letters from an American Farmer" by Saint-John de Crèvecoeur. © 1782.

"Life Saving Nantucket" by Edouard A. Stackpole. © 1972 Nantucket Life Saving Museum.

"The Madequecham Wigwam Murder" Bulletin of the Massachusett Archaeological Society—Volume 42, Number 1. © The Massachusett Archaeological Society.

"Marine Disasters of Nantucket" compiled by B.W. Luther. © Life Saving Museum.

"Miriam Coffin or The Whale-Fishermen—A Nantucket Novel" by Joseph C. Hart. First published 1834. Reprinted in new edition 1995 Mill Hill Press.

"Nantucket Argument Settlers—Island History at a Glance." Edited by Marianne Griffin Stanton. © 1994 The Inquirer and Mirror.

"Nantucket Conservation Foundation, Inc. Property Booklet" © 1970 Nantucket Conservation Foundation.

"Nantucket Farming" by Aimee E. Newell. © 2000 The Nantucket Guide, Anderson Publishing. Nantucket Historical Association, Edouard A. Stackpole Research Center.

"Nantucket—A History" by R.A. Douglas-Lithgow, M.D., LL.D. © 1914 G.P. Putnam's Sons.

"The Nantucket Indians. Legends and Accounts before 1659." by Meredith Marshall Brenizer. © 1976. Printed by Poets Corner Press.

"Nantucket Island: An Analysis of the Natural and Visual Resources" by Holzeimer et al. © 1974 Harvard U. Department of Landscape Architecture.

"Nantucket Landfall" by Dorothy C. A. Blanchard. © 1956 Dodd, Mead & Company.

"Nantucket Lands and Land Owners" by Henry Barnard Worth. © 1906 Nantucket Historical Association. Re-published 1928.

"Nantucket. The Last 100 Years" © 2001 The Inquirer and Mirror.

"Nantucket! Nantucket! Nantucket! An Insider's Guide" by Dick Mackay. © 1981 Sankaty Head Press.

"Nantucket Odyssey" by Emil Guba. © 1965 Emil Frederick Guba.

"Nantucket Only Yesterday" by Robert F. Mooney. © 2000 Wesco Publishing.

"Nantucket In Print" by Everett U. Crosby. First published 1896. Reprinted 1946. Ten Pound Island Book Company & Maurizio Martino. Nantucket Registry of Deeds.

"The Nantucket Scrap Basket" by William F. Macy. © 1930 The Riverside Press.

"Nantucket Summers" by Katherine Stanley-Brown Abbott. © 1996 Pinniped Press.

"Nantucket—Then and Now" by John W. McCalley. © 1981 Dover Publications, Inc.

"The Nantucket Way" by Robert F. Mooney and André R. Sigourney. © 1980 Doubleday & Company, Inc.

"The Nation of Nantucket—Society and Politics in an Early American Commercial Center, 1660–1820" by Edward Byers. © 1987 Northeastern University Press.

"Naturalistic Landscaping for Nantucket. An Ecological Approach" by Lucinda Young. © 1992 Nantucket Land Council, Inc.

"The New Columbia Encyclopedia" edited by William H. Harris and Judith S. Levey. Third Edition © 1975 Columbia University Press.

"The New York Times" various editions from microfilm.

"Old Nantucket—The Faraway Island" by William Oliver Stevens. © 1936 Dodd, Mead & Company.

"Old-Time Nantucket—The Present Town" by Edouard A. Stackpole. © January, 1988 Historic Nantucket, Nantucket Historical Association.

"The Philadelphia Inquirer" article by Steve Stecklow. © June 23, 1990.

"The Prehistory of Nantucket" by Bernard H. Stockley. © October, 1969 Historic Nantucket, Nantucket Historical Association.

"Privateer Ahoy! A Story of the War of 1812" by Edouard A. Stackpole. © 1937 William Marrow & Co.

"Quaint Nantucket" by William Root Bliss. © 1869 The Riverside Press.

"Quaker Nantucket" by Robert J. Leach and Peter Gow. © 1997 Robert J. Leach and Peter Gow. Published by Mill Hill Press.

"Rambling Through The Streets and Lanes of Nantucket" by Edouard A. Stackpole. © 1951 Reynolds-DeWalt Printing, Inc., New Bedford, MA.

"Remains of Old Sherburne" by Sharon N. Lorenzo. © January, 1989 Historic Nantucket, Nantucket Historical Association.

"Sconset Cottage Life—A Summer On Nantucket Island" by A. Judd Northrup. © 1881 C.W. Bardeen, Publisher.

"Sconset Heyday" by Margaret Fawcett Barnes. © 1969. Revised and reprinted by The Inquirer and Mirror.